A NEW AMERICA

The Awakening

ROBERT HOSTETLER

ABOUT THE COVER

The sacred lotus plant was used to represent the God consciousness. The U.S. flag was used to represent America. The white doves represent messengers of peace. This is the trinity of a new American Spirit for Peace.

Without peace there can be no prosperity. Without prosperity there can be no peace. Think and speak of war and a greater menace of destruction evolves. Think and speak of peace and a greater gift of prosperity evolves.

This book is dedicated to all the good people in the world desiring to have love in their hearts. Special thanks to the heavenly Angels. Without their guidance and encouragement this book would not have been possible.

INTRODUCTION

Turn on the TV news and one may see images of people rioting or demonstrating in the streets around the globe. One will see images of the American flag being burned not just in America but across the world. American troops are being killed almost daily in a never ending war in two countries where the Pentagon generals are claiming the conflict will last many more years. Major corporations in the past two decades have shipped the higher paying jobs overseas for cheaper wages. The rising unemployment has been spiraling out of control. People are losing their homes and vehicles. Many businesses are folding daily to include many large corporations. Lower paying retail jobs are replacing the higher paying manufacturing jobs. America has become a debtor nation with a decade of record breaking deficits. America is a consumer nation no longer a producer nation. Corporate and government corruption is at an all time high.

The major political parties, Republicans and Democrats, are embattled in gridlock. Both parties are creating a great divide throughout America. America and the world are trying to revive a lagging economy from what is now known as the Great Recession. Many parts of America and other parts of the world are experiencing a Depression with no end in sight. The world's energy resources are rapidly depleting. America and other nations are facing many challenges from global terrorism and where other nations want to become nuclear nations; threatening the United States and their neighbors. The world is experiencing catastrophic natural disasters. And to make things worse, many are predicting that December 21st, 2012, will bring in the End of Days. One wonders if the world has gone insane.

There are some in the U.S. Government, who are political and government leaders, who feel that the U.S. Constitution is 'cumbersome'. As a former public candidate in the Texas 21st Congressional District, I address the U.S. Constitution in the first chapter. This sacred document has been under attack from both, the right and the left. The U.S. Constitution has been the bedrock and foundation for American democracy. However, there is good news. This book addresses these issues with viable and common sense solutions. This book will show how humanity is on the cusp of global peace and prosperity. We can make a difference. We can expect a better tomorrow. Sit back, relax and let me take you on a journey and show how we can all experience the pursuit of happiness not just in America but across the globe. Together we can end worldwide poverty and hunger. Together we can bring a lasting peace to the world free of tyrannical governments and global terrorism. The first steps start now.

America will rise again to higher heights surpassing the advanced civilization of Atlantis. America will once again become a beacon of light shining brightly as they walk together with their fellow neighbors across the globe. The choice and the opportunity are here to seize. The angels are standing by, raising our consciousness, for a better tomorrow full of love. There are some who do not want peace and prosperity. Nevertheless, they are in the vast minority. We can end worldwide poverty, hunger, and disease.

We can make America great again. We can restore the Republic. We can bring in the people from the federal, state and local government agencies as an integral part of We The People. Government does not need to be in opposition to the desires and dreams of people. As citizens it is our civic duty to ensure that those who serve the people in the public sector do so with competence and integrity. Without competence and integrity, corruption will run wild and out of control. Those who cling to power and control over others in this country serve no one but themselves. Their actions threaten the existence of a free society.

America is in serious peril. The rights and freedoms that we all cherish are in jeopardy. To remain apathetic will allow those forces to continue their quest to control our mind, body and soul. They want all of us to fear the government. Fascism is at our doorstep. We can open the door and let it in or we can remain strong by letting liberty prevail. To do nothing, a free and open society will perish.

Together we can make America great again. The first step starts now. Working together for a brighter future will reap unparallel peace and prosperity for the American people and others across the world. With your determination and dedication the will of God and the Angels will usher in a new era for humanity.

CHAPTER 1 – CONSTITUTIONAL RIGHTS

"The sacred rights of mankind are not to be rummaged for, among old parchments, or musty records. They are written, as with a sun beam in the whole volume of human nature, by the hand of the divinity itself; and can never be erased or obscured by mortal power."
Alexander Hamilton, 1775

In the early morning hours of April 30th, 1789, thirteen guns representing each Colony were heard across Manhattan, preceding the inauguration of America's first president, George Washington. President Washington in his inaugural address in the Senate chamber called upon "that Almighty God, who rules over the universe" to help the American people find "liberties and happiness" under "a government instituted by themselves" and he urged a spirit of moderation in the years ahead.

Moderation is discussed in Aristotle's Doctrine of the Mean. His writing on ethics works around finding the mean, or middle ground, between excess and deficiency. George Washington had wanted a proper balance between the Legislative, Judicial, and Executive branches of the government, whereas no particular branch would have excessive or deficient power in managing the government and leading the nation.

The original intent of our founding fathers was to have each branch of our government focused on their specific responsibilities to the people. The Legislative branch is to write the laws. The Executive branch is to execute these laws and the Judicial branch of our government is to ensure the laws fall within the parameters of the U.S. Constitution, mediate disputes in civil matters, and to render fair judgments' in both civil and criminal matters. Today we find the Judicial branch legislating new laws and the Executive agencies cherry picking the laws to enforce or adhere.

It is time for our political, governmental, and judicial leaders get back to the basics and start honoring the original intent of our Constitution. Every year that our legislatures are in session, rather it is at the federal, state or local levels. The citizens of this nation are losing more and more of their rights, freedoms and liberties. It is the responsibility of every citizen to hold those who are in a political office accountable. The reasons' politicians get away with a lot is because many people are apathetic and don't want to know what is happening in their federal and state capitals. Many people think they can't do anything about the corruption and incompetence by government and political leaders. As a citizen one MUST get involved. It is everyone's civic responsibility to do so.

It becomes very disturbing that many people when they go to the voting booths vote according to their political affiliation and not the individual. It's time to stop voting straight party lines and be discriminative on who they are electing. America needs a new breed of legislatures, which truly represent the desires of the people and not the desires of back-room party leaders. Many of our political leaders seemed to have forgotten that they are in public service to the People and not the other way around. Today's public servants and political leaders feel that they should be governing the citizens. The original intent of the Constitution was that elected officials and public servants are responsible to, We The People. Our elected officials and public servants should be governed by We The People.

The first ten amendments to the U.S. Constitution are referred to as the Bill of Rights. These rights are sacred and cannot be infringed upon. The Constitution of the United States under the 1st Amendment states "Congress shall make no law respecting an establishment of religion, or prohibiting the free exercise thereof..." The Courts have interpreted this to mean that the state can interfere with individual rights of freedom to express their religious and spiritual beliefs. God has been legislated out of the schools, the work places, and the public places for the establishment of a non-religion. The courts have misinterpreted the Constitution in denying this most basic right.

There have been many instances throughout the country where public Nativity scenes were banned. Banning these public displays is an infringement upon the Peoples most basic rights. People should always be allowed to exercise their religious beliefs as long as it doesn't interfere with the rights of others. One needs to have respect for other religious or spiritual beliefs rather it be Christianity, Judaism, Islam, Hindu, Buddha, New Age and other religions. They are all paths that one can follow to find God.

Several years ago there was a southern county courthouse in Georgia that was forced to remove a statue depicting the Ten Commandments under the Separation of Church and State ruling. The Ten Commandments does not depict a particular religion. If there ever were a place where it is appropriate to list the Ten Commandments it would be in a courthouse. Because in these Commandments from God is where "Thou shall not steal"; "Thou shall not kill"; "Thou shall not bear false witness"; and "Thou shall not commit adultery"; it should be seen and read by every individual entering a courthouse rather it be defendants, witnesses, and the lawyers and judges who work in those courthouses.

Several years ago an Appeals Court in California had ruled that children in the public school system couldn't say the words "under God" when saying the Pledge of Allegiance. That ruling was so wrong. Not only did that court ruling violate the First Amendment pertaining to the exercising of the right to say God, but it also violated the First Amendment right to free speech. This country was originally founded when people came to the New World to escape religious persecution. No court or legislative body should diminish that most basic principle and right. Prayer or meditation in the classrooms should not be banned but encouraged by educators. Under the U.S. Supreme Court ruling of Separation of Church and State, where is it that the public school system is a state governing body? The people through their property taxes fund the public school systems. Public schools do not have the power or authority to legislate laws or deny the rights of students exercising their rights to pray.

Is it wrong to use an Amendment to the U.S. Constitution in restricting the rights of an individual or groups of individuals? In the Constitution, WE THE PEOPLE granted the legislative bodies certain responsibilities for the betterment of all. There are many in today's legislatures at the state and federal levels whom have forgotten that they are in public service to the People. Sometime ago former President George W. Bush, had wanted to restrict and prevent gay couples from being married, and he wanted to accomplish that type of restriction in proposing a Constitutional Amendment banning marriages to gay couples. That was so wrong on his desire to restrict ones right to pursue Life, Liberty and Happiness. That is an issue that is better left to the states and the people in those states to determine. The Constitution should not be abused in restricting the rights of people in pursuing Life, Liberty and Happiness. One may not personally approve of the lifestyle of the gay community because that lifestyle is not for them. However, just because an individual lifestyle may not be appropriate or desired by other people, those rights should not be infringed upon. When it comes to matters of moral behavior those are issues that the churches and the family should address instead of legislative bodies. What a person does behind closed doors, as long as it

9

doesn't interfere with the rights of others, shall be of no concern to the State.

With the many abuses of the First Amendment to the U.S. Constitution this first amendment needs to be better clarified, and the actual rights better spelled out to prevent additional abuses to the People. The Constitution should be amended that clearly states that this Nation was founded under God, and no legislative body or Court cannot restrict one's right and privilege to pursue their religious and spiritual beliefs in their own pursuit of Life, Liberty, and Happiness. The Constitution should be amended to clearly state that public schools are non-governing bodies, and the students should be allowed to exercise their right to prayer or meditation and display their religious beliefs in the public schools. These rights cannot be infringed upon so long as those beliefs do not interfere with the rights of others in exercising their spiritual beliefs. Rights contrary to what the U.S. Congress thinks cannot be legislated away. That is why they are called rights.

Another right that was granted by the First Amendment is the right of citizens to petition the Government for a redress of grievances. Unfortunately, over the years since our country was first formed those rights have been corrupted by bodies of the Judicial, Legislative, and Executive branches of the U.S. Government. Many of the States within the Union have state immunity laws to protect the states from lawsuits. There have been many court decisions that have come about in limiting the rights to address grievances in the court system where one cannot sue the federal government, unless specifically allowed by Congress.

Personally, I had a particular lawsuit that I will discuss in a later chapter against the federal government where I was denied my 1st Amendment right for redress of my grievance where the 6th Circuit Court of Appeals upheld the District Court decision where one cannot sue the government. The People have the right under this 1st Amendment to sue the government. In my particular case, corrupt federal and state employees had willfully violated federal and state statues. The U.S. Attorney's office in Columbus, Ohio wasn't interested in doing their jobs in ensuring compliance of federal laws pertaining to the job protection rights of veterans while this country was engaged in two wars, Iraq and Afghanistan.

Our republican form of government needs to become accountable for their actions to We The People.

We The People ought to take back our country from the

corrupt politicians, corrupt judges, and the corrupt bureaucrats at the local, state and federal levels. Where there is light and the ability of the People in addressing wrongs and injustices and holding those accountable in a just judicial system, corruption by public officials will fade away. The U.S. laws needs to be amended to clearly state the rights of the People under the Constitution in suing the government at the local, state, and federal level when there is a violation of law or other misconduct or legitimate grievance. No court or legislative body should be allowed to diminish these most basic rights. The people are the fourth tier of a republican government. They have final oversight over the government. However, the politicians and the government leaders have thought differently where they feel they need to control the masses. Our government has eroded where they are now 'control freaks' and feel they have the omnipresence to control as much as your life as possible. It is all about a greed and lust for power over others.

Back in the days of the Old Wild West there were only two laws that people needed to heed. Those two laws were "Do not Steal and Do not Assault another person". There is another law or rule and that is the Golden Rule – Treat others the way you would like to be treated. If only people could lead their lives according to the Golden Rule and two laws from the Old Wild West, just think what life could be like in this world. Why can't people start living in harmony with one another? Isn't that what God really wants us to enjoy? God wants us to enjoy the fruits of our labors in living a life of abundance and its many treasures.

CHAPTER 2 – STATE OF THE UNION

Each year the country witnesses a gathering of political and government leaders in Washington DC where the President of the United States speaks to the nation and world in a Joint Session of Congress regarding the state of the union. The president states the goals and objectives that the Executive Branch of the government desires to implement. In this gathering are members of the primary political parties, the Democrats and the Republicans. Whoever is the opposition party this is the time where they begin concocting their schemes to defeat the President's objectives regardless of their merit. Both parties have been guilty of this. In each election, many of the issues are a repeat of previous election campaign issues. The candidates claim they have the answers to bring about change but once elected or reelected those claims fall to the wayside only to be drudged up at election time again.

In getting back to the State of the Union speech; what does or should it really mean? What it does entail is more of a highly charged political evening instead of the real current state of health of America. Instead it should be more reflective of what all has transpired the previous year(s). It should be a time where what went well and what went not so good should be objectively brought out into the open. Isn't this supposed to be a Republic? The State of the Union should be an honest appraisal of the actual state of the union.

Unfortunately, what we find in the political mainstream is where our elected officials are in many instances more concerned of what is good for them instead of what is good for the nation as a whole. The politicians when conducting the people's business are Republicans or Democrats and at the end of the day are Americans. America needs strong political leaders who serve their nation and constituents first and their political party lastly at the end of the day. Politicians in attendance who are texting their fellow colleagues and friends on Twitter during the State of the Union is unprofessional and makes a mockery of a democratic society. During the 2009 State of the Union several Republican members of Congress showed disrespect to the President and the American people by texting on Twitter. These members of Congress need to grow up and be a true representative of their constituents.

The State of the Union gala should be less of a political event and more of an event where political differences and ideology are set aside for one evening, and the nation's business is on the platter for Americans and the rest of the world to witness. The United States is made up of a union of the states united. So why is that not reflected in the State of the Union gala event? The House and Senate are divided that night, and it shouldn't be. The U.S. Congress is divided this evening along political ideology; "Conservatives versus liberals and Republicans versus Democrats." The State of the Union event should be a reunion of the states where the political leaders in attendance are representative of their respective states. They should be seated during the State of the Union accordingly by their respective states and not seated as a Democrat or a Republican or other political party member but as an American citizen. This is a night where the President of the United States appears not as a party leader but as President of the United States for all of America in a "union of the states" event and not as a union of republicans and democrats. Would not more be accomplished by that one night than all the days of the year? Cannot political differences be set aside for one evening to bring about a united nation and a united world? What our government and political leaders do or not do in this country impacts the rest of the world. Instead of disunity but pursuing a path of unity so much more can be accomplished throughout America and the rest of the world.

America has the power and the opportunity to change the world for the betterment of mankind to bring about world peace, end the proliferation of nuclear weapons, end worldwide poverty, end civil wars, eradicate many diseases, end terrorism throughout the world, end human oppression and suffering, and to end repressive governments. There are many powerful good people in this country, if united as a just cause, whom can help bring about a new golden direction. In quoting Edmund Burke, who said it best "The only thing necessary for the triumph of evil is for good men to do nothing." It's time the good people throughout America as well as the rest of the world to stand up and be heard. The synergy of these people while working instead of independently but as a group could make astronomical positive changes throughout the world.

CHAPTER 3 – BIG BROTHER

The League of Nations after World War II evolved into what is now called the United Nations. Recent U.S. presidents have used the United Nations as an authority to go to war. The original purpose of the United Nations was to maintain peace and stability throughout the world. No doubt the United States exerts much power over the United Nations. This world body has been misused in giving authority rather right or wrong to the United States in entering armed conflicts.

Early in American History, a group of individuals which were labeled 'patriots', formed together to bring about a major change in the thirteen colonies by breaking away from the Throne of England. Of course across the pond, the Throne of England had labeled these patriots as traitors. These individuals risked both life and limb in a belief of a better way of life and political structure in the thirteen colonies by their determination and perseverance. These individuals risked it all in manifesting a new and independent nation built on a solid foundation of values where all people were created equal in the eyes of God to pursue life, liberty and happiness. The group as a whole drafted the Declaration of Independence and from that a new nation was born. The synergy of this small group was so overpowering they couldn't be defeated by the largest army and the navy that the world had ever seen at that time. Later this small nation grew and prospered into a major world super power. The United States became the 'melting pot' of the world and a beacon of light for many to follow. Many of you may have read the book 1984 written by George Orwell. This book was written in 1949.

George Orwell later died of tuberculosis at the age of 46 in 1950. What he left us was a fictional tale of a corrupt one party system that had taken over the minds and actions of the populace. This political party was called Big Brother who had a vast domestic spying program. Big Brother had surveillance cameras in every building and on every street.

In this fictional tale, there were three major world powers that controlled the world. Those were Oceania, Euroasia, and Eastasia. In this story that had taken place in London, Oceania, that country was allegedly at war with Euroasia. When Oceania was at war with Eastasia, there was peace with Euroasia. The party Big Brother had depicted a Jewish man named Goldstein that everyone hated. Big Brother fueled this hatred to control the population to serve Big Brother. They had this person

Goldstein as a person to hate and incite rage within people; so that they would support Big Brother in its war against Goldstein and Euroasia. The people had willingly given up their civil liberties to Big Brother so that Big Brother would have the tools necessary to fight this menace to their society. Big Brother laid all the blame of the suffering within the country to this despicable Goldstein. However, this was just a fictional tale or was it maybe a warning to what this country and the world could face in the future?

Now here in the United States, the land of the free and the brave, could this happen? Well, for starters, the costs would be astronomical, in installing surveillance monitoring cameras at every intersection. Who would pay for it? How can our elected officials' sell this concept to the public? I suppose they could tell us it is for our own safety.

Perhaps they could capture the license plate numbers of cars to catch people running red lights. That would pay for the costs of the surveillance equipment. My friends, 1984 has arrived, and it has been thriving.

Today, here in America, there lays the National Security Agency (NSA). The NSA, with the help of our elected representatives in Washington DC in passing laws favorable to the NSA, are conducting domestic surveillance programs to monitor American citizens. This agency uses data mining in monitoring our e-mails and phone conversations under the auspices of protecting American citizens from terrorists. Federal laws had required NSA to obtain a surveillance warrant from a special court and show probable cause that the person they wanted to monitor was, in fact, communicating with suspected terrorists overseas. However former President George W. Bush had been quoted, as claiming the process of obtaining such warrants under the 1978 Federal Intelligence Surveillance Act were, at times, "*cumbersome*".

A recent Justice Department IG report says the FBI abused the use of national security letters to collect personal data on its citizens. The FBI has been criticized in the past for its abuses of anti-terror investigative tactics by a federal judge as being unconstitutional. Americans had a person to "hate and loathe". That person was Osama Bin Laden and the Al-Qaida terrorist network. Each year Americans are rapidly losing their civil liberties so that our government could catch this bad guy. There have been opportunities to catch this madman by our military but those efforts have been thwarted by those in power. Having Osama Bin Laden on the run instead of capturing or killing him was giving those in power the justification to establish more elaborate surveillance means and more civil liberties restrictions. Even though Osama Bin Laden has been killed and if his terrorist network were also all captured and killed; would this surveillance monitoring and the restrictions on our civil liberties be lifted? I really think neither political party in Congress, the Democrats or the Republicans have the gumption or resolve neither to restore lost liberties nor to end domestic spying over non-terrorist related activities.

After serving in the United States Air Force for over 20 years I know our military can win the war on terror. However, because of political and bureaucratic blunders our military has been fighting this war on terror with its hands tied behind their backs. America has taken a downward spiral away from being the land of the free and brave to a land of fascism and Big Brother. 1984 has arrived and George Orwell's fictional tale is becoming a reality every day. The paranoid mindset within our government is where the average American citizen is feared as being the enemy and needs to be watched. It is in the interest of national security to refocus on this war on terror and to win it. If terrorist organizations are not willing to lay down their arms and join the people of the world then the people of the world needs to take the battle to the terrorists, wherever they are.

CHAPTER 4 – U.S. POLITICAL TURMOIL

The United States needs a new breed of representatives in the U.S. Congress as well as a president who will fight for the civil rights and liberties of all Americans, and who will take us away from possible future government atrocities and tyranny against its citizens. As citizens if we do nothing, evil will flourish and all will be lost. In order to safeguard our republic; individuals should heed a higher calling in forming a major political party to strengthen our nation within our borders and to seek peace with our neighbors throughout the globe.

America needs a new major political party that can see more than just both sides of an issue. I watched a trial lawyer in court talking to the jurors. That attorney raised his arm and showed the jurors the palm of his hand. He asked the jurors a rhetorical question. Do you see this hand? The jurors nodded positively. He then told them "but you only see one side of this hand". He turned the palm of his hand around for them to see the other side. He told them "there are always two sides to a story". This is where we need a political party that can look objectively at all sides of a story or issue. I am not talking about compromising but to take a different perspective or outlook, a three-dimensional look at the whole instead of the two-half sides. If you take an empty glass and pour milk half-way into it some people will think it as being half-full while some people will think of it as being half-empty. We need a new political party to see it as it is, in the whole, which is a glass of milk. Let's take a look at Social Security and Universal Health Care but looking at in the whole, three-dimensionally.

The path to fix Social Security and provide Universal Health Care to the many people with no health care coverage is to start by taking a <u>non-partisan</u> approach. In the past Congress has tried to take a bi-partisan approach but failed. Why did they fail? Politics has always persevered and then nothing gets accomplished. When Congress takes rather a partisan or bi-partisan approach to an issue, politics is in the equation. If Congress and our state legislatures would learn to take a non-partisan approach to an issue then politics is no longer in the equation. Our legislatures need to learn to be an American, first and a politician lastly. As it now stands, neither major political party, the Democrats and the Republicans wants the other party to take credit. They are both strong opposing forces. The U.S. Congress and the White House needs to do what is in the highest good for all of America and not necessarily what is good for their political parties. America and its citizens need to come first.

Social Security and Universal Health Care is an insurance plan, plain and simple. Social Security needs to be regulated by an outside entity as an insurance plan. Insurance companies are required to set up reserves to pay out future claims. Social Security needs to be regulated and not mismanaged, which is currently what is happening. Reserves need to be set up to pay out future claims. Currently, premiums collected from the American workers exceed what is paid out in benefits. The surplus funds from Social Security have been borrowed with IOUs to run other programs within the federal government. That practice needs to stop and the surplus funds set aside in reserves. If that practice doesn't end then later down the road Americans will be taxed heavily in higher premiums because of this mismanagement. Legislation needs to be introduced where Social Security has to be managed as an insurance plan for Americans with mandatory reserves set aside to pay current and future claims. A better Universal Health Care system can become a reality in this country if the major political parties come together as Americans and set up a non-partisan approach task force. This task force could consist partly of insurance executives 'on loan' from the insurance industry. This task force should look at other industrialized nations which have Health Care Coverage for its citizens, and use those ideas as benchmarks. There has been much talk about making Health Care coverage mandatory for all Americans and criminalizing those who cannot afford this insurance by paying heavy fines. The logic behind those thoughts is that car insurance is mandatory in many states. Congress is trying to compare apples to oranges. If a person drives out of their driveway and hits the neighbor's car, that neighbor incurs a financial loss. That is why we all need car insurance to pay for damages that we inflict upon others. Now if one would walk out of their house and suffer a heart attack, would one's neighbor incur a financial loss? Of course not! Making Health Care coverage mandatory with a criminal penalty is ludicrous to say the least. Mandatory Health care for everyone would put a heavy burden on small business owners. Some businesses might have to be closed with widespread job losses. In 2011 American workers have found that the premiums their employers pay are now taxed as taxable income, thus driving up the costs for health insurance for working families so that a few could benefit. This Health Care program that passed through the U.S. Congress was set up with the Robin Hood syndrome. Take those who work hard for a living so that the less fortunate will have better care.

To fix Social Security and to provide Universal Health Care coverage, politics needs to be taken out of the equation, to do otherwise; this problem and issue will persist for several more decades with nothing being accomplished. Our country already has a National Health Care plan. That plan is called Medicare/Medicaid. Medicare/Medicaid should be expanded to offer low cost insurance coverage to more Americans. Why create a whole new government agency to manage or mismanage healthcare when the federal government already has the infrastructure in-place? Get the many lawyers in Washington DC out of working on Health Care and bring in the actuary's from the insurance industry to do the number crunching. Why spend over a trillion dollars on a program that will take years to set up? After the Wall Street bailout money and the Economic Stimulus plan our country is nearly bankrupt, and heavily in-debt. Affordable health care coverage can be better provided under Medicare/Medicaid by expanding that program to cover many of the nation's uninsured. Would it not be better to open up free clinics versus opening up new Universal Health Care administration offices?

This mandatory Health Care that was signed into law was a compromise between the two political parties. The Democrats had to concede some issues to please a few Republican Senators. Those concessions were made that members of Congress knew would be unfavorable to the American people. The Republicans coined this Health Insurance plan as ObamaCare. President Obama was willing to sign any piece of legislation pertaining to Health Care regardless of the merits of the plan. The Republicans insured this program was broken so that they could vote against it and put the blame on the Democrats. This piece of legislation needs to be repelled and replaced with a workable solution. The American people need to demand action by their Representatives and Senators in Congress. The Republicans will use ObamaCare as a political football without doing anything to fix this piece of legislation. It serves their party goals. The more Americans suffer, the more the Republican Party will flourish according to their logic. People we need to change that mentality. The people will need to challenge the politicians to put politics aside vice the people will put those politicians aside and work on a plan that will make quality health care and health insurance premiums affordable to Americans. It can be done.

Congress needs to start doing what is best for America.

Our elected representatives at the federal, state and local levels need to serve WE THE PEOPLE and not those with a hidden personal agenda and focus on non-partisan solutions. Political parties are mostly necessary to get politicians elected into public office but when doing the people's business, the party hats need to come off, and our elected officials and government bureaucrats need to act as an American citizen for all the people that they are supposed to serve. When I was running for the U.S. Congress, I attended a Tea Party rally in San Antonio, Texas where I had spoken briefly. I later listened to several other speakers from the Tea Party movement. This party movement had gathered much speed across the country. A lot of that can be attributed to former Fox News Commentator Glenn Beck, Sarah Palin, and Rush Limbaugh. Tea Party members claim to be We The People. Nevertheless, to them We The People mean everyone who agrees with them and who is not a Liberal or a non-conservative. The Tea Party movement and the Republican Party propagates a hate campaign against liberals and Democrats. The liberals would like to see many of the Tea Partiers tossed into Boston Harbor. They (Tea Party) claim that President Barrack Obama is a Socialist, who wants to do away with capitalism. All the problems in this country and the world are being blamed on President Obama. This political war machine uses half-truths and political rhetoric to create as much instability and chaos in the United States to win voter support and to regain power over the American people. If enough lies are repeatedly told people will start believing in them. That is happening in America.

The Republicans in Congress would like nothing better than to see America and the global economy to slip into a great depression. They are doing everything they can to prevent an economic recovery that could help the cause of the Democratic Party and President Obama. They have many people believing that Obama is the cause of their problems. The Republican Party and the Tea Party movement do not want people to remember that under the leadership of President George W. Bush and the Republican controlled Congress the United States and the global economies suffered an economic collapse. Many of the northern states in the United States have been experiencing an economic depression.

Shortly after Barrack Obama became President, the Democrats in the U.S. Congress had an historic opportunity to quickly bring about much needed reform and an economic revival. However, because of internal party bickering and inaction they lost that opportunity to do what is right for America. The political division gap has widened where both major political parties have gone to extremism. Neither party is representative of mainstream America because of their far-left and far-right views. Neither party has the solutions to build a greater nation and world. The Democrats in Congress lack the resolve and leadership to build a better tomorrow. Extremism in both parties is not representative of mainstream America. The Tea Party movement is evolving into the militant arm of the Republican Party. Their aim is to divide and conquer the nation and its people.

For many years, I had been a conservative Democrat. When I made the decision to run for public office I couldn't run as a Republican because I didn't believe in the leadership or the causes of the Republican Party and running as a Democrat I would have been tagged as a liberal. I always believe in taking the middle ground as a Moderate taking hold of Idealism for the highest good of the people. That is what America needs, political leaders and a political organization that hold true values of being Idealists in support of, We The People. America and the world needs new leaders who are not self-serving and seeking destructive greed for power but in-service to others which hold an idealistic, visionary and futuristic outlook that peace and prosperity can evolve for the greater good of the world's inhabitants. Former Presidents Kennedy and Reagan were idealists.

"I'm an idealist without illusions – John F. Kennedy"

CHAPTER 5 – ABORTION

When it comes to abortion, there are two opposing forces, Pro-Choice and Pro-Life. This has been an emotional issue that has hit at the heart of America. There are two sides to this issue but let's take a look at it as a "whole hand" and take an objective and non-partisan viewpoint for a possible solution. Let's examine abortion and the rights of the unborn child and the rights of the mother in making a choice taking a step away from and distancing ourselves from an emotional or moral stance.

In 1973 the U.S. Supreme Court ruled in Roe v. Wade and Doe v. Bolton giving the right to abortion for any reason until viability (into the sixth month), and for any health reasons to include emotional health during the final three months of pregnancy. Previous state laws became invalidated pursuant to the Supreme Court rulings. In 1992 in the case of Casey v. Planned Parenthood, the Supreme Court reaffirmed its rulings in Row v. Wade where they stated that any law placing an undue burden on access to abortion would be struck down. Legislation such as the Unborn Child Pain Awareness Act (H.R. 3442, S. 356) requires that any mother considering an abortion first must be provided with clear and accurate information about the capacity of an unborn child to feel pain, and about possible alternatives to lessen or avoid the pain. There is scientific evidence that abortion methods used beyond the fifth month such as dilation and evacuation (dismemberment) method, and the partial-birth abortion method, causes excruciating pain to the unborn child. Any medical procedure that is used to cause excruciating pain to an unborn child, in my opinion, should be banned by law or at the minimum by the American Medical Association (AMA).

Several years ago a well-known murder trial took place in California where the Defendant, Scott Peterson, was found guilty of murdering his spouse and unborn child in a double-homicide case. So if it is murder when someone kills an unborn child of a mother why is not considered a murder when an abortion takes place? However, one does have to respect and take into consideration the U.S. Supreme Court decisions with regards to abortions. Prior to the 1973 rulings by this Court, abortions were being conducted "underground" or by the mothers themselves"; where many women died as a consequence of these abortion butchers. Personally, I would not like to see this country go back to those days. I believe there can be other ways to reduce the number of abortions performed in this country that can follow the intent of the Supreme Court.

One should believe in the rights of the unborn child. One also should consider the rights of the mother "to choose" as was granted by the Supreme Court. A woman considering an abortion should make the decision based on getting all the facts and considering all other alternatives. Abortion should never be used as a method of birth control. Since the Roe ruling, there have been roughly 50 million abortions performed in the United States. Of all U.S. women getting abortions, about 54 percent are doing so for the first time, while a staggering one fifth has had at least two previous abortions. A third of the women getting abortions have had a previous abortion performed. Half of the roughly 1.2 million U.S. women who have had abortions each year are 25 or older. Only about 17 percent are teens. The abortion rate among women living below the federal poverty level is more than four times higher than among women from middle-income and affluent households.

There should be federal legislation that will require all women seeking an abortion attend mandatory counseling classes prior to the performance of an abortion. When requested, mandatory counseling should and must be made readily available, without delay. State or federal certified instructors should conduct these classes. Counseling should be provided for other alternatives such as adoption. Ultrasounds should be conducted for each woman so that the mother can view the images and hear the heartbeat of the unborn child. There should be no coercion of the mother in making a decision as well as those who want to picket in front of an abortion clinic. People should have the right to picket provided that right does not interfere with the rights of others. Picketing in front or near an abortion clinic does interfere with the rights of others.

The states' levy "sin taxes" for the consumption of alcohol and tobacco products. Perhaps another type of "sin tax" could be levied called an abortion tax based on the income of the mother to deter but not heavily restrict abortions as an alternative birth control method. This tax could be a progressive tax levied for two or more abortions performed. No public funds should ever be provided for abortions except in rape and incest cases. Public funds should be made available should a woman decide to have her tubes tied. More education and counseling should be provided and wider availability of contraceptives along with federal and state funding for the intrauterine device, or IUDs, that don't require attention as frequently as condoms or birth-control pills. There should be no restrictions on females to include young teens that choose the "morning after pill" without a prescription. With all the birth control methods available there really should be no reason for a person to use abortion as a birth control method.   Men also have a duty and responsibility in preventing unwanted pregnancies. A female friend of mine had suggested that men should be castrated. However, though that idea might have some merits, I don't subscribe to that theory.

When people have unprotected sex, they are playing Russian roulette, in contracting a STD or a pregnancy. Federal or state funding for abortions and requested counseling should be granted to all victims of reportable rape or incest. A woman has a right to choose based on Roe v. Wade but those choices and decisions should not be taken lightly.

Now does having an abortion constitute a sin against God? God has given us all 'free will' to live our lives. Of course with this 'free will' comes responsibility.   Shortly after a woman becomes pregnant, in the heavenly worlds, a soul is chosen to be born.   Doreen Virtue, writes in 'Messages from Your Angels' "Children, who are aborted don't blame their parents, and they don't realize that they're dead either.   In fact, the souls of children who don't grow to full-term births because of abortion, miscarriage, or stillbirth stay by their mother's side. Those souls then have 'first dibs' on the next body that the mother conceives. So, if you've lost an infant or fetus and have since had another child, chances are good that this is the same soul. If the mother doesn't conceive additional children, that soul then grows up next to the mother and acts as a spirit guide. Or, the child's soul may enter the physical world and come into
its mother's family in another way, such as adoption, or by becoming the woman's niece or nephew." The child's soul wants to be born into a happy and loving family and is willing to wait for the right circumstances to manifest. Before a mother makes a final determination to abort a pregnancy, she must consider not only her needs but also the needs of the child soul. Fathers equally important consider your own responsibilities prior to and after the act of conception. A few moments of pleasure can wreck havoc in the lives of others. Are you willing to accept those responsibilities?

CHAPTER 6 – RIGHT TO BEAR ARMS

A hot issue that should have a non-partisan approach taking in respect to the Second Amendment to the U.S. Constitution is the right to bear arms. Proposed gun control legislation by our elected officials is many times geared to the wants and desires of the National Rifle Association (NRA) and not what is good for America as a "whole". The Second Amendment to the U.S. Constitution reads "A well regulated Militia, being necessary to the security of a free State, the right of the people to keep and bear Arms, shall not be infringed".

It is my belief that the government shall never infringe upon the rights of individuals that have been granted by the U.S. Constitution. It is also the responsibility of each citizen to be responsible and law abiding citizens from both the public and private sectors in not to forcibly interfere with the rights of others. Every citizen has the right to protect themselves and their families from violent assault – both in and away from the home.

Earlier I had written where it is important to take a look at the "whole" picture objectively and non-emotionally. I have always, personally favored a gun ban within the District of Columbia. Recently, that ban was proven unconstitutional. A reason for a gun ban in the District of Columbia is because that is the center of our nation's federal government. We have numerous high ranking officials who reside and work in Washington D.C. However, even though one may feel very strongly and emotionally in support of a gun ban within the District of Columbia, one needs to step away from their prejudices and emotional feelings and look at the big picture, the whole. Under the U.S. Constitution, there are rights granted to ALL citizens of the United States. If our government is successful in stripping away the rights of certain citizens because of where they reside what will prevent the government in taking away other certain rights. By looking at the big picture it is more important to preserve our Constitution.

In 1996, Congress enacted a gun ban known as the Lautenberg Domestic Misdemeanor Gun Ban. This ban covers misdemeanors; it disarms otherwise law abiding citizens for life – for offenses as slight as spanking an unruly child or grabbing a spouse's wrist. This legislation needs to be repealed. If a person hasn't acted irresponsibly with a firearm that person should not be denied the rights granted by the Second Amendment to the

Constitution.   Legislation should be granted for ownership of firearms of any individual convicted on either a misdemeanor or felony provided that the citizen wasn't convicted in committing a crime with a firearm. Now on the reverse side, or the other hand figuratively speaking, if an individual has committed a criminal act while using a firearm then they should forfeit their rights to bear Arms.

Commercial businesses and industrial entities have the right to ban any and all weapons from their place of employment or business. Likewise, federal, state, and local governments also have the right to ban all weapons on their property. It is the right of citizens to be protected from those who will cause them harm. In 2004, the gun control legislation allowing a seven day waiting or "cooling down" period had expired. The waiting period or cooling down period needs to be reinstated to prevent violent acts of passion. That piece of legislation also banned the sales of heavy assault or offensive weapons.   Owning these types of weapons goes way beyond protecting ones personal life and property.   Cop killer bullets should be banned in the United States.   Exceptions should be made for an individual which is a gun collector to own any type of firearm to include banned firearms provided that the firearm has been modified not to cause harm to any citizen.   Any type of legislation that will allow instantaneous background checks should not be allowed. There needs to be a mandatory waiting period.

Background checks should always be made to prevent individuals who cannot act responsibly in owning a firearm.   A person should be allowed to register for a permit to purchase a firearm after a background check has been made. This type of written permit should be good for 60 days to allow that person to purchase a legal firearm rather it is through an authorized gun dealer or at a gun show.

If Congress bans a certain type of assault weapon then Congress should authorize a subsidy to be made to the firearm manufacturer to cover their economic loss, within reason.   The bottom line is that guns do not kill people. People kill people. Our country needs to keep firearms away from those who seek to kill people. Along the Southwest border, many criminals are able to legally purchase automatic weapons in large numbers from gun dealers.   Those weapons are then exported to the drug cartels in Mexico.   Exporting of these heavy assault rifles are being used to kill political and government officials who are trying to restore order in Mexico. Members of Congress receive millions of dollars in campaign contributions from the National Rifle

Association and arms manufacturers to allow this ungodly practice to continue. People have the right to pursue Life, Liberty and Happiness. The U.S. Congress needs to do whatever is necessary to keep the heavy assault weapons out of the hands of the "bad guys" while preserving the rights of law abiding citizens to bear arms.

There has been talk in Washington DC, where the Obama Administration wants to use the military to confiscate all firearms in direct violation of the Constitution. Congress or any Executive Order shall never allow this to occur. The federal government has increasingly become a corrupt and militant bureaucracy, who is actively engaged in curtailing the constitutional rights of its citizens. Those who demand their constitutional rights or who are in disagreement with the corruption in government and politics are now being labeled domestic terrorists by the Justice Department.

The President and members of Congress are sworn in to protect and defend the Constitution. When a member of Congress or the President is unwilling to perform their Constitutional duties, then they shall be removed from office or impeached. The Bill of Rights granted under the U.S. Constitution is NOT negotiable.

In the following chapters, if one would connect the dots one might come to a conclusion that the current administration is laying the groundwork for having President Obama, the last U.S. President elected by the people. If they are successful, there will only be the Executive branch of the government. The Judicial Branch and the U.S. Congress might still be operating but only under the wishes and desires of the Executive branch.

CHAPTER 7 - HOW INCOMPETENCE CAN LEAD TO CORRUPTION

Incompetence and corruption go hand and hand. One leads to the other. Corruption will lead to incompetence, and incompetence will lead to corruption. We see that every day in our governments and corporate entities. Now I didn't write this book as an expose of my own personal battle with government incompetence and corruption. I'm writing this to show how a little mistake or an incompetent person or employee can get the ball rolling where many people along the way instead of fixing a problem will close their eyes or add to this snow ball rolling down a hill. This is a story about how many government employees had the power and the authority to fix a problem but instead of doing what is right decided to take a path to harm others. Keep in mind many of these people are no longer employed within federal agencies of the United States Government as well as some elected officials who had closed their eyes to corruption are no longer in public office. However, the problems these people left behind, their legacy continues and the problems continue to mount and compound. Pray that God and the many angels may help us all.

In writing this book I'm making an effort to show that major changes in our laws need to be made to end this culture of corruption in America. Without major changes in our laws, our leaders' perspectives and moral compass are doomed to follow a history in a rapid decline of our culture and values. America could become a country no longer the conqueror of injustice and oppression throughout the world but a nation conquered by self-injustice and self-oppression. I want to show the readers here how a simple mistake or incompetence, eventually over a period of time, lead, to a major case of corruption that traveled to the highest levels within the United States government. Is America doomed to suffer the same fate of the mighty Roman Empire? The path America is on if it stays on its course then, yes, America's brilliance in the world will crumble and vanish never to rise again. When America becomes weak because of this vicious cancer of corruption, the strong across the globe and within this country will conquer her and split America apart.

In September 2002 I had completed over twenty years of service in the United States Air Force and the Air National Guard. In leaving the service, I had to fight my own personal battles of incompetence and corruption by many government employees.

I should not have to do so if people would have performed their jobs within the service regulations in regard to my pay and reemployment rights under U.S. federal laws. This is a story so that people can get a real understanding of what our veterans have to endure when leaving the service and to show how many government bureaucrats are in many cases sticking it to the veterans because of their service to their country. The Defense Finance and Accounting Service (DFAS) had gotten involved when a payroll clerk at Randolph AFB, Texas royally messed up my final separation pay and grossly miscalculated the amount of disability severance pay I was entitled to receive. This pay transaction had rejected in the military payroll system and instead of researching the problem, she forced that transaction to take into the system by creating a debt of $66 thousand in my name to the Air Force. A few months later officials at DFAS informed me that they were able to correct that debt where I now only owed them $19,995 and to please remit the full amount. This corrected debt amount was for federal tax withholding. I was outraged in receiving this news. Now I could write numerous chapters on how that all impacted my life. Doing so in this book will be taking away the spirit and intentions of these writings.

The reason DFAS withholds federal income taxes on those receiving a disability severance payment are because they (DFAS) refuse to make a minor coding change in their computer system. Military disability severance pay is considered non-taxable income. In my particular situation since the military office at Randolph failed to deduct federal taxes DFAS should have just left that issue alone.

In St Clair v. United States, the Appellant Court in 1991 upheld a federal statue granting tax exemption to veterans receiving a disability severance pay. DFAS and the Internal Revenue Service didn't agree with the U.S. Congress and the federal court in regard to a federal statue. Since DFAS was not a party to that Complaint, DFAS had continued to withhold federal income taxes and leave it up to the service member to find a way to claim that as non-taxable income. It took months of writing letters and making phone calls to find a resolution. The only way for a service member to get that tax withholding as a refund is by submitting the court decision with the tax return. However, by doing that; it will also generate an automatic tax audit by the IRS. Since the IRS owes the veteran money, it will be many months before the IRS gets around completing their audit. So what I had to do was write to the IRS Taxpayer Advocate in

Austin, Texas where I had requested that they clear this audit. A service member should never have to go through all that bureaucratic red tape just because the IRS did not agree with the Appeals Court decision.

A year after this entire nightmare started, the Taxpayer Advocate in Austin contacted me and advised me that my tax refund was in the mail. I was excited, elated and relieved that this was all behind me. The day I was expecting my tax refund, I was literally waiting by the mailbox. Nevertheless, instead of receiving the expected refund check, I was in for a bigger surprise. I received a letter informing me that my tax refund was seized by DFAS to pay a federal debt for income tax withholding. I had already lost my business and much of what I worked for my whole life to achieve. In my case DFAS seized my income tax refund by fraudulent means to what later turned out to be a bogus debt that was created by DFAS. What should have happened was for DFAS to find an employee who was proficient in the use of a calculator and who knew how to prepare a simple payroll calculation. Unfortunately, in my case they were unable to perform that task. This is a federal agency that manages over a $600 billion dollar Department of Defense budget.

In response to a Congressional Inquiry DFAS advised U.S. Representative Mike Oxley, May 2003, that they will need till August 2003 to research this problem. Later that September they would respond to the Congressional Inquiry in an elaborate scheme to what the FBI would later classify as a Conspiracy to Commit Fraud and Theft. Previously, DFAS had advised me that the previous entitlement of the disability severance was miscalculated, and it should have been 66K and that I owed them $19995. If DFAS had originally taken the time to actually calculate what the disability severance payment should have been they would never have come up with 66K, which is why DFAS needed more time.

The response they made to Congressman Oxley was that I was only entitled to receive 61K, but I still owed them $19995 plus interest accumulating at 3% per month. In order to come up with the same amount of debt they had to make many changes to tax withholding and other deductions. They advised me through the congressman that I could seek a waiver through DFAS provided, I signed a Promissory Note acknowledging my agreement to that debt. Obviously, since I suspected they were trying to scam me, I refused to sign the Promissory Note; to get them off the hook. Later I filed a lawsuit in a U.S. federal court after being threatened with legal action through the Justice Dept.

In this Federal Court it came out that every individual that has ever received a disability severance payment, that entitlement was miscalculated in favor of DFAS. There are maybe thousands of veterans who have been cheated out of their entitlements by DFAS. It would also come out that there are thousands of military members, who have received corrected W-2s that have not been reported to the Social Security Administration and the IRS. These problems are still on-going with no corrective action planned. I had provided this evidence to the IRS, but they refused to take further phone calls from me in regard to these issues. How do you think these "black" secret programs are funded in the government? No elected official no matter how corrupt would ever consider funding for some government programs and operations that go beyond a civilized nation.

Much of this evidence of possible criminal misconduct by DFAS employees and senior management had been submitted to DCIS, AFOSI and later the Department of Defense Inspector General. Because these allegations involved senior level personnel, the DOD Inspector General dropped the case. I had been fighting very powerful bureaucrats who personally manage over a 600 billion-dollar defense budget. Because this possible criminal activity involved DOD personnel, the FBI lacked the jurisdiction to investigate and prosecute. The DOD does a fantastic job when investigating fraud and other criminal acts that are committed against the DOD. However, when they themselves commit criminal acts, they rarely investigate if there are high level individuals involved. The laws need to be enforced when those who work in the public sector commit criminal acts against its citizens.

There are many individuals within the Department of Defense who hold a contemptuous attitude towards America's men and women who are in harm's way. Their actions are in a way sabotaging the war effort in Afghanistan and Iraq. When they take the law into their own hands because of their federal employee or government statue, they are being traitors to their own country. The end result of my legal battles with the corrupt business practices of DFAS was where I did receive my tax refund; that fraudulent debt was extinguished; DFAS kept the federal and social security taxes that should have been remitted to the U.S. Treasury; and DFAS kept my final separation pay.

On November 14th 2003, President George W. Bush sent a Memorandum for the Heads of Executive Departments and Agencies. The subject of this memorandum was the "Return of

Activated Military Members to Federal Civilian Employment. In this memorandum, the president stated *"The Federal Government will continue to be the model for employer support to the Guard and Reserve. We are guarantors of the rights of returning service members under the Uniformed Services Employment and Reemployment Rights Act, and I am personally committed to providing each of them with our full support, recognition, and assistance. Accordingly, I hereby direct you to grant Federal employees under your authority who are returning from active duty 5 days of uncharged leave from their civilian duties, consistent with the provisions of Federal law."*

Federal agencies responded to the president's memorandum by denying reemployment rights to returning Reservists where since February 2005, one law firm alone had represented 1,802 Reservists in federal USERRA cases. Undoubtedly federal agencies did not share in President Bush's vision as well as his directive to immediately reemploy returning Reservists. In an Oct 31st, 2007 hearing Senator Daniel Akaka, D-Hawaii, Senate Veterans' Affair Committee chairman expressed his frustration with the volume of federal public sector claims related to federal military service by stating *"It is simply wrong that individuals who were sent to war by their government should, upon their return, be put in the position of having to do battle with the same government in order to regain their jobs and benefits. "*

On Mar 1st, 1999 I was recalled to extended active duty from the Ohio Air National Guard and reassigned to the Air Force Personnel Center to work on a joint project involving the Air Force, Air Force Reserve and the Air National Guard. I was a dual status Air Technician with the Ohio Air National Guard. While on active duty I incurred a service connected disability where I was later separated on 29 September 2002. I had an agreement with my employer, the Ohio Air National Guard, that upon completion of this project I would have job restoration rights to my civilian federal employee position under the Uniform Services Employment Reemployment Rights Act (USERRA). When I was separated by the Air Force, I was denied reemployment by my former employer. I was advised to apply for reemployment with the Office of Personnel Management. Several months went by with no response. Eventually, I had to seek the assistance of Republican U.S. Representative Mike Oxley. The Office of Personnel Management responded that they were waiting for an answer from the National Guard Bureau (NGB). The NGB never responded. Later I would seek assistance from the U.S. Department of Labor/VETS and the U.S. Attorney's office in Columbus, Ohio. Several months went by with no resolution.

My next step is where I wrote a letter to the White House seeking assistance. The White House later wrote me back and advised me that the Department of Defense will address this matter. The Pentagon did meet with officials at the National Guard Bureau. NGB refused to comply with the provisions of the USERRA and their orders to reemploy me. I was forced to file a Complaint in U.S. Federal District Court since the U.S. Attorney's office didn't want to pursue this matter in Court against the state of Ohio Adjutant General. The U.S. Attorney's office in their Motion to Dismiss cited state sovereignty and that they (the state) could not be sued. In their Motion to Dismiss, the Dept of Justice's lawyer filed as evidence a personnel action form, Standard Form 50, which showed my full social security number, place of birth, residence address, and date of birth in direct violation of the Privacy Act of 1974. I filed several Motions regarding this unlawful act. Knowing that they (Justice Dept) could lose this case of that wrongful action enlisted the aid from the State of Ohio Attorney General. The Ohio Attorney General's office filed a Motion to Dismiss claiming state sovereignty that the state of Ohio has immunity from lawsuits.

The State of Ohio was not a party to this suit, but they intervened to obstruct justice. The Justice Dept lawyer then tampered with that evidence to cover up the misdemeanor. By tampering with that evidence; he committed a possible third degree felony. The District Court dismissed my lawsuit and ignored all my Motions as well as my Motion for a Protective Order that I was seeking to prevent identity theft since all of my personal information to include my social security number became a public record for the world to view. It was not until I filed an Appeal did the District Court removed that document that was exposing me to worldwide identity theft from evidence.

The district court reaffirmed state sovereignty over the Ohio National Guard. I was quite shocked and taken back that the U.S. Attorney's office in Columbus would allow a state to have sovereignty over a U.S. federal military installation. Later efforts by the attorney that co-authored this legislation and efforts made by President Bush, Secretary of Defense Donald Rumsfield, and Ohio Governor Bob Taft were fruitless in convincing the National Guard Bureau and the Ohio National Guard to comply with U.S. federal laws. The National Guard is the beneficiary of the USERRA.

CHAPTER 8 – MINI-PENTAGONS

The major problem that I had encountered was where the National Guard Bureau and the state Adjutant Generals did not support the provisions of the USERRA when it applied to its full-time technician force. So I ended up doing battle with both the state of Ohio and the United States government where they have been vigorously defeating USERRA claims. My lawsuit in U.S. Federal District in Columbus, Ohio was against the United States Office of Personnel Management and the United States Ohio National Guard. However, since there was a violation of the Privacy Act by the opposing counsel with the U.S. Department of Justice, the state of Ohio Attorney General entered this complaint in an apparent criminal act to obstruct justice. Later I would re-file this Complaint in U.S. Federal District Court in San Antonio, Texas against the Ohio Adjutant General and the Human Resources Officer as an individual action. I was still a resident of Ohio. The state Attorney General again reentered this lawsuit, even though the state of Ohio was not a defendant, to represent the defendants in this case.

Again I had to deal with the state immunity laws in Ohio. In my experience, the Ohio National Guard was intentionally violating federal law because it is extremely difficult to bring a state entity into Court because of the state immunity laws. The U.S. Attorney's office was unwilling to enforce U.S. federal laws that were grossly being violated by a state entity. These state immunity laws are a breeding ground for corruption by state agencies. State immunity laws encourage public sector employees to run afoul of the laws without accountability to the citizens of the States. A State cannot and should not be able to claim immunity from U.S. federal laws. However, that practice occurs all the time. Claiming immunity under state statues is one thing but a State should not be allowed to claim sovereignty over U.S. federal laws. The state of Ohio has been successful in doing so. The U.S. Justice Department is sleeping on the job.

When I was originally a civilian Department of the Air Force employee with the Ohio Air National Guard, the military chain of command extended from the Wing, to the state headquarters (Hqs Ohio Air National Guard, at Rickenbacker ANGB), to the Air National Guard Support Center, to the National Guard Bureau, the Department of the Air Force and the Department of the Army, the Secretary of Defense and finally rests with the President of the United States. However, today, that chain of command has been changed.

Lt Gen H. Steven Blum, former Chief of the National Guard Bureau (NGB), was ironically in Columbus, Ohio explaining his vision for a more efficient and accessible force at the nation's adjutant generals meeting on May 18th, 2003. General Blum on that day ordered the state headquarters for the state Air National Guard and Army National Guard headquarters to merge with the state Adjutant Generals. The states were ordered to complete this transformation on October 1st, 2003. Prior to this May 18th meeting, the Hq Air National Guard had merged with the National Guard Bureau. What did that action accomplish? General Blum, a three star general who later had his position upgraded to a four star general, was successful in seeking autonomy for the National Guard from the Armed Forces of the United States.

The military chain of command now rests with the state Adjutant Generals in each state. The governors of each state have very limited control over the day to day operations of the Guard. The President of the United States no longer has authority over the National Guard of the United States by that reorganization. The real day to day commander-in-chief is now the Chief, National Guard Bureau. The Air National Guard is ranked as the fifth largest air force in the world. The Army National Guard has the 8th largest army in the world. This is a highly lethal force and combat ready force without the control of an elected civilian commander-in-chief. Former President George W. Bush was asleep on the job in relinquishing his command over the Guard.

The states now have sovereignty over the Guard bases on U.S. military installations. Why would a state governor need assets of tactical fighter planes and the B-2 bombers for state emergencies? Now I can only speak about Ohio's claim to sovereignty over the U.S. military installations that host the National Guard. The state Attorney General's office was successful in their claim with the assistance of the U.S. Attorney's office in Columbus. President Obama or the next president, someday, will have to resolve this issue as a possible national security issue. The corruption that I encountered with the Ohio National Guard and NGB poses a grave danger to this nation. One can conclude this is a very serious matter when you had General's defying a state governor, former Republican Governor Bob Taft, former Republican U.S. Representatives Oxley and Regula and President George W. Bush. A host of other agencies to include the Pentagon and the U.S. Dept of Labor were also involved in restoring the rights of service members under the USERRA.

The action by NGB, on May 18th 2003, created mini-pentagons within the states, which brings up a Constitutional question. Article I of the U.S. Constitution bars states from maintaining troops and ships. Tanks and warplanes had not yet been invented. Article I, Section 10 of the U.S. Constitution states: "No State shall, without the Consent of Congress, lay any Duty of Tonnage, keep Troops, or Ships of War in time of Peace, enter into any Agreement or Compact with another State, or with a foreign Power, or engage in War, unless actually invaded, or in such imminent Danger as will not admit of delay." Since the states are maintaining troops, tanks and warplanes and since the chain of command no longer resides with the President, that brings up a Constitutional question; are they in direct violation of Article I of the U.S. Constitution?

In that May 18th 2003 meeting with the state adjutant generals, General Blum talked about his plans to "transform the National Guard, both Army and Air Force side, into a more agile force that would better be able to team with the other five services – the Army, the Navy, the Air Force, the Marines and the Coast Guard, so that the American public gets the best of all the services capabilities that a joint team can provide." Those were colorful words but so was the Declaration of Independence. This is a case where the NGB and the state adjutant generals had really sought their own independence from the Armed Forces of the United States and the President of the United States. This civil
case in U.S. Federal Court brought out a possible national security issue and the possible threats this issue poses to the people of the United States, in my briefs to the Court. Later I would pose a question to the State Inspector General of Ohio to determine if this meeting was a possible Act of Treason against the people of the United States. Predictably, that office never responded to the evidence of possible Treason that I provided.
In this case, I had brought up some possible criminal violations of law that had been committed by some individuals at the state and federal level. Attorneys at the U.S. Department of Justice and the State of Ohio Attorney General's office were more concerned about defeating a valid USERRA claim and Privacy Act of 1974 violations versus a possible national security threat. They had the evidence of this possible Act of Treason but the lawyers were more dedicated to winning the civil case at any expense. The best interests of the country and the worldwide war

on terror as well as the reemployment rights of Iraqi war veterans were of no concern to these government lawyers. Doing what was right for the veterans took a back seat in favor of corruption.

Under United States Code Title 32, the National Guard of the United States falls under a federal executive agency. By the efforts made at NGB on May 18th, 2003, the National Guard of the United States was disbanded where the command and control rest with the state Adjutant Generals versus the President of the United States. However, the Department of Defense is maintaining the funding from U.S. taxpayers for the states to maintain a large and heavily armed force. Obviously, I voiced my concerns to former Ohio Governor Bob Taft and to former President George W. Bush, in late 2005 and early 2006.

In the John Warner Defense Authorization Act of 2007 there was a federal statute that granted the president to take control of the National Guard of the United States in a national emergency. That piece of legislation was later repealed in 2008 in a letter to Congress where all 50 governors opposed the increase in power of the president over the National Guard. It could make someone wonder on how all 50 governors agreed on an issue. No doubt this legislation to repeal the authority of the president originated through the National Guard Bureau and the state Adjutant Generals. There has been prior legislation granting the president control of the National Guard.

The Militia Act of 1903 organized the various state militias into the present National Guard system. In the National Defense Act of 1916 this act abandoned the idea of an expandable Regular Army and firmly established the traditional concept of the citizens' army as the keystone of the United States defense forces. It established the concept of merging the National Guard, the Army Reserve, and the regular Army into the Army of the United States in time of war. The act further expanded the National Guard's role, and guaranteed the State militias' status as the Army's primary reserve force. The law mandated use of the term "National Guard" for that force, and the President was given authority, in case of war or national emergency, to mobilize the National Guard for the duration of the emergency.

The National Guard Mobilization Act of 1933 made the National Guard a component of the Army. The Total Force Policy, in 1973 requires all active and reserve military organizations be treated as a single integrated force; reinforced the original intent of the founding fathers (a small standing army complimented by citizen soldiers with the right to bear arms).   Government lawyers from NGB, U.S. Attorney (Columbus, Ohio) and the State of Ohio Attorney General's office with the assistance of the U.S. Federal Court in Columbus ignored all this prior legislation. This was a case of government lawyers 'gone wild!'

The National Guard is wrong in asserting their autonomy from the Armed Forces of the United States. Under Ohio Revised Code 5919.05 commissioned officers of the Ohio National Guard shall take and subscribe to the following oath of office: "I ...., do solemnly swear that I will support and defend the constitution of the United States and the constitution of the state of Ohio, against all enemies, foreign and domestic; that I will bear true faith and allegiance to the same; that I will obey the orders of the president of the United States and of the Governor of the state of Ohio; that I make this obligation freely, without any mental reservation or purpose of evasion, and that I will well and faithfully discharge of the duties of the office of .... in the National Guard of the United States and of the state of Ohio, upon which I am about to enter, so help me God."

National Guard members have a dual status at both the state and federal level authority. Under Section 1002.57 (VBIA, Public Law 108-454), "The National Guard has a dual status. It is a reserve component of the Army, or, in the case of the Air National Guard, of the Air Force. Simultaneously, it is a State military force subject to call-up by the State Governor for duty not subject to federal control, such as emergency duty in cases of floods or riots."

In a legal brief to the 6th Circuit Court of Appeals, I had argued "The Plaintiff would like to draw attention to 10 U.S.C. Subtitle E, Part 1, Chapter 1011, Section 10501 which states: "(a) National Guard Bureau. – There is in the Department of Defense the National Guard Bureau, which is a joint bureau of the Department of the Army and the Department of the Air Force. (b) Purposes. – The National Guard Bureau is the channel of communications on all matters pertaining to the National Guard, the Army National Guard of the United States, and the Air National Guard of the United States between (1) the Department of the Army and the Department of the Air Force, and (2) the several states." I then argued "The individual military units (Guard) within the states are a composite of the Air National Guard of the United States and the Army National Guard of the United States.   The governors of each state have limited authority over the individual Guard units.   The state Adjutant General is a federally recognized military officer, appointed who is appointed by the state Governor. The Pentagon funds the National Guard Bureau which in turn funds, the Air National Guard and the Army National Guard."

But unfortunately I lost that case where prior U.S. Supreme Court rulings were overturned. So on that day, May 18th, 2003, where the state adjutant generals and the National Guard Bureau had sought out autonomy from the command and control of the President of the United States; our country now has a massive Guard Air and Army forces no longer under the control of the Pentagon, which is a very serious threat to our national security and every citizen and elected official should be concerned. Our Democratic form of government is in possible jeopardy. A question that I keep asking myself, if the National Guard Bureau does not support the provisions of the laws pertaining to the USERRA, which are laws designed as being the cornerstone for the Guard and Reserve, then what other laws are they not supporting? I had to deal with numerous DOD employees who have been waging their own "personal war" against those who are serving our nation at a time when this country is at war defending civilization and our democratic form of government.

In November of 2006, I had sought out assistance with Republican U.S. Representative Lamar Smith requesting Congressional Hearings in regard to the corruption at NGB and DFAS. I provided extensive documentation in regard to this corruption. Congressman Smith has been a long-term member of Congress. His office later replied to me *"That since the Democrats have taken control of both houses of Congress this is a problem that the Democrats need to fix."* Congressman Smith dropped the ball. The American people need to elect representatives who are willing to work hard in preserving our rights and the American dream that are fading away.

I had argued in the District Court *"Under Sec. 1002.305(b), if an action is brought against a state by a person, the action 'may' be brought in a State Court of competent jurisdiction according to the laws of the state. It is the admonition of the U.S. Supreme Court that courts should give a liberal interpretation of the USERRA in favor of the service member. Using a liberal interpretation as pertains to this case, if under 1002.305(b) where an individual 'may' bring an action into a state court it sounds to reason that an individual 'may' also bring an action into a district court. Since the Office of Personnel Management in addition had a responsibility to fulfill under the USERRA then bringing this action into this Court under Section*

4324 was proper by the Plaintiff.

The State of Ohio is claiming state sovereignty. However, they have not indicated what specific state sovereignty issue is involved. If there are no state sovereignty issues when the U.S. Attorney General brings an action against a state in a district court then it sounds to reason there should be no state sovereignty issue if an individual brings an action against a state.

State agencies have an obligation to comply with federal laws, and they should not be immune from prosecution to willfully violate federal laws. Now what could be especially troubling is when heavily armed military forces such as the Guard are allowed to violate federal statues as well as defying Presidential Memorandums with no accountability. Allowing the state of Ohio to infringe upon federal sovereignty is setting a very dangerous precedent in having a large military organization to pick and choose what laws they decide to comply with when it is in their best interest to do so. Granting the State of Ohio's Motion to Dismiss can have a serious and grave impact as well as a threat to the national security interests of the United States was as evidenced in this case, senior guard military officials were willfully defying directives issued by the Department of Defense.

The USERRA is a piece of legislation that is vital to the national security interests of the United States. Any action by government officials in weakening these statues should be a cause for serious alarm. The USERRA has over 70 years of federal legislation by the U.S. Congress in strengthening the nation's armed forces to defend against threats to our democracy and freedoms both domestic and foreign. The long-term best interests of what is best for the national security of the United States should outweigh any state sovereignty issue, if any. The efforts by the Ohio Attorney General's office to consider as unconstitutional in having the Ohio Air National Guard to comply with federal statues is appalling and their action poses a grave threat to the United States as well as to future presidents, where military officials are free to do as they please under the disguise of state sovereignty.

At the conclusion of the Constitutional Convention, Benjamin Franklin was asked, "What have you wrought?"
He answered, "…. A Republic, if you can keep it."″

When the District Court in Columbus and the 6th Circuit Court of Appeals ruled in favor of the Defendants, that was a day of victory for government crime and corruption. On March 11th, 2008, the district court in San Antonio ruled in favor of the

Defendants which was a day of victory for government crime and corruption. On March 11th, 2008, the district court in San Antonio ruled in favor of the defendants in my second lawsuit against the individuals. The state attorney general in Ohio fought vigorously in defending these corrupt business practices. My legal battles ended that day after a long four-year battle. The result because of these corrupt business practices was that I was denied my reemployment rights granted under a federal statue; I lost 20 years of federal civil service time; I was unable to seek my federal retirement; and I lost all of my FERS contributions that I made over the years; and the Courts had legitimized the May 18th 2003 possible Act of Treason against the people of the United States.

As I stated earlier in another chapter The Department of Defense had met with senior officials from NGB in getting them to comply with U.S. Federal laws. NGB resisted all efforts made by the Pentagon by asserting their new autonomy from the president and the Pentagon. In the final analysis, had the NGB not restructured in their apparent Act of Treason, the laws pertaining to the USERRA would have been complied with not only for me but the many other Iraqi war veterans who have been denied reemployment rights.

With the new restructuring of the Army and Air Guard units, the nation's part-time forces would undoubtedly curtail the response time of the National Guard to respond to emergencies at home and abroad. This restructuring that has already taken place could slow down the mobilization process to deploy in future conflicts; such as deploying in the aftermath of Katrina.

In the Federalist papers No. 4 dated November 7th, 1787, John Jay had written a discussion on militias. He stated "It can place the militia under one plan of discipline, and, by putting their officers in a proper line of subordination to the Chief Magistrate, will, in a manner, consolidate them into one corps, and thereby render them more efficient than if divided into thirteen or into three or more distinct independent companies."

It was the intention of our founding fathers that the state "militias" would be consolidated into one corps hence the creation of the National Guard of the United States. But May 13th 2003 changed all that into separate military guard entities no longer under the command and control of the President of the United States. The state of Texas as well as a few other states maintains their own "state militia" in addition to the National Guard.

The term "militia" stood for "military force" when the

Constitution was ratified. John Jay later writes in The Federalist "What would the militia of Britain be if the English militia obeyed the government of England, if the Scotch militia obeyed the government of Scotland, and if the Welsh militia obeyed the government of Wales? Suppose an invasion; would those three governments (if they agreed at all) be able, with all their respective forces, to operate against the enemy so effectually as the single government of Great Britain would?" When the United States was first formed, there was not a central military force. The states did need a military force to protect them from invasion from other nations. The governors needed a force for civil strife and insurrections.

The National Guard in the past has been used to assist victims of natural disasters. A question that should be asked is "How much force is required for natural disasters?" Do the state governors need the assets of air-refueling tankers, bombers, and tactical fighters for natural disasters or civil unrest? Would these assets pose a danger to the country should a state decide to secede from the Union? The U.S. Congress should look into this matter and determine if those assets to include personnel would be better utilized being transferred to the Air Force and Army Reserves. With the repeal of the John Warner Defense Authorization Bill of 2007 the president lost control of the Army and Air National Guard to the state adjutant generals.

There has been speculation that should the United States suffer another terrorist attack or other grave national emergency on our shores that the U.S. Constitution should be abandoned. I disagree wholeheartedly with that type of talk. It is so imperative that our Constitution is strengthened and adhered too.

The U.S. Constitution grants the establishment of three pillars of the government, the Executive Branch, Legislative Branch and the Judicial Branch. Should the U.S. Constitution ever be abandoned or free elections denied then there would be no authority to maintain the three branches of our government. Our government would turn into a military junta or a civilian dictatorship where the American form of democracy will be toppled since there would be no succession of power in the Office of the President. Those voices who speak of abandoning the U.S. Constitution in the event of another national emergency from a terrorist attack, those voices should be considered and questioned for a 'hidden' personal agenda.

When military officers (NGB) feel they are above the laws of this nation and do not support the president as being the

Commander-in-Chief of the total force structure; as granted in over 100 years of legislation. Those actions put now at risk the American form of a Republic. I don't think the Iraqi people will come to the aid of the United States in liberating Americans by reestablishing a Republic as a form of government.

CHAPTER 9 - TEXAS SECESSION

When I was running for the U.S. Congress, I started coming across people from the Tea Party movement that were talking about Texas seceding from the union. They were claiming that under an agreement made with the U.S. government in 1845, Texas retained the right to secede. These people really believed that they would be better off with Texas being an independent nation. My first thoughts were that 'here I am running for the U.S. Congress and if these Tea Party members are successful, I'll be out of a damn job.' The U.S. Supreme Court ruled in Texas v. White 1869 that no state has the right to unilaterally secede. In 1861 Texas did secede from the union and joined the Confederate States of America. We all see how that worked out. After the American Civil War and subsequent restoration to the Union, Texas entered a long period of economic stagnation. Mexico controlled the Texas territory until 1836 when Texas won its independence, becoming an independent Republic.

In April 2009 Governor Rick Perry appeared to endorse a resolution supporting Texas sovereignty at a Tea Party in Austin Texas, following a question from a reporter. Gov Perry stated *"There's a lot of different scenarios. Texas is a unique place. When we came into the union in 1845, one of the issues was that we would be able to leave if we decided to do that... My hope is that America, and Washington, in particular, will pay attention. We've got a great union. There's absolutely no reason to dissolve it. But if Washington continues to thumb their nose at the American people, who knows what may come of that? But Texas is a very unique place, and a pretty independent lot to boot."* Governor Perry is correct of the different scenarios. If President Obama, a Democrat, does get reelected then the American people will see Texas, and other Republican states attempt to secede from the union.

On February 17th, 2009, House Concurrent Resolution 50 was introduced and on May 30th, 2009 the resolution passed in the House with amendments. The resolution reads in part:
RESOLVED, That the 881st Legislature of the State of Texas hereby claim sovereignty under the Tenth Amendment to the Constitution of the United States over all powers not otherwise enumerated and granted to the federal government by the Constitution of the United States; and, be it further:

RESOLVED, That this serve as notice and demand to the federal government, as our agent, to cease and desist, effective immediately, mandates that are beyond the scope of these constitutionally delegated powers; and, be it further

RESOLVED, That all compulsory federal legislation that directs states to comply under threat of civil or criminal penalties or sanctions or that requires states to pass legislation or lose federal funding be prohibited or repealed.

The conservative state legislators do not fully understand is that Texas did secede from the United States and joined the southern Confederacy; but Texas reentered the union after the conclusion of the American Civil War thereby making any prior agreements to later secede mute.

Governor Perry and many of the conservative state legislatures somehow believe that if they are successful in leaving the union, there will not be any repercussions from the U.S. government. Do they really think if they act upon their desires to secede, the U.S. government will tell them 'Sorry things didn't work out, and we wish you well?'

As of the later part of 2010 the unemployment rate in Texas is much lower than the rest of the country. Texas enjoys a striving business climate where many experts rank Texas number one as being conducive to commerce and business. It is expected that the San Antonio/Austin corridor will be the first region to pull out of the current Great Recession. Texas enjoys a healthy federal employee workforce, with numerous military installations and VA centers. Many corporations have relocated their main corporate offices to Texas. The construction business in Texas is still robust.

However, Governor Perry and the Republican majority in the Texas legislature want to change all of this. The greed and lust for power are a driving force behind this movement. This greed and lust for power, if left unchecked, will lead Texas into an economic stagnation and depression. When the Economic Stimulus plan that President Obama was trying to push through Congress, Gov Perry commented that Texas will not take a dime. Later Gov Perry demanded that money and that money were not spent towards creating jobs or reviving the lagging economy. It was spent to balance the state budget in Texas.

Should these forces be successful in breaking apart from the United States, America will no longer be a global super power. Terrorists cannot harm America; any attacks from them will only make America stronger and united. America, however, could fold from within.

If Texas is successful in seceding from the union, Texans can expect to have their social security, and the many federal employee pension benefits frozen or eliminated. Texans could experience a major federal employee layoff putting additional burdens on the state. Texans would be witnessed to the massing of federal and state forces in a possible clash, setting off civil strife and another civil war.

The United States could also experience other states joining the cause of the Lone Star state. Texans would no longer enjoy the liberties granted under the Bill of Rights in the U.S. Constitution. The new currency from the Texas treasury would be highly devalued and worthless. As Texans we may not agree with all the nonsense that comes out of Washington DC but this is our country, and we must demand accountability and positive change in Washington, as well as at the state capitals. Anarchy and civil unrest are not the answer.

Sometimes politicians, business, and government leaders come up with some bonehead ideas and make decisions without really thinking of the consequences of their actions. Texans and the citizens across the U.S. spectrum needs to Reclaim America. American citizens for too long have given up their power to the corrupt politicians and government bureaucrats. American citizens have already seceded their power; it is time, to reclaim what is right and just, and reclaim that power. The pursuit of life, liberty, and happiness is a just and divine cause.

CHAPTER 10 – ENERGY FUTURES

The Roman Empire was one of the world's largest empires in the world that was spread among numerous countries and continents. What remains of that great empire is now a tiny nation in Europe, Italy. So what happened to this vast empire that eventually crumpled away? One word – CORRUPTION. What was once a powerful and mighty empire became a weak nation with no moral compass to keep on track. It is very possible that a nation can make headway when its leaders are corrupt. History shows us that. But that corruption eventually becomes the downfall of a nation. Corrupt business practices will also become the downfall of a major corporate empire.

We saw that at Enron. Enron became America's largest corporation. It got there because of the corrupt business practices of its greedy leaders. Even so, then look what happened, almost overnight, it crumpled and fell. A corrupt entity rather it be a government or a corporate entity eventually will not be able to sustain itself over a long period of time. It will start to unravel at the seams. But the legacy that Enron left the world was speculative trading in oil futures on the New York Mercantile Exchange, which would later drive-up oil prices forcing the United States economy and the many other nations around the globe into a deep recession.

In April of 2008, the United States Department of Energy under the Bush Administration released a prediction that gasoline prices will hit four dollars per gallon by the summer. By them issuing that statement became a green light for oil prices to rise. Three weeks later prices at the pumps surged beyond four dollars per gallon. The primary drivers in the rising price of gasoline at the pumps are the oil speculators. Prior to Enron, Commodity producers primarily traded futures contracts to maintain stable prices for products of crude oil, corn and soybeans.

Because of the falling dollar investors have rushed into the oil commodity market. These investors are large investment banks, mutual funds and private hedge funds. As of June 2008 it was estimated that half of the investment dollars came from pension fund managers. So every time the U.S. Dept of Energy, pulls out their crystal balls, and makes a prediction of rising crude oil prices, the oil commodity futures will rise drastically. Now when there is a drastic fall in oil futures, American workers can expect to see their pension funds dry up.

American greed for investing in oil futures has driven up the prices of gasoline not only for Americans, but it has also impacted countries throughout the world. Many European countries are paying well over $9 per gallon at the pumps. It is not just OPEC causing these rising fuel costs but also American investors. Many OPEC nations are sitting back and enjoying this greed for oil speculation. Iran and Venezuela must love the investors in America for driving up the price of crude oil for them. Those OPEC nations are getting richer every day while America is losing their standard of living each day.

This victory for OPEC is even sweeter because Americans are doing it to themselves. Iranian officials are laughing all the way to the bank thanks to Wall Street. The United States and the European Union have been demanding that Iran stop their Uranium Enrichment Program. The European Union had offered Iran cash incentives that were rebuked by Iran. Because of the greed on Wall Street, they don't need those cash incentives that were offered by the European Union. As a matter of national security the U.S. Congress needs to ban market speculation in oil futures on the New York Mercantile Exchange. Maybe if the U.S. Congress bans market speculation in oil futures that will lower the price of oil; then maybe Iran would be willing to talk nuclear disarmament.

Since the year 2000, the United States has lost millions of manufacturing jobs. American corporations are closing plants to have goods manufactured in China to take advantage of cheap labor costs. China's factories are notorious for being energy inefficient where they are steadily consuming increasingly amounts of crude oil. The wars in Iraq and Afghanistan have been weakening the dollar where the United States has become a major debtor nation to China and Japan. Industries across the board had felt the pinch of rising fuel costs. Economically, this has impacted the United States and other industrialized nations into a vicious cycle. American corporations need to bring the manufacturing jobs back to America. If they do not they will perish.

The war in Iraq has created massive deficits for the United States. The United States now owes China and Japan well over a trillion dollars in funding for the occupation of Iraq. This massive war debt, because of the prolonged wars, has dwindled the value of the dollar. The enemies of the United States do not need to conquer America. All they need to do is sit back and watch how greed, corruption, lust for power, is gradually bringing about the fall of America.

CHAPTER 11 – ENERGY DRIVES ECONOMY

Energy is what drives the global economy. Without reliable sources of energy the whole world economy and economic society would slide to a screeching halt. This is not negotiable and that is exactly what is happening today. People are negotiating America's and the planet's future to meet selfish self-interests. As an alternative to oil the United States and other countries are in the process of building new nuclear facilities. Building a nuclear power plant may take well over ten years to complete. Nuclear power is not an alternative energy solution. The fuel that is used to power the nuclear power plant is uranium. Many scientists are predicting that the fossil fuels such as coal, oil, natural gas, and uranium is rapidly being depleted. It is estimated that in fifty short years all of these sources of energy will be depleted. The human race will then have to wait a few billion years to extract the fossil fuels. If mankind does nothing to curb the consumption of fossil fuels then the children being born today will be left with a global energy crisis.

The United States and the world need to look for renewable sources of energy. Green energy sources such as the wind and solar is where mankind needs to pursue further. There are major disadvantages and future problems with nuclear power. A byproduct is nuclear weapons to obliterate mankind from this planet. When it comes to waste disposal, the byproducts of the fissioning of uranium-235, remains radioactive for thousands of years, requiring safe disposal away from society until they lose their significant radiation values. A problem that is looming ahead is that in a few years the world's existing power plants will begin to decay and breakdown. In a few years across the world, there will be more "Three Mile Island and Chernobyl" disasters looming over everyone's heads.

It is very possible for America and the world to become energy independent. We already have the technology to accomplish this goal. One aspect of solar energy is 'concentrating solar power' (CSP), a technique of concentrating sunlight using mirrors to create heat, and then using the heat to raise steam and drive turbines and generators, just like a conventional power station uses by burning coal. It is possible to store solar heat in melted salts so that the electricity generation will continue through the night or on cloudy days. This technology has been generating electricity successfully in California since 1985 and half a million Californians currently receive their electricity from this source. CSB works best in hot deserts. It is feasible and economical to transmit solar electricity over very long distances to anywhere in the United States. A portion of the Mojave Desert would be sufficient to meet the entire U.S. demand for electricity.

Construction of concentrating solar power could meet the energy demands of Mexico. Iran has entered the nuclear age by the construction of a nuclear power plant even though they are sitting on a major reserve of oil. They want to use the nuclear power plants to supply the electricity to their country allegedly for just peaceful purposes. They have plans to build additional nuclear power plants. With construction of concentrating solar power built in the hot desolate deserts of Saudi Arabia, Kuwait, Iraq and the Sahara Desert, the electricity demands for the entire Middle East to include Russia and Europe could be met. With this would bring much needed jobs to the Middle East. This could spread an economic resurgence in the Middle East where unemployed people instead of joining terrorist organizations, who have been used as pawns to commit evil acts, could be employed bringing a better life for themselves and their families. Now I have worked at construction in Texas during their hot summers. I can sympathize that building these types of solar facilities out in the hot desert could be very grueling to the construction workers. Using space age technology, clothing to cool the workers could be easily developed. Producing these types of 'hot weather gear' could generate a whole new industry.

Governments across the globe must impose laws, rules and regulations whereby utility companies must comply with a fair "Net Metering" (the buying of excess energy generation from the consumer). The technology to power our cars is already here where the cars of the future instead of being a major consumer of energy resources and pollution outputs, will be a major producer of energy resources where at the end of the day, people will plug in their hybrids to "download" the excess energy created into the power grid. The world needs to pursue the renewable green energy technologies such as Solar-Photovoltaic, Geothermal, Wind, and Biofuels. The internal combustion engine is a dinosaur and should be replaced with a more energy efficient engine, external combustion engine that can be powered by natural gas, gasoline, diesel, powdered coal and other source.

Global oil executives and automakers do not want energy efficient automobiles. Many of you will recall the automotive engine with the carburetor. The oil industry bought the patents for the 100 mpg carburetor engine so that consumers will spend more money purchasing and consuming gasoline. Automakers no longer produce the automobiles with carburetors. The oil industry has brought to the world climate change and environmental disasters such as the one in the Gulf of Mexico.

In March of 2009, I founded a business entity, Satgaud Energy (meaning God's energy), with the intention of developing the Next Generation Electric Hybrid Vehicle (NGEHV). Satgaud Energy is committed to natural energy research that will later be shared with many others across the globe. Sometime ago I had communicated to the Obama Transition Team, prior to the inauguration of President Obama, in regard to this project where the vehicles of tomorrow can be powered by harnessing the energies of the wind and sun.

Today that is quite possible. The technology used to power the NGEHV can also be used to power small aircraft. The rising cost of aviation fuel and other costs have been detrimental to general aviation. If produced this new type of aircraft could revitalize the general aviation industry. The NGEHV encompasses three sources of energy; the sun, the wind, and recyclable energy. Many components of this vehicle generate electrical energy while at the same time serves as a mode of transportation. This 'green hybrid' is a moving electric power generator.

Many of the electric cars being produced today have a maximum range of 135 to 200 miles. By recycling the energy used in propelling this type of vehicle, the driving distance would be unlimited. The same applies to small aviation aircraft. Electricity is a source of energy that can be recycled. At the end of the day instead of recharging the batteries, the owner will plug in the NGEHV; to drain off the excess energy back into the electric grid. Many automobile manufacturers have spent millions of dollars in promoting their hybrid vehicles as green. Even so, those vehicles still consume gasoline, and the electric engines have to be recharged by electric utility companies which burn coal and natural gas. Nuclear energy is by far not green energy since the radioactive waste that is buried will present environmental hazards for many centuries.

The vehicles of tomorrow do not have to be powered by the world's rapidly depleting fossil fuels. The NGEHV is a concept of a completely reengineered vehicle from bumper to bumper. Most of the components and parts for this vehicle do not exist in today's automobiles. The automobiles, trains and airplanes of today consume massive amounts of fossil fuels to power them, but the automobiles, trains, and airplanes of tomorrow could be massive producers of alternate sources of energy.

Today's automobiles are designed to absorb the massive energy forces from a collision, thereby causing extreme bodily injuries to the occupants. Every consideration was made to design the NGEHVs as a safe mode of transportation. There needs to be a zero tolerance for death or serious injury from vehicle accidents. Because of the light weight of the NGEHV, not requiring an internal combustion engine, there is a better way to design a vehicle where instead of absorbing the energy forces in a collision the NGEHV can be produced to 'deflect' those energy forces away from the colliding vehicles.

I reside in the San Antonio area, and I've witnessed several horrific crashes where the occupants were severely injured or killed. The safety concepts from the NGEHV could have saved those people. I had written Ford, General Motors and Toyota in regard to the technology pertaining to all of this and neither automaker were interested in eliminating the internal combustion engine or the safety concepts from this type of vehicle.

The Obama Administration has been pouring billions of dollars to finance the production of electric vehicles claiming this is an investment in Green Energy. Replacing gasoline, as a fuel, by using electricity from power utility companies that burn coal and natural gas is not 'green energy'. They are just exchanging one fossil fuel for another. The public utility companies are excited about seeing electric vehicles on the road. They see dollar bills in their eyes. A greater demand for electricity usage increases due to this pseudo green energy, business and residential customers will see skyrocketing energy costs. Utility companies have enjoyed the 'free energy' from wind turbines and solar panels; however, those cost savings haven't been passed along to the consumer. The U.S. Congress needs to introduce legislature directing those cost savings to the consumers.

As a side note, nearly a year ago I had sent a fax to a White House staff member, requesting their assistance in making this type of vehicle available. Predictably, they never responded or showed interest. When people start paying over four dollars a gallon for gasoline, if not more, you have the White House to thank. The major insurance companies and major auto manufacturers are not interested in having safer vehicles on the roads.

Now as many of you recall in 2008, there was an economic collapse on Wall Street. The Federal Reserve and Treasury Department had to intervene to prevent a global economic depression.   The banking industry has blamed the problem on the huge amount of foreclosures. The blame for this economic collapse was the housing bubble that busted where people who were in high interest rate mortgages could not make their house payments. It all became a vicious cycle. The high rate of mortgage foreclosures brought about a glut of housing on the market where the demand for new home purchases was much less than what was available on the real estate market which brought about a deflation in home market values. People's homes were worth less on the market than their mortgages. The banks had been packaging these new home loans as derivatives. By doing so when people gotten behind on their mortgage payments due to a loss of a job, or other economic hardship, the loans could not be refinanced. This was partly responsible for the economic collapse on Wall Street.

There were many other factors involved in this collapse that have been overlooked.   One was the outsourcing of good paying jobs overseas.   When people are unemployed their purchasing power of goods and services are greatly reduced. This leads to many more manufacturing job losses. The real catalyst for this started back in the summer of 2006.

The oil companies were successful in raising the price of gasoline at the pumps; aided tremendously by the oil futures investments.   The oil industry boomed at the detriment of the global economy.   By the summer of 2008, gasoline prices in America soared past four dollars per gallon. Transportation costs in providing goods and services became exorbitant. People had less disposable income, which leads to many more plant and job layoffs in an unending cycle.   It was not until the prices of gasoline at the pumps' fall; did the economy begun to stabilize. Affordable energy is what drives the economy. A thriving global economy requires stable and reasonable energy costs to the consumer.

OPEC nations may not totally agree to what I have said. Many OPEC nations would like to see the price of oil to continue to rise so that they may prosper. However, those actions will only wreck havoc right back to them. They will not prosper if the world slips into a global depression.   The world is now (2011) as a result of the turmoil in Northern Africa and the Middle East; is facing steadily increasing oil prices.   Long term effect could trigger another economic collapse of colossal proportions.

As of the writing of this book, the world has witnessed a nuclear tragedy in Japan. I'm not an engineer but it has become apparent that once a nuclear energy plant becomes operational, it cannot be easily shutdown. What will the world experience when the current nuclear plants across the world become aged and needs to be safely shut down? Until this question is answered there should be a worldwide moratorium on building anymore nuclear power plants. Any politicians who promote nuclear energy should be considered a snake oil salesman.

There are many other alternatives to energy. Even Nikola Tesla's many electric energy projects should be considered before nuclear energy. In the Appendix to this book, there are discussions on other forms of energy; one in particular is Thermal Energy. Another concept to consider is using the oceans to generate electricity to power the cities. Along the oceans in the world are the largest cities. Harnessing the energy that is created by the oceans could meet the entire electrical power needs for the world. The tides come in and the tides go out. This is hundreds of thousands of tons of a push/pull energy that is scheduled by the moon, it is forever. With the emerging economies in the world there will not be enough coal and natural gas to meet the growing future energy demands. We have all been witness to the dangers of nuclear power plants.

CHAPTER 12 – IRAQI INVASION

In March of 2003 the United States with the patronage of other countries launched an invasion to disarm Iraq and remove Saddum Hussein from power. Previously, in September 2002, President Bush addressed the UN in regard to Iraq, requesting that the UN move to send weapon inspectors back into Iraq. The United States had difficulty getting the cooperation of other members of the UN Security Council to agree. Many countries were fighting and stalling the sending of weapon inspectors into Baghdad. It wasn't until several months later, in December of 2002 that the UN Inspectors arrived in Baghdad thus giving Iraq three-month advance notice. Now if I were an evil dictator sitting on top of a pile of weapons of mass destruction knowing that the UN will be looking for my pile, what would I do if I was that evil dictator?

"After all the denials that I have made in regard to my stockpile, I sure wouldn't want to be caught with those weapons and give the United States a reason to send over their bombers again. So who would be my friends in the world besides France? Syria is right next door to me. We both loathe and hate the United States almost as much as we hate Israel. If it wasn't for the United States, Israel may not have survived. My other Arab neighbor Jordan has close ties to the United States. Kuwait, Saudi Arabia, and Turkey all have friendly ties to the United States, so they are out. Iran hates America but we did fight a war with them. Iran cannot be trusted like I cannot be trusted, so my only option is Syria.

So what I would do is by piecemeal in not drawing attention from the American spy satellites; I would move those weapons out of this country. France and other countries are helping me in delaying the arrival of the UN Inspectors. They can buy me time. I'll be sending cars and trucks in small numbers across the border into Syria so as not to draw attention. Should it later be discovered that Syria is assisting me, America will not want to expand their threats or military involvement into Syria. So America will keep it quiet and classified. If I can I'll try and bury as many weapons as possible in the sand. Since I have members loyal to me in this effort, they could also tell of their activities. I would have all of them executed. Dead men tell no tales. So that is what I would have done if I was an evil dictator in Iraq."

Now rather that scenario actually happened, no one living

in Iraq would know or be willing to publicly speak about it. It has come out that Saddum Hussein made billions of dollars in the UN Food for Oil Program. He became quite wealthy from his kickbacks. He had the money and the means to bribe many people. If the United States had backed off in invading Iraq, eventually he and his sons would have obtained nuclear weapons or dirty bombs on the black market, and he would have been willing to use those weapons. America has many enemies throughout the globe. Sometimes our friends in the world, if the price is right, will betray us.

There was a former Iraqi general who had appeared on Fox News telling the reporters who were interviewing him that prior to the war starting and before the UN Inspectors returned to Iraq, that stockpiles of WMD's were trucked over into Syria. The Iraqi dictator was confident the UN Inspectors would find nothing because they were all sent to Syria. The Germans, French, Russians and other countries with their stall and delay tactics gave this dictator time to hide those weapons. President Bush at the time with the disclosure by this Iraqi general should have capitalized on those facts to continue to get the support of the nation behind him. That was a missed opportunity to at least justify the war, unless our intelligence agencies already knew that in advance of when hostilities began.

During the first Gulf War, in the liberation of Kuwait, the Coalition should have finished the mission when there was a positive world opinion. The 100-Hour Ground War should have been a 100-Day Ground War to finish the job. We had the military forces not only from the United States but also from all of our allies. The Iraqi Army suffered heavy bombardment, and they were surrendering to reporters traveling with the Coalition troops. Didn't matter who they surrendered to, they just wanted out of where they had been while trying to dodge America's non-stop bombing raids. American military forces were within forty miles of Baghdad. When I was in the Air National Guard, I had the opportunity to talk too many of the returning troops and many of them expressed their disappointment and remorse that the job was not finished. They all knew that eventually our country would need to return to finish the job. The mission was not complete. Invading Iraqi troops occupying Kuwait were killed but the Iraqi dictator was allowed to remain in place

In February 1991, the hostilities had ended but the war never ended. The United States established a No-Fly Zone over northern and southern Iraq to contain Saddum Hussein. Because of this and the continued threat that Saddum Hussein might regroup and launch another invasion against one of its neighbors, the United States had to maintain a large military presence in the Gulf. One has to wonder what would have happened if the White House under President George Herbert Bush had allowed our troops to finish the job by capturing or killing Saddum Hussein and his closest advisors while the United States had the support of the world. Patriotism was strong in America at an all time high since World War II. The rest of the world respected us and were in shock and awe of the capabilities of our military. If we had completed the mission, we would have been able to draw down our military to a pre-Kuwait level. By the United States maintaining a large post-Desert Storm military force in the Gulf; this later became fuel to inflame Islamic radicals to form terrorist organizations.

The miscues of the first Bush Administration lead to the birth of new terrorist organizations such as Al-Qaida. These terrorist organizations now had a real cause. September 11th may not have happened if we had finished the job back in 1991. However, in defense of the United States; if terrorist organizations want to blame someone on why the United States remained in the Gulf, they should be blaming Saddum Hussein. He is why the United States remained in the Gulf States after Operation Desert Storm.

CHAPTER 13 – Part 1 WINNING THE PEACE IN IRAQ

The occupation and conflict in Iraq continue to this day (March 2011) with no signs of being over. The Democratic presidential candidates in the 2008 elections pledged responsibly ending the war immediately, if elected. They were elected but the wars continue. Other candidates wanted the United States to be in Iraq for a hundred more years. The United States invaded Iraq with a small number of boots on the ground as an occupying force. This occupation festered outrage among many throughout the world where an insurgency grew and festered. Where we had once stayed not long enough we are now staying too long. There was no insurgency in Iraq prior to the March 2003 invasion. As long as there are American boots on the ground in Iraq, there will always be an insurgency. For this insurgency to end, American troops need to be back on U.S. soil.

The American military destroyed the infrastructure when invading Iraq only to be replaced with a government based on ethnic origins and not political beliefs. One has to wonder what the second Bush Administration was thinking in forming this type of government. That would be like our political parties; here in the United States as being formed under, for example, the White Party, the Black Party and the Hispanic Party, or it could be the Southern Party versus the Northern Party. If those types of parties existed in our government, we would all be in civil strife, but that is what we have done to the people of Iraq.

The second Bush Administration installed a government guaranteeing the people of Iraq civil unrest for many years to come. Under a democratic form of government in Iraq, the Shiites will always rule as an ethnic and religious majority party. Ethnic or religious origins should never be allowed as a political entity in a democratic form of government. We have all heard the phrase, politics and religion do not mix. The current form of government in Iraq, installed under the Bush Administration has got to be one of the biggest blunders our country as ever achieved in recent history. History will eventually judge America harshly as being wrong and incompetent invaders and occupiers. Iraq needs a government that speaks for the entire nation based on beliefs and culture and not ethnic or religious origins and one that is not oppressive to its people. I do not think many will argue that this current conflict in Iraq is a sequel to the first Gulf war from 1991. Sure Kuwait was liberated but Saddum Hussein allowed to remain in power. The threat from him was far from over. The Russians wanted the conflict to be over but with Saddum Hussein still in power. Prior to this conflict, they had lucrative trade relations with Iraq. They saw that the reconstruction from this conflict would be very beneficial to them. The first President Bush buckled with pressure from Russia in not finishing the job. Now had the first President Bush been willing to finish the job so that all of our troops could come home, most likely he would have been reelected to a second term in office. At the time our country had world support in liberating a foreign power from Kuwait. This support came from many nations by sending troops as well as funding for the war. He was happy and satisfied declaring victory with a 100-hour ground war.

Prior to the invasion of Kuwait, Iraq had amassed troops along the border ready to strike. They felt they had a right to take Kuwait as a former province. Their main concern would be how would the United States respond? Former Secretary of State Madeline Albright gave them the response they wanted to hear. She expressed a deep and grave concern but also told the world that the United States did not have any military partnerships with Kuwait. At the time the president was vacationing. Now this is where a president has to be decisive. Do you take a diplomatic initiative or do you use a military option first? Now had the United States responded immediately by sending fighters and bombers to that region in the early hours of that conflict, Saddum Hussein would have backed off and there wouldn't be a need for our country to go to war. Thousands of lives, including the lives of many American soldiers would still be living today had President Bush been decisive in the early hours of that conflict. The September 11th attacks would never have happened since the United States would not have had a major military presence in the Middle East.

Now if the United States had finished the first Gulf War and removed Saddum Hussein from power, there would have been stability in the Middle East instead of what we find happening in this volatile region. Gulf War II erupted because there appeared to be strong evidence where Iraq still had weapons of mass destruction and there was a growing fear that Iraq would use those weapons against their own people or other neighboring Arab countries. Another strong fear was his capability of obtaining nuclear weapons that could be used against Israel and the United States.

Nevertheless, we are still in this conflict with no end in

sight. This conflict in Iraq has lasted longer than World War II. Think about that for a moment. During World War II, our country was on a war footing in the Pacific against Japan and Germany in Europe. The United States was united in fighting their foes. The people back home labored in factories producing war munitions for our men and women wearing the uniform. Our nation was focused on ridding the world of the evils of Japanese imperialism and Nazi Germany. Americans back home put their soul and passion in fighting for a just cause. The world was in serious peril from the aggressive actions that were undertaken by Japan and Germany. The people back then during World War II were in synergy with one another. The combined energies of the people in our country were united against Japan and Germany.

Synergy occurs when two or more elements are brought together and joined to bring about increased energies than what would not occur if those elements were acting independently. Synergy can work in both a negative and positive way. Synergy in the medical healing process can be best be summed up where the benefits of using two or more different medicines together are greater than if used independently.

So what is happening in this prolonged conflict in Iraq is that our country lacks the synergy to bring about an end to hostilities. The former Bush Administration had been determined to "stay the course" in Iraq thinking that things might eventually improve. This "stays the course" mentality has cost the needless loss of life of many young service members as well as many innocent Iraqi citizens. The mindset had been to throw billions of of dollars at a problem without really examining and pursuing a strategy to end hostilities. Greed has taken over where it was more important to satisfy defense contractors under the Bush Administration. There are many individuals and corporations which have been reaping the financial benefits of having this conflict prolonged as long as possible.

The Halliburton Corporation has obviously reaped many benefits from this war as well as the first Gulf war. Halliburton Corporation was awarded many lucrative defense contracts that were not opened to competitive bidding. The greed for oil rich Iraq has been the primary driver in why we went to war and why our country will remain in Iraq. The needs of the Iraqi people and what is good for them have taken a low priority. Our government, political and military officials have made numerous mistakes and numerous bad decisions, and they have all been steadfast in not wanting to fix their mistakes or change their course. Now rather the new Obama Administration can responsibly bring peace to the region remains to be seen. The Obama Administration has withdrawn its combat forces but that nation is still in political and economic turmoil. The people want equal representation.

This nation allegedly went to war to end the corrupt regime of Saddum Hussein and to remove weapons of mass destruction. By doing so, the Department of Defense (DOD) and the Bush White House planners destroyed unnecessarily the infrastructure in Iraq. Democracy was forced upon the people of Iraq. The people of Iraq had little to say about what type of government would be best for them. So a puppet government instituted by the United States and Great Britain was forced upon them.

The mistakes that the former Soviet Union made in their incursion and occupation into Afghanistan are in many ways the same mistakes the United States has undertaken in Iraq. This war in Iraq is not really another Vietnam but another "Soviet Afghanistan". The former Soviet Union lost many young soldiers due to an insurgency designed and created by the U.S. Central Intelligence Agency (CIA). The CIA made a pact with the devil in supporting Bin Laden in his efforts to rid Afghanistan of the Soviet menace. The CIA played a part in the birth of the current Al-Qaida terrorist organization. It's ironic how things have gone full circle. We have all heard the phrase "what goes around comes around" i.e. karma.

After the Soviets retreated from Afghanistan, this was an opportunity for America to do the right thing by providing economic assistance to war-ravaged Afghanistan. The United Nations blew an opportunity in filling a void in the political structure after the Soviets left the country. Instead two opposing groups, the Northern Alliance and the Taliban fought a lengthy civil war which continues to this day (2010). If the United States had earlier made non-military financial support to that region in an effort to provide stability that investment would have paid off. So instead of the United States providing a multi-million dollar economic aid package, after the Soviets left, the United States has now been providing billions of dollars with no end in sight in assistance to a country that attacked America on September 11th.

CHAPTER 14 – Part 2 – WINNING THE PEACE IN IRAQ

By December 2003, the Iraqi dictator was captured. His sons were previously killed many months before and most of his henchmen either killed or captured. The United States allegedly went to war to remove weapons of mass destruction (none found) and to topple the Iraqi regime. With the capture of Saddum Hussein the "mission was complete". The United States should have begun troop withdrawals from Iraq. The insurgency was minor at that point in history. Granted a complete troop withdrawal from Iraq could have created a vacuum.

Earlier the world body was willing to assist the United States with the reconstruction and rebuilding the infrastructure of Iraq. But, there was money to be made in lucrative contracts and the powers to be in the United States didn't want those contracts awarded to other countries. American greed prevented and blocked the assistance from many nations. This greed has prevented alternative peaceful solutions from taking hold. The United Nations could have sent peacekeeping troops from Middle Eastern nations to fill the potential vacuum of withdrawing American troops.

This greed and corruption have led to the deaths of many more American soldiers and Iraqi civilians. The greed gave fuel to a stronger insurgency – evil begot more evil. Corruption is like a vicious cancer that spreads. It is so important that senior leaders, rather they are in private industry or the public sector needs to exhibit ethical and integrity standards and a moral compass. When they fail to do so, those who report to them will either lose respect for their leader or accept that it is moral behavior, which leads to corruption.

In January 2007, former President Bush announced that additional more troops would be sent to Iraq to curb the violence. The move for this troop surge was many years too late. The Pentagon and White House have maintained a long-term strategy of remaining in Iraq for many years to come. There has been very little real interest in developing strategies on ending this war responsibly in Iraq. President Bush held the belief that Iraq was the "central war on terrorism" even though America was attacked by a terrorist group in Afghanistan.

The Bush Administration preoccupation and obsession over Iraq overshadowed a much greater threat to the national security. North Korea became a nuclear power with Iran on their heels in their own nuclear program development. Iran has been very successful in dragging their feet buying more time to get their nuclear program up to speed. Both countries view the United States as being bogged down in a winless strategy in Iraq and Afghanistan. Iran has taken advantage of the lack of border security along the Iraqi and Iranian border. Foreign fighters have easily slipped into the country with the financial support of Iran and Syria. The past winless strategy by the United States will continue to bring instability to the region for many years to come. The intentions of the United States in remaining in Iraq for many years have manifested into such that. Now had there been a strong effort to win the war quickly peace would have had a chance to manifest itself within the region. The opportunities for peace were there, but the Bush Administration was wearing blindfolds.

There is still a chance to bring peace to this region. In order to do so corruption needs to be eradicated and replaced with competent leaders who maintain the belief that 'the good of the country takes precedence'. Our country needs a president who is a statesman versus a politician. Our country needs a president who is President of the entire United States and who will work for what is good for the country and the world instead of what is good for their political party or hidden personal agendas.

There is a solution to the war in Iraq where the United States can still leave with honor while at the same time curtail the on-going insurgency. The United States needs to win the peace in Iraq. This war has been very costly in terms of dollars and the many lives lost. The Shiite's and Sunnis have been fighting for centuries. The only viable solution for a lasting peace is to divide Iraq into three main provinces to separate the Sunnis, Shiites, and the Kurds. The ethnic and religious groups need to choose their own form of government whatever that may be as long as that government is not repressive to the people. The United Nations need to come in with peacekeeping troops from other Arab nations to fill the vacuum.

The generals at the Pentagon have all claimed that it will take several more years before they can restore order in Iraq. It is imperative that the White House finds some generals who can restore order and peace in Iraq. Maybe it is time that Arab nations enter the picture to restore the peace in Iraq since the United States has been claiming they are unable to restore order in Iraq. Countries such as Saudi Arabia, Jordan, Kuwait, Egypt,

Lebanon and other nations within the region need to step up to the plate. This multinational force under the command of the United Nations could enter the country at the time that U.S. forces are withdrawing from the region to the levels of pre-1990 Iraqi invasion of Kuwait. The United States could maintain air bases as a small military presence with a non-combative mission.

The United States won the war in Iraq the day Saddum Hussein was captured by U.S. troops. That is when there should have been a concerted effort to withdraw American forces. Now some may argue that we had to stay because of the foreign fighters that crossed over the Iraqi borders. These foreign fighters were there to kill American troops and those Iraqi citizens who were assisting Coalition forces. Most likely, with the absence of American troops to shoot at, these foreign fighters will no longer have a "cause" and just might have to go back home to find a "real" job.

Now there are many that have benefited by this conflict in Iraq. For example, former Vice President Dick Cheney has profited immensely from this war with his large portfolio of stocks in the Halliburton Corporation. The American taxpayer has funded this war so that others may become very wealthy. The longer it takes for the American forces in Iraq to remain in-place, the wealthier these people become. Due to incompetence, greed and corruption this war is lacking serious tactical strategies in ending this conflict.

The path to peace in Iraq is for a concerted effort to be made to bring about a lasting political solution between the Kurds, Sunnis, and Shiites. If they are divided into three separate provinces with their own separate legislative branches in each province peace may have a chance to take hold in this country. With three separate provinces or states the political parties will be founded on political principles not ethnic divisions. There will be a need for an Executive branch or body to oversee the interests of the country of Iraq. At one time before Saddam Hussein there was a Monarchy that ruled the nation. Possibly, in order to establish national pride to bring the country together a Monarchy could be reinstated not to rule or govern but to unite the diverse people in that region much along the same lines as the current British Throne.

The Executive Branch of government within Iraq could manage the oil revenues to share among the three governing provinces. Diplomatic efforts should be made with the Kurdish rebels in accepting their border between themselves and Turkey. Multinational forces made up of Arab nations could maintain the borders from Syria and Iran and get the cooperation of Syria and Iran in not interfering with the internal security of Iraq. Intermediaries between the Arab multi-national forces and those organizations which are raging attacks against the citizens of Iraq need to come into play in trying to get these militias in laying down their arms.

There are many factions in Iraq, who are trying to destabilize the country with violence. They are killing one another not only because of centuries old hatreds and feuds but also as a protest to the U.S. occupation of Iraq. Those actions are only keeping the U.S. troops' presence in Iraq much longer. Extremist radical groups love the presence of the U.S. troops in Iraq so that they can kill American soldiers. This conflict in Iraq is helping Syria and Iran in developing their own weapons of mass destruction to be used against Israel while America is distracted.

The previous Bush Administration was not willing to change course, but it is something that the Obama administration will have to seek a lasting solution least America remains in Iraq indefinitely. Until that day arrives for peace many more lives will be lost. Greed and corruption over oil revenues and military contracts has prevented and will continue to prevent a peaceful solution to the problems and conflicts in Iraq. It will take President Obama and those who follow him to undo the damage and harm caused by the Bush administration in both domestic and foreign affairs. America will need to earn the trust and respect of foreign nations. That will be an uphill battle, but it can be accomplished.

There is no reason why all U.S. troops that are in harm's way back on U.S. soil by September 11th, 2011. Since World War II the United States has been involved in numerous civil wars starting with Korea, Vietnam, Afghanistan, and Iraq. Americans have shed much blood in these civil clashes without learning anything from these conflicts. With the exception of Vietnam, U.S. troops are still struggling in these conflicts.

In Korea there have been minor skirmishes' with a ceasefire in-place. The war has not ended. U.S. troops still remain. This has been a tough struggle. The United Nations needs to take on a leadership role in the world. The United Nations has to intervene to win the peace in Korea, Iraq and Afghanistan. The UN has been silent too long. The world body needs to come together as one for global peace and prosperity. Most of the power within the United Nations rests with the UN Security Council instead of the General Assembly.

The UN should revise its charter and give broader power to the General Assembly. Having all the power with just a few countries has brought turmoil, wars and misery throughout the world. Many times the UN Security Council has become a bully pulpit. The UN needs to use the collective power of ALL nations to end the menace of destruction and poverty to seek a peaceful resolution in Korea, Iraq and Afghanistan. The likelihood of the Pentagon in Washington DC pursuing a path of winning the peace in these conflicts is slender. A passion for peace does not exist in Washington. The nations of the world have the power to end these regional wars and oppression for the highest good of the earth's inhabitants.

The next chapter is about winning the peace in Afghanistan. A thought that you should keep in mind when reading this chapter is this: If your neighbor's dog comes over into your yard and kills your cat; do you go over and shoot your neighbor?

CHAPTER 15 - PEACE IN AFGHANISTAN

"To announce that there must be no criticism of the president, or that we are to stand by the president right or wrong, is not only unpatriotic and servile, but is morally treasonable to the American public." – President Theodore Roosevelt

In October 2001 the world witnessed U.S. forces, in response to the September 11th attacks on U.S. soil, conducting aerial bombing raids against suspected Al-Qaeda training camps and Taliban strongholds in Afghanistan. The Taliban is a banafi Islamist political group that governed Afghanistan from 1996 to where it was overthrown by U.S. and NATO-led International Security Assistance Forces (ISAF). This extremist group is believed to have been organized a decade ago with the help of Pakistani intelligence to fight the Indians in disputed Kashmir. The Taliban had been officially recognized by Pakistan, Saudi Arabia, and the United Arab Emirates.

The origin of the Taliban and Al-Qaeda was constructed by the CIA and the ISI (Pakistan's Inter-Services Intelligence Agency). There are claims that the CIA and ISI provided arms and money, and the ISI recruited radical Muslims from around the world to fight against the Soviet invasion of Afghanistan. Osama Bin Laden, a former CIA operative, was one of the key players in organizing training camps for the foreign Muslim volunteers.

Bin Laden had forged a relationship with the CIA funded Al-Qaeda and Taliban. The leader of the Taliban is Mullah Omar. In the early weeks of this war in Afghanistan, U.S. forces had the opportunity to kill or capture both Osama Bin Laden and Mullah Mohammed Omar, but because of incompetence and some bad decisions by the Bush Administration, that opportunity vanished; and both men were allowed to 'escape'.

A real American hero is Army retired Col Terry Cook. In the book "Looking for Trouble' written by Ralph Peters he writes of Col Cook: "Terry Cook was one of the great behind the-the-scenes soldiers of our time. A literal cowboy born on the edge of the North Dakota badlands, he joined the Army as an enlisted man and surfaced as a staff sergeant on a beefed-up Special Forces A-team in Angola, seventeen Green Berets pitted against 17,000 Cuban troops and East German advisors; after that, the excitement picked up. Despite a wound to his left eye, he became a Mohawk surveillance-aircraft pilot, then learned to fly helicopters, and as a officer, hovered on the Honduran/Nicaraguan border, where he navigated over unmapped jungle and arrived at his first destination to find nothing but "fire, smoke, and bodies on the concertina wire." Then there was El Sal. Terry flew night missions into every country where we officially weren't, delivering arms and calling in fire support for battles that never the official dispatches. For a break, he turned to Pakistan, studying at the Quetta staff college and kicking off his long series of cross border-border excursions into Afghanistan, where he soon gained access denied to our diplomats by playing *buzkashi*, the bone breaking Afghan version of polo, on horses borrowed from warlords. Assigned to our embassy in Islamabad, his genius for making personal connections on every side aroused jealousy from a series of ambassadors; his prescient reporting infuriated the apparatchiks of the Clinton administration; he penetrated the Pakistani nuclear testing program only to see his messages spiked; he tapped into the Taliban and, even after the State Department forced him out of the country for calling things right too often, he brokered a deal in the wake of 9-11 for terrified Taliban moderates to hand over Mullah Omar – but the Bush Administration rejected the offer. (Mullah Omar remains at large.) His final job on active duty pitted him against terrorists in the Philippines; they're dead, Terry's a retired bird colonel."

The U.S. government financial support for the Afghan Islamic militants was substantial. Aid to Gulbuddin Hekmatyar, an Afghan Mujahideen leader and founder and leader of the Hezb-e Islami radical Islamic militant faction, alone amounted to $600 million. Hekmatyr worked closely with Bin Laden in the early 1990s. In addition to hundreds of millions of dollars of American aid, Hekmatyr also received substantial sums from Saudi Arabia. There have been claims made where the CIA supported Hekmatyr's drug trade activities by giving him immunity for his opium trafficking that financed his militant faction. There are estimates that from 1985 to 1992, 12,500 foreigners were trained in bomb-making, sabotage and urban guerrilla warfare in Afghan camps the CIA helped to set up.

The Soviet Union finally withdrew its troops from Afghanistan in 1989. After the collapse of the Marxist government, tribal leaders were unable to agree on a structure for governance, and chaos and civil strife ensued, leaving the country devastated. The United Nations sat by idling without bringing stability to Afghanistan once the Soviets vacated. With the withdrawal of Soviet troops, American interest in Afghanistan ended; until September 11th. Another key player in driving out the Soviets was Ahmad Shah Massoud. Moussad at the age of 48 was the target of a suicide attack by two Arab extremists. He was killed by Al-Qaeda on September 9th 2001. It is believed that Moussad's killing was linked to the September 11th attacks.

Moussad by 1999 started training police forces, specifically in order to keep order and protect the civilian population from the Taliban. By early 2001, one million people had fled the Taliban to Massoud's areas to which he commanded. Early 2001, Massoud and a French journalist described the bitter situation of the refugees in Afghanistan and asked for humanitarian assistance in front of the European parliament in Brussels, Belgium. Massoud went on to warn that his intelligence agents had gained knowledge about an imminent huge-scale terrorist attack on U.S. soil. The president of the European Parliament, Nicole Fontaine, in 2001 called him the "pole of liberty in Afghanistan".

By the end of 2008, U.S. intelligence officials estimated there were approximately one hundred Al-Qaeda members still in Afghanistan. In 2009 President Obama expanded America's involvement in this civil war to go after the Taliban, an extremist Afghan political group. The enemy in this engagement is unknown where many of the Taliban hide behind women and children, much like the Viet Cong did in Vietnam. America has learned nothing from its involvement in the civil war in Vietnam. America is fighting an enemy in Afghanistan that they created. To the members of the Taliban and Al-Qaeda in Afghanistan and Pakistan, war is employment and peace is unemployment. The leaders of the Taliban and Al-Qaeda have an ego-centered thirst for power, much like many U.S. government leaders and politicians.

Two major super-powers started this mess in Pakistan and Afghanistan, the United States and the former Soviet Union. The Soviet Union dissolved as a direct result of this conflict. The United States is not far behind if America continues its journey in this conflict. The engagement of the United States is beneficial to its enemies across the globe by being in Iraq and Afghanistan. Should there be a real threat to the United States in the future, future presidents will have their arms tied because of this lengthy involvement. American government and political leaders believe that if its citizens demonstrate and speak out against either conflict 'that action provides aid and comfort to the enemy'.

The majority of people being killed by U.S. soldiers are Iraqi and Afghan citizens. Foreign fighters are in the minority. How can peace ever blossom with a raging war with no end in sight? Are not the previous actions by the government on why American service members are losing their lives daily in these two wars more treasonous to the American people? You cannot fight darkness with more darkness to obtain peace. Fighting evil by committing evil acts by a government entity turns that government agency on the road to corruption and destruction. By the U.S. opposing the Soviet excursion into Afghanistan created a greater menace of destruction – global terrorism.

The Taliban has become known internationally over their harsh treatment of women. Women are not allowed to work nor be educated beyond the age of eight, and only permitted to study the Quran. They were not allowed to be treated by a doctor, unless accompanied by a male chaperone. They faced public flogging in the streets and public execution for violations of the Taliban laws. One of these laws includes adultery. Instead of taking it out on the male they punish the female because they view the female as the weaker sex. The Taliban men are obsessed that their spouses might cheat on them. The Taliban men feel that if they control all aspects of a woman's life, they will be faithful.

Nevertheless, that is a problem men face globally. The real culprits are men. Men do not respect other men. For example, in the United States if a man sees a very attractive woman and, even if that man knows she is engaged or married, he will try to steal her away from the other man. If he would be successful in winning that woman over, he will possess her and do everything possible to keep her away from other men, since he knows what goes around comes around. That happens to be a vicious cycle. Men you need to start establishing values and leave the women who are in relationships alone. Establish a guy code and do not infringe upon another. If guys would learn to do that, the dating scene would all go much smoother.

When Jesus walked the earth, he came across a mob scene of men in the process of stoning a woman who was accused of committing adultery. They came to Jesus asking him what they should do. He told them "You without sin cast the first stone." They dropped their rocks and walked away. They didn't try to punish the man involved with this adultery. Men do not take your grudges out against another woman. Be respectful to those in relationships. Do not covet thy neighbor's spouse. The Taliban in Afghanistan and Pakistan will brutalize another woman whom they feel is the weaker sex instead of another man. Whenever a man strikes another woman, for whatever reason, that man is weak and insecure.

The Taliban and Al-Qaeda have been on an anti-Muslim crusade. Most recently on November 5th 2010, seventy worshippers were killed in attacks on Pakistani mosques. Pakistani Taliban claimed responsibility for these attacks. These mosques have just been one of many more that will be attacked to kill Muslims around the world. Global terrorism is not just against Judaism and Christianity. It's against all civilized nations and its people. This is a global problem requiring a global solution. The people of the world need to unite in order to preserve civilization and eradicate global terrorism.

The United Nations needs to stop sitting on its "duff" and protect the citizens of the world. The United States should not be doing this alone. Terrorism impacts the entire globe, both economically and politically. Osama Bin Laden and Mullah Mohammed Omar can best be characterized as being the Anti-Mohammed.

Both individuals are determined to destroy the Islam religion by carrying out their extremist beliefs. Their followers are only pawns into their wicked and evil business. They do not carry out the peaceful wishes and desires of God. If the world does nothing, evil will flourish and destroy mankind. God has given mankind "free will". Mankind to survive cannot give up their "free will" to the darkness. The planet's citizens should not be willing to give up their "free will" to repressive governments and organizations. Some of the current Afghan and Pakistani Taliban were children eight or ten years old on September 11th. They were still in their "sandbox days". Not knowing any better they have joined the Taliban for employment and to rid their country of foreign occupation.

Now having said all of this, does the Taliban pose a grave threat against the United States? Do Americans need to worry about the Taliban traveling to the United States in fishing boats and hurl rocks at American citizens? Undoubtedly, the Taliban have been on the wrong side of history by allowing Al Qaeda a safe haven in Afghanistan prior to Sept 11th. When America was attacked that fateful morning were there any Taliban or other Afghan nationals on those planes? No most of the terrorists on those planes were Saudi nationals. So why didn't the United States bomb Saudi Arabia instead? The Saudi's were bankrolling the Taliban and Al Qaeda. Osama Bin Laden was a former terrorist informant under the Clinton years. When the money dried up, he retaliated by attacking America.

When the weather breaks in Afghanistan (spring 2011), the Obama Administration plans to make massive attacks against the Taliban for being extremely creepy. What this will amount to is genocide against a people who do not pose a threat to America only to themselves. The CIA created the Taliban and Al Qaeda. Most Afghans have not heard yet about Sept 11th. They see a massive foreign troop presence in their country that is dropping bombs on them. The only thing the Bush and Obama administrations have accomplished is festering hate from people towards America around the world.

What the Obama administration should have done when they came into office was try to bring the Taliban into the Afghan government. This has been a prolonged civil war between the Northern Alliance and the Taliban. The Taliban are prohibited from being in the Afghan government. Peace will not manifest until the Taliban are brought into the government. That is common sense.

You cannot end violence with more violence. Instead of dropping bombs to kill people, send over teachers to educate the people. The United States Congress needs to stop this needless genocide by stopping the funding of the war and bring our troops home. Many of our troops have been on five or six combat deployments to Iraq and Afghanistan. Many of them have been shot or seriously wounded, the doctors patch them up and they are sent back into the killing fields. I have talked with several returning veterans and they have all told me, this is a war without end.

The United States won the wars in Iraq and Afghanistan but lost the peace. The Obama administration has put the nation on the same path as the prior administration. Under Bush, the central war on terror was focused on Iraq. Under Obama, the central war on terror is focused on Afghanistan. But the Al Qaeda network of terrorists who attacked us are scattered about the globe. To win the war on terror you have to go where the terrorists are located and hunt them down. Wasn't that the original plan? The U.S. taught the Taliban a lesson for providing a safe haven for terrorists. Now finish the job and stay focused on Al Qaeda. Al Qaeda receives comfort in knowing the war on terror is focused on others.

As long as this war on terror goes on indefinitely there is justification for the U.S. government to engage in unlawful wire tapping and other restrictions on Americans. Is it all about gaining absolute power over every aspect of the lives of

American citizens? Is it all about global absolute power for a New World Order? Were the Bush and Obama Administrations trying to fulfill the dreams of Hitler, Stalin and Lenin?

There may be some who wonder why the United States is still so focused on Afghanistan as well as Pakistan. For the most part, Al Qaeda has been defeated in Afghanistan. The Taliban and the Northern Alliance (now the Afghan Government) have been in a civil war since the Soviets left that country. Why all the interest not just from the former Soviet Union but the United States and China. What is attracting the attention of these world powers to include also NATO? Are they all concerned about the abuses and violence being caused by the Taliban? Afghanistan is not the only nation on the planet experiencing a civil war. There are many other nations fighting regional conflicts and internal civil strife. Why is not the United States liberating those people? For thousands of years Afghanistan has been occupied (never successfully) by the military forces of Persians, Greeks, Mongols, Britons, Soviets, and now American and NATO forces. What is there that has drawn the interests of many empires?

Hundreds of billions of dollars worth of iron, copper, rare earth metals, zinc, mercury, tin, fluoride, potash, talc, asbestos, magnesium, lithium, silver and gold are buried beneath this country's deserts and mountains. J.P. Morgan and the Pentagon are heavily involved in this Gold Rush. However, there are many risks involved. The Taliban are killing Westerners and they are attacking companies involved in mining. Another problem is that Afghanistan has the second most corrupt government after Somalia. Because of this corruption many Afghans are siding with the Taliban. There is much money to be made by Western mining companies. The downside is that the American tax payers have to foot the bill for the presence of American troops which amounts to over $10 billion a month.

Is this investment worth the thousands of American lives and billions of dollars funded by U.S. taxpayers so that others can become wealthier? President Obama thinks the risks and costs are worth the investment. China and Russia also has its sights on Northwest Pakistan. So does the United States. The U.S. wants to get there before the Chinese or Russians. This greed may eventually cause a military showdown between China, the U.S. and Russia. Obviously, the U.S. would rather see the showdown between China and Russia.   .

We all know that the Bush Administration was focused on the oil wealth in Iraq. The Obama Administration is focused on the natural resources of Afghanistan and Pakistan. The end result of this Gold Rush is that the mounting deficits could trigger a worldwide global depression and a possible nuclear confrontation. The beneficiaries are the military/industrial complex, some banks and mining companies. The military/industrial complex needs to have regional conflicts and wars to survive. Without endless wars they could perish. This greed and insanity will cause America to crumble much like the Roman Empire. History has a way of repeating itself. Insanity occurs when the same solutions are applied to a problem expecting different results.

President Obama is this the 'Change' you were seeking when running for president?

CHAPTER 16 - 911 CONSPIRACY

An Associated Press Writer, Ali Akbar Dareini, writes on September 23rd, 2010 that the U.S. delegation walked out of the U.N. speech of Iranian President Mahmoud Ahmadinejad, and rightly so, after he said some in the world have speculated that Americans were behind the Sept. 11 terror attacks, staged in an attempt to assure Israel's survival. Iranian President Mahmoud Ahmadinejad spoke of three possible scenarios or conspiracy theories on 911. These theories were:

"That a powerful and complex terrorist group penetrated U.S. Intelligence and defenses."

"That some segments within the U.S. government orchestrated the attack to reverse the declining American economy and its grips on the Middle East in order also to save the Zionist regime. The majority of the American people as well as other nations and politicians agree with this view."

"The attack was the work of a terrorist group but the American government supported and took advantage of the situation."

The Iranian president is giving way too much credit to the 'intelligence' of U.S. Intelligence agencies prior to the attacks of September 11th. These conspiracy theories started before the dust and smoke was settled at the twin towers of the World Trade Center. As mentioned in a previous chapter where I discussed my own personal battle of corruption that I endured by several governmental agencies. This corruption was a direct result of bureaucratic incompetence. The aftermath of the Sept. 11th attacks resulted in the formation of the Department of Homeland Security and the installation of an Intelligence czar. Certain intelligence agencies had bits and pieces of intelligence of an upcoming attack in America but that information was not relayed and gathered among other agencies. The men and women who work within the various intelligence agencies are outstanding citizens and workers who all undergo extensive background checks.

Not one person or a small group of people within these agencies could have pulled off the allegations being made by the conspiracy theorists claims. Most Americans do not trust the U.S. government, and many believe that the political and governmental leaders engage in corrupt practices but these practices stem from bad judgment calls and just plain incompetence and in many times their careers take precedence over what is good for their agency or the American citizen.

There had been some claims made by demolition experts who claim that the collapse of the World Trade Center was as a direct result of explosions placed inside these buildings prior to the attacks and that somehow a rogue fraction of the U.S. government was responsible. When viewing the images of the Twin Towers collapsing, the government's viewpoint appears to be accurate. The collapse started at the base of the fires and the weight of the building created a pancake effect on the way down. It did not appear to be imploded within by demolition experts. Popular Mechanics and U.S. Institute of Standards and Technology and the mainstream media have rejected the 9/11 conspiracy theories.

Among the Civil Engineering establishment generally accepts that the impacts of jet aircraft at high speeds and in combination of the resulting fires, rather than controlled demolition, led to the collapse of the the Twin Towers. The 7 World Trade Center, another skyscraper in the vicinity of the WTC shows a much different picture which has added fuel to the 9/11 conspiracy theories. Videos of Building 7 show where there were no fires or falling debris on this building. The videos show that it was imploded within. Video shows that no external forces would have caused that building to collapse.

It has been claimed that Israeli agents may have had foreknowledge of the attacks. Four hours after the attack, the FBI arrested five Israelis who had been filming the smoking skyline from the roof of a white van in the parking lot of an apartment building, for 'puzzling behavior'. The Israelis were filming the events, and one witness stated that "they acted in a suspicious manner: "They were like happy, you know...They didn't look shocked to me. I thought it was very strange." The Forward, a New York Jewish news magazine, reported that the FBI concluded that two of the men were Israeli Intelligence operatives; a spokesperson for the Israeli Embassy in the United States said that they had not been involved in any intelligence operation in the United States. The FBI later concluded that the five Israelis had no foreknowledge of the attacks.

Iranian President Mahmoud Ahmadinejad firmly believes that Americans are passionate about the survival of the Jewish state. Obviously, the Iranian president doesnot know much about Americans. Many Americans are apathetic towards America. The dominate religious faith in America is Christianity. Most Americans are tolerant of the Muslim and Jewish faith. Americans feel everyone has the rights to their own beliefs.

Now most Americans will favor the Israeli cause over the Palestine cause and the reason for this is that Americans feel every ethnic group has the right to exist and let's face it Americans have seen many images of the hatred towards America by seeing Palestinians chanting "Death to America" while burning the American flag. By the Palestinians doing so, does not create any sense of empathy by Americans to the plight of the Palestine people.

Most Americans all in all have apathy to the Zionist regime. The feeling in America is that both people need to eventually work out their problems themselves. This hatred towards one another goes back to the biblical days. However, in getting back to the theory that a rogue element of the CIA was responsible, for the incineration of the World Tower; the CIA made many blunders in identifying the terrorist threat. I was on active duty with the Air Force on Sept. 11th.

Prior to that date U.S. intelligence agencies identified, numerous times potential threats to U.S. Embassies' and U.S. military installations across the world. None of those threats ever materialized. After the Sept 11th attacks those threats increased, and they never materialized. Undoubtedly, the terror networks organized a misinformation campaign to divert attention away from the real threats as a decoy and to test intelligence agencies across the globe. The U.S. government has committed numerous blunders in this country and in across the world but for them to be behind the attacks behind the September 11th attacks is ludicrous.

Mr. Ahmadinejad firmly believes that U.S. government elements perpetrated this attack to reverse the declining American economy. At the time of these attacks the Bush Administration was in its early days. The stock market was bullish, with no end in sight. The economy was in full bloom as a direct result of the Clinton Administration fiscal policies. The Treasury Department was reporting record tax revenue surpluses. On September 11th, the economy took a fast dive. The airline industry has never fully recovered.

There is one nation that has benefited, indirectly, from extreme Islam fundamentalists holy war against America. This one nation has the most competent global intelligence gathering network. The new hatred towards America has diminished the hatred from Islam to this nation where many global U.S. interests have been attacked. There is probably not a nation across this world that could mirror the intelligence gathering of this agency. This nation knew in advance of the planned attack by Arab nations in 1967, which quickly defeated the opposing forces. Israel has gained the most from this attack on the United States. Now I am not in any way suggesting that agents from the intelligence agency, Mossad, had planted explosives in the Twin Towers or at the 7 World Trade Center to fuel anti-Islam sentiments, dramatically, in the United States. Even so, something of this magnitude and intense attack against America, if there were any advanced intelligence of this attack, presumably would not have slipped through the Israeli intelligence agency, Mossad.

It is interesting to note that the Bush Administration submitted the 342-page USA Patriot Act to Congress on September 24th, 2001, just 13 days after the attack. Most of the policies enacted in the name of the War on Terror were accomplished via Executive Orders. Two U.S. Senators who attempted to slow the the passage of the Patriot Act received letters containing Anthrax.

There have been many allegations that U.S. officials had knowledge of these attacks but did nothing out of incompetence or corruption. Former British Environmental Minister, Michael Meacher, has stated that the United States knowingly failed to prevent the attacks. Author David Ray Griffin alleges that the 9/11 conspiracy was considerably larger than the government claims and that the entire 9/11 Commission Report "is constructed in support of one lie: that the official story about 9/11 is true. An FBI supervisor involved in the investigation into Zacarias Moussaoui sent a message to his superiors in Washington that he was "trying to keep someone from taking a plane and crashing into the World Trade Center." Some of the FBI agents involved in that investigation felt they were being thwarted by the government.

The Chairman of the 9/11 Commission commented "Sixteen of the nineteen shouldn't have gotten into the United States in any way at all because there was something wrong with their visas, something wrong with their passports. They should simply have been stopped at the border. That was sixteen of the nineteen. Obviously, if even half of those people had been stopped, there never would have been a plot." Khalid al Mihdhar and Nawaf al Hazmi had both been identified as al-Qaeda agents by the CIA, but that information was not shared with the FBI or U.S. Immigration, so both men were able to legally enter the U.S. to prepare for the attacks.

Five of the alleged hijackers may have received training at U.S. military facilities. The Defense Department confirmed that three of the hijackers, Mohamed Atta, Abdulaziz al-Omari and Saeed al-Ghamdi, "have the same names as alumni of American military schools." A Mohamed Atta attended the International Officers School at Maxwell Air Force Base in Alabama; an Abdulaziz al-Omari went to the Aerospace Medical School at Brooks Air Force Base in Texas; and a Saeed al-Ghamdi was at the Defense Language Institute at the Presidio in Monterey, California.

The World Trade Center was a collection of seven buildings in lower Manhattan, including the Twin Towers, which at the time were once the tallest buildings in the world. On September 11th, 2001 all seven buildings were either leveled or severely damaged and gutted, including Building 7, which was located on a separate block. Washington D.C. is the most heavily defended city in the world. On September 11th, the Pentagon was damaged in the attack. Brave citizens' flying over Pennsylvania thwarted further attacks against the Capital or the White House. NORAD monitors all air traffic in North America in real time. The 9/11 attacks amounted to be the worst criminal act on U.S. soil. No forensic testing was ever conducted.

The aftermath of the attack began immediately and continues through today. This attack has been exploited as a pretext for wholesale violations of civil liberties, the disappearance of government accountability, and a series of invasions in the world, Iraq and Afghanistan.

Earlier in this book I speak about taking a total look, a 360 degree viewpoint, on an issue. I stated earlier about a personal viewpoint that the Twin Towers had fallen as a direct result of the airplanes which is the same viewpoint shared by Popular Mechanics, the mainstream media and the U.S. government. Incidentally, Popular Mechanics is owned by a large media corporation, the Hearst Corporation. The weakened steel structure was caused by high extreme temperatures in the heat which created a pancake effect.

A fallacy in my personal beliefs where no one could have planted explosives is that each floor of the Twin Towers disintegrated creating huge plumes of cement dust. The pancake effect would not have caused an entire building disintegrate into dust particles. Many firemen had stated they heard explosions. Obviously, the government considers these firemen as crackpots as well as all the other conspiracy theorists since their evidence and statements do not agree with the official government version.

The FBI should have been more proactive in investigating these attacks to seek the real truth of what happened. Since the Capital Building was a target, these attacks might have been a plot to overthrow the government, specifically the legislative branch. Those senior government officials who have blocked efforts in fully investigating the 9/11 attacks, should be criminally charged with obstructing justice. With the legislative branch out of the picture, the executive branch of the government would be free to operate with no oversight.

The Patriot Act has allowed abuses to Constitutional Rights to embolden the federal government with broader powers over the people and to launch invasions against other nations for their natural resources and fossil fuels. Someday the truth will be told and justice served for crimes against humanity.

CHAPTER 17 - REDEMPTION

In writing these words the 112th Congress of the United States has been sworn in. The previous Congress has dropped the ball because of party bickering. Many of you managed to either get reelected or elected into public office to serve your constituents. You need to remind yourself in this new Congress that you need to either start or continue to serve all the people in your state or district. This new Congress needs to start making some Progress for the highest good of the nation and world. Do not confuse Progress with the Progressive Movement.

Each member of the House and Senate need to make a solemn pledge to your God that you will be steadfast in your work for the preservation of the Union and to restore an open and free society. Democracy and the greatness of America are at stake. Some of you may not be willing to come out of the darkness. It is redemption time. In this time of American history the opportunity in working together is here. The time of party bickering and trying to divide America are over. You need to come to the light and shed old worn out ideas. It is time to develop American solutions. The problems in this country will not go away with conservative or liberal solutions. Corporations are not run by utilization of conservative or liberal practices. Corporations are or at least should be run by solid business practices.

The world is going through some historic times never seen before. This is the time for all members of the 112th Congress to shed your party hats and work for the Union of America. There needs to be unity in America, not red or blue states. Americans are frustrated at the leadership in Washington. Candidate Obama is a different person as President Obama. Where did the candidate Obama run off too? Members of Congress can choose to go to the dark side or towards the light. You will manifest your own destiny. You have the free will to work for the good of your party or work for the good of the American people. That choice is yours.

U.S. House Minority Leader John Boehner has claimed that he wants all legislative bills pending before Congress on a public website so that Americans can view them prior to coming to the floor. Candidate Obama claimed the same thing. Why couldn't this have been done prior to the 2010 General Election? Mr. Boehner as House Minority Leader you had the power to do so before the election. American people do not want to hear what

The wars in Iraq and Afghanistan have played havoc with the budget of the United States. America has seen record breaking deficits that are bankrupting America for the good of the Super Elite, the military/industrial complex. Some have profited immensely by these two wars, and they want to see us involved in both wars as long as possible. The generals at the Pentagon need to bring themselves to a winning the peace strategy. It is time to bring our troops home least America falls into decay, and the American dream vanishes.

The United States is in peril. Leaving America engaged in a civil war in Iraq and Afghanistan has worked to the advantages of Iran and has added fuel to worldwide terror. These prolonged wars have provided aid and comfort to our real enemies across the world. The 112th Congress needs to end the funding of the wars in Iraq and Afghanistan for fiscal year 2012. Congress needs to make progress by funding "winning the peace" in both countries. Demand from the generals at the Pentagon to develop a strategy to bring the troops' home to manifest peace and economic stability to America. Demand from the generals at the Pentagon to do their job, they were hired to perform. Many people in life will go through great lengths in not performing their jobs. The solution in Iraq and Afghanistan is not a protracted war. The solution is peace with the support of the world body, the United Nations.

Federal and state agencies have done a miserable job in supporting the men and women who serve their nation. There have been many government lawyers who have gone through great lengths in defeating claims under the USERRA. The thousands of veterans who have served us all have had to wage battle with the state and federal government to comply with the provisions of the USERRA. Many of these veterans were defeated in court by government lawyers. That is an atrocity of the worst type of corruption and governmental treason against our troops.

The U.S. Congress has held many hearings but nothing was ever done. Legislation pertaining to the USERRA needs to be strengthened. Those federal lawyers who have fought against the provision of the USERRA or other federal legislation should be terminated. The U.S. Congress needs to provide a solution and fund compensation for lost wages to veterans who were denied reemployment rights by a federal or state agency. For those state agencies that were successful in defeating USERRA claims should have federal funding for lost wages taken out of the federal funding to state budgets. They will cry and whimper, but they were wrong in not supporting the laws of this nation.

Thousands of veterans have been denied their rights under the USERRA by federal and state agencies. It is redemption time.

Since the National Guard was successful in their efforts in seeking autonomy from the Armed Forces of the United States, those assets, both in equipment and military personnel, need to be transferred to the reserve units of the Army and Air Force that are pledged by allegiance to support the U.S. Constitution and the President of the United States. When this country was first founded there were no local or state police forces during the early settlements' days. Today the states can provide their own forces to handle disasters and civil strife that doesn't require tanks and warplanes. This can be an employment opportunity for many veterans. The state governors and adjutant generals desire their own military forces; in case they need to do battles with federal forces so let them have it, without the federal funding. The National Guard's unwillingness to comply with federal statues and the Pentagon's orders to comply with the provisions of the USERRA began with the Ohio National Guard. The Ohio National Guard is no longer a federal entity and should not be funded as such. They won their independence.

Let the National Guard survive without federal tax dollars. Under the U.S. Constitution, state militias are prohibited from possessing ships. This is why there is no Naval Guard. If tanks and warplanes been invented when the Constitution was ratified, they (tanks and warplanes) also would have been prohibited.

Earlier I discussed the possibility of a worldwide energy crisis that could manifest with the dwindling supplies of fossil fuels. The world will run out of fossil fuels someday at the current rate of energy consumption. Energy is what drives the global economy. The decisions made today will determine the global outcome. But there is another threat to the free flow of oil from the Middle East.

Since 1979, Iran is still holding America hostage. Iran is becoming a nuclear nation that can threaten its neighbors and the free flow of crude oil. Iran poses a threat not only to Israel but to Saudi Arabia and Kuwait. U.S. political leaders for decades have been talking about America's addiction to foreign oil. Iran soon will have the capability to bring America to its knees by going cold turkey without foreign oil. The subsidies that Congress has provided to petroleum companies need to end, and those funds should be made available in grants for further energy research in developing natural energies and bio-fuels least we all go back to the horse and buggy days.

Further research dollars should be provided in further developing the external combustion engine. The external combustion engine is more efficient and is capable of burning bio-fuels, natural gas, powdered coal, diesel and gasoline. Should there be a deficiency or shortage in one fuel; alternative sources of fuel can be utilized. The external combustion engine outputs less carbon exhaust into the air. The future has arrived; the external combustion engine with further development could someday be burning a person's own garbage.

One of the most unpatriotic acts that the U.S. Congress and former President Bush bestowed upon the American people is the Patriot Act. The idea for this Patriot Act must have come right of the book by George Orwell, 1984. The Patriotic Act gave the U.S. government broad powers to invade the privacy of all Americans not just those who want to harm its citizens. The government engages in wiretapping, monitoring emails, and monitoring telephone conversations. The government knows what books you are reading. This is a way for them to monitor dissent from the people. In essence, the Patriot Act hinders one's right to free speech.

People now have to be careful what they say to others on the internet and over the phone because Big Brother is watching and hearing everything. This act is unconstitutional. Your elected officials in Washington gave away your rights under the auspices of "we want to protect you". What they are really saying is "we want to enslave you".

Benjamin Franklin stated "They, who can give up essential liberty to obtain a little temporary safety, deserve neither liberty nor safety."

Abraham Lincoln stated "Those who deny freedom to others deserve it not for themselves."

Congress gave away many freedoms that Americans have enjoyed to the federal government under the auspices of protecting Americans from the terrorist threat. The Patriot Act became the breeding ground for another type of terrorism - 'governmental terrorism'.

The story in the next chapter is a harrowing tale of governmental terrorism and the dire need for federal civil service reform and the need to overturn the Patriot Act. Remember people that work for your government have become ego-centered where they want to control you. By controlling you it gives them broader powers to do just about anything they desire. Who is going to prosecute the prosecutors? Who is going to protect you from armed thugs of the government? As a former federal employee I know that most employees of all the agencies are good and decent people. But there is a criminal element in many agencies that operate outside of federal and international laws with no accountability. The government classifies many criminal and wrongful acts against its citizens and other citizens across the globe as top secret. They have rendered Whistleblower Protection Act impotent.

Many people are questioning why a natural herb, commonly referred to as marijuana, cannot be legalized. Remember the War on Drugs is big business to law enforcement agencies. This war will go on indefinitely. The United States has a porous border where drugs arrive daily. Many times law enforcement agencies make drug busts, and by doing so, they confiscate airplanes, homes, automobiles, boats and large amounts of cash. They confiscate anything of market value.

I had briefly talked once with someone who was busted for growing marijuana in her basement for personal use. During that drug bust the agents were upset that they couldn't find any cash or anything of value to confiscate. The only thing they could walk out with was a refrigerator and a few plants. It isn't about taking drugs off the street; it is about seizing money for law enforcement agencies. How did you think America became a police state? It was financed in part by drug trafficking.

America imports drugs into the country and exports heavy assault weapons to Mexico. Why do you think the borders go unprotected? Several years ago the Arizona Attorney General had prosecuted several National Guardsmen who were using military vehicles to transport illegal drugs into the country. Do you really think the "shadow government" really cares about your health and well being? They do so only when it is in their best interests. Don't believe me. I have some beachfront property in Arizona I would like to discuss with you.

As Americans we can and we will reclaim our nation from the armed thugs and restore integrity within the government. We can no longer be apathetic to what is going on in our country. Read on so you can take back your basic rights of freedom and liberty that is being trampled upon. Make your voice heard in the upcoming 2012 elections while we are still able to vote.

The government does not like criticism. Senator McCain (R) introduced Senate Bill 3081 that coined a new term...Enemy Belligerent. In this bill if a person made any type of unflattering comments against the government that person could be detained, indefinitely, with no legal representation. That bill is now dead. U.S. Rep Diane Feinstein (D) has introduced legislation denying federal pensions to federal employees for disclosing unclassified information. If passed, a federal employee would not be able to disclose fraud, waste and abuse and criminal acts against the American people by the intelligence agencies. There are traitors among us.

CHAPTER 18 - GOVERNMENTAL TERRORISM

Corruption is a primary barrier to peace and prosperity. This is a tale of a federal officer, Julia Davis, formerly with the Department of Homeland Security, who discovers a national security breach related to the entry of 23 aliens from terrorist countries into the United States. These thugs are still employed with the U.S. Government. One individual to escape the arms of a federal judge for "obstruction of justice, fraud, waste and abuse" has been transferred to the U.S. Embassy in S. Korea by this administration. The "shadow government" controls the politicians and the American people.

Fleur De Lis Film Studios launched several projects from their expanding production slate, including TV Series "I Fight For My Life", "Whistleblowers - The Untold Stories" and "Rogues in Robes". Production of these projects is spearheaded by screenwriter/ investigative reporter Julia Davis, CEO of Fleur De Lis Film Studios, Producer/Director BJ Davis, President of Fleur De Lis Film Studios and Spice Williams-Crosby of Make Believe Entertainment.

Julia Davis is a member of the Academy of Arts & Sciences, Executive member of Women In Film, member of the Independent Film Producers, Screen Actors Guild and the Independent Filmmakers Alliance. During her 15 years in the film industry, Julia Davis served as a stunt double to Angelina Jolie, wrote the screenplay for an award-winning feature film and authored teleplays for TV Series/ documentaries. Her investigative reports and photographs been prominently featured by various publications and news outlets. Julia Davis is now a FOX-News-contributor.

Now Julia Davis' own story is coming to the forefront of public attention, as she recently settled a multimillion dollar lawsuit against the Department of Homeland Security. Her historical case reflects unprecedented acts of reprisal by the Department of Homeland Security, perpetrated in retaliation for Julia's whistleblowing disclosure that embarrassed the corrupt elements within the beleaguered agency. While serving as a Customs and Border Protection Officer, Julia Davis fulfilled her duty to protect American citizens from terrorism by making a report to the Federal Bureau of Investigation's Joint Terrorism Task Force (FBI/JTTF). Her report exposed serious shortcomings in the processing of aliens from terrorist countries seeking to enter the United States.

In retaliation for Julia's heroic actions that embarrassed the Department of Homeland Security, the agency dispatched a Blackhawk Attack Helicopter and a Special Response Team to storm the Davis' residence by 27 Agents armed with assault weapons in a commando-style raid. Julia Davis was baselessly declared a "domestic terrorist" and listed as "armed and dangerous" in law enforcement databases. 27 DHS Agents and a US Marshal Andrew Haggerty conducted an extended warrantless search of the property. While in the house, DHS Agents went out of their way to send another message to Julia, by crossing out the date of the raid on her office calendar and writing "Boo!" straight across. In the course of the raid, Julia's parents have been attacked, brutalized and unlawfully detained.

Immigration and Customs Enforcement (ICE) Agents, Herbert Kaufer and Jeffrey Deal coordinated series of unlawful actions that included throwing Julia's father, Mykola Kot, face down on the cement with such a force that it broke his finger. He was then handcuffed, dragged down the steps away from the house and kept in full sun for an hour, wearing only boxer shorts. Mykola Kot repeatedly asked agents to bring him into the house from the 114 degree desert sun, telling them that he was having a heart attack and needed medical assistance. DHS Agents laughed in response to his pleas for water and heart medications. Their own reports reflected the extreme heat that was expected that day and advised ICE personnel to carry and drink a lot of water. Their actions towards Mykola Kot were apparently designed to cause serious harm, as the Agents were aware of his prior heart condition before the raid. While Mykola Kot suffered a heart attack, writhing in pain while his hands were still twisted behind his back in handcuffs, agents laughed at him and sent away the ambulance that was stationed across the street on standby. They left the injured couple in the ransacked house with a broken door, without any means of transportation to the hospital.

These and other related actions by DHS personnel contributed to Julia's father untimely death at the age of 61. Having immigrated to the United States just months before the raid, Julia Davis' father had his American dream shattered by the corrupt agents within the Department of Homeland Security. While the agency settled the wrongful death lawsuit, nothing could ever correct Mykola Kot's death, caused by the egregious *wrongs to which he was needlessly subjected - an innocent victim in the DHS' plot to destroy his daughter, Julia Davis.*

Department of Homeland Security wasted millions of dollars of taxpayers resources in retaliation for Julia Davis' national security reports. The agency targeted and harassed Julia Davis, thereby prompting her involuntary resignation. ICE Agents Kaufer and Deal opened 54 investigations against Julia, conducted warrantless searches of the Davis' residence and office, subjected Julia Davis and her husband, renown filmmaker BJ Davis, to two false imprisonments, two malicious prosecutions, years of warrantless surveillance, wiretaps and other egregious privacy violations. BJ and Julia Davis have been falsely charged with felony crimes and twice imprisoned.

Prior to the raid, Julia and BJ Davis have been subjected to aerial surveillance with the Customs and Border Protection Air and Marine Unit (by a Blackhawk helicopter and a fixed-wing airplane), followed by as many as eight ICE agents at each given time, their medical and insurance records have been inappropriately disclosed by the Screen Actors Guild, SAG Producers Health & Welfare Program and Directors Guild of America illegally with voluminous materials seized in a warrantless search of BJ Davis' office.

While Katrina victims were drowning due to the shortage of evacuation resources during that national catastrophe, Department of Homeland Security was wasting helicopters, airplanes and enormous manpower resources on following and harassing Julia Davis and her family. During their admittedly "social" meetings with a porno actress and members of the Bonanno crime family, Agents Kaufer and Deal boasted of abusing Patriot Act provisions that were improperly used for "keeping close tabs" on the Davis family, conducting wiretaps, sneak and peak intrusions. Agents Kaufer and Deal have also illegally disclosed highly privileged TECS printouts and classified details of FBI investigations to third party civilians and the Bonnano Mafia organized crime associates.

Documents produced by the government in discovery outlined daily efforts of Kaufer and Deal to "get" Julia Davis by soliciting as many as nineteen (19) Assistant US Attorneys, State, County and City prosecutors with fifty four (54) investigations, to include the IRS, FBI, Los Angeles Police Department, California Department of Justice, Firearms Divisions, Central and Southern Federal Districts of California, Federal District of Arizona, Arizona Attorney General Terry Stoddard, San

Diego, Los Angeles, San Bernardino County District Attorney offices. Kaufer and Deal enlisted the San Diego Police Department, Chief William Landsdowne, Lt. Caroline Kendericks, Lt. Shay, Sgt. Steve Webb and others to make an illegal and unconstitutional traffic stop of Julia Davis, in a ploy to make her unable to attend her EEOC hearing.

In the end, federal prosecutor John Lee admitted that the Davis's should have never been prosecuted in the first place. Judge Bryan Foster issued a finding of factual innocence, ordering that arrest records be sealed and destroyed. Additionally, Judge Foster ordered the government to return the proceeds of both warrantless searches. The DHS has defied that court order and refused to return the television series "Medal Of Honor" television series hosted by Burt Reynolds and the book, "Confessions Of A Hollywood Stuntman", by former celebrated Stuntman BJ Davis with items unlawfully taken estimated in the millions of dollars.

In another court order, Judge Daniel Leach ruled that Julia's resignation was "involuntary" and was caused by the Department of Homeland Security's "illegal conduct", "unnecessary harassment" and "impermissible discrimination" against her. CA Superior Court Judge Margaret Woods issued a restraining order to protect Julia Davis against unlawful harassment and stalking by DHS personnel. Former Department of Homeland Security, Acting Inspector General Elizabeth Redman ordered an investigation that affirmed allegations in Julia Davis report to the OIG. The DHS hid the report until ordered to release it in a legal proceeding. To date, no one was disciplined, in spite of court orders that the perpetrators be held accountable. Central Federal District Court of California, federal Judge Stephen Larson commented, "I am amazed at what the government is not denying in this case." (Emphasis added).

Perhaps the most damning commentary was issued in the court order by federal Judge Virginia Phillips, who ruled as follows on January 28, 2010: "On August 10, 2005, ten DHS Internal Affairs Agents, a United States Marshal, seventeen SRT members, eight unmarked cars and a Blackhawk helicopter arrived at the Davis's residence in Yucca Valley to execute warrants for the Davis's' arrests...Plaintiffs [BJ and Julia Davis] have produced significant evidence about the August 2005 raid and search of their residence... This evidence is sufficient to create a factual question as to whether federal agents committed an abuse of process when they conducted that search pursuant to the arrest warrant... In light of the substantial evidence presented by Plaintiffs as to the magnitude of the search, and the

Government's failure to identify undisputed facts in support of a contrary finding, the Court holds that a reasonable fact finder could find the extreme nature of the search and raid of the Davis's Yucca Valley home was "not proper in the regular conduct of the proceedings." Throughout their opposition, Plaintiffs have identified evidence that suggests the degree of force used in the search was severe, particularly in light of the nonviolent nature of the charges against the Davis's. The reports of the Agents involved suggest no attempt to arrest the Davis's in a more peaceable manner was ever even considered. According to Julia Davis's parents, in the course of the search, Agent Deal told them that Mrs. Davis was a "domestic terrorist," a statement without any support... At some point on the day of the raid, someone scrawled the word "Boo!" and crossed out the date on Julia Davis's calendar, located in her home... As discussed above, several witnesses have testified that documents and other items were seized from the home, though no receipt was given. The search of the home continued long after it was determined the persons named in the arrest warrant were not present. Together, this evidence creates a question of material fact as to whether the manner in which the arrest warrants were executed was proper. There is also sufficient evidence for a reasonable fact finder to conclude the OPR Agents had an ulterior, improper motive: retaliation for Julia Davis's successful EEOC complaint... In addition to the unusual degree of force used in executing the arrests, the arrest warrants were executed two months after the EEOC ALJ issued his initial decision in Julia Davis's sexual harassment case, which was in her favor and highly critical of CBP, ICE, and their internal investigators. Agents Deal, Kaufer, and Wong had all been involved in Julia Davis's EEOC and MSPB proceedings. One week after the search, CBP moved to hold the ALJ's decision in abeyance based on the federal criminal charges. The sum total of these facts is sufficient to allow a fact finder to infer a retaliatory or malicious motive in the execution of the search... Plaintiffs have therefore produced sufficient evidence to allow a reasonable fact finder to conclude the August 2005 search was an abuse of process."

Julia Davis' husband, filmmaker BJ Davis stated with the regards to the settlement, "Due to the criminal actions of Agents Kaufer and Deal, lives were lost, careers destroyed and other irreparable damages were inflicted. The TV Series and the upcoming feature film will tell all, to ensure that such egregious acts don't happen to anyone else. We will continue to lobby in DC with Congress to have these individuals, terminated from federal service and prosecuted. We are also seeking permanent amendment of the Whistleblower Protection Act, which is toothless at the present and completely incapable of protecting whistleblowers. Julia Davis prevailed in her legal battles without any assistance from the agencies and organizations purportedly created to provide support to whistleblowers."

In addition, Julia Davis revealed that the agency had lied to Congress in its reports filed under the "NO FEAR" Act, forcing Department of Homeland Security to correct its fraudulent report and re-submit corrected information to Congress. Government corruption and the use of a Blackhawk helicopter are immortalized as well as the untimely deaths surrounding the case... Julia Davis stated, "Things like these should never happen in America. We intend to hold corrupt government elements and individuals accountable, as the American public will be the ultimate judge and jury in this case. By holding the perpetrators accountable, together we can eradicate corruption from the ranks of those sworn to protect us."

Government and elected officials with personal, direct and legal knowledge of the events declined to participate in on-camera interviews or to answer any questions about this matter. Julia Davis recently held extended discussions with head of the DHS Committee Chairman Benny G. Thompson and will return to Washington, DC to testify before Congress.

A book, documentary and feature film are in the works in addition to the ongoing episodic television series as Julia Davis' heroic deeds in the performance of her duties is far more than just whistleblowing. Davis aspired to these monumental achievements without any support from any organization or advocacy groups.

Davis was asked recently during two broadcast interviews, if she would report the national security breaches again - knowing what she knows now. Without hesitation, Davis responded, "I swore an oath to protect the United States in the performance of my duties as a federal law enforcement officer and as a citizen of this great country. Instead I had to protect myself from the government corruption, Kaufer and Deal. My answer is "yes". I would still make that report, as it was the only right thing to do. I would still protect and serve my country with the same zeal and determination. I will continue to do so by educating, entertaining and enlightening people with these true stories that should be of concern for every American citizen."
This story is a clear example of abuse of the U.S. of concern for every American citizen."

This story is a clear example of abuse of the U.S. Constitution and the Patriot Act. The original intentions of the Patriot Act were to give law enforcement additional tools in pursuing international terrorism within the United States. Unfortunately, law enforcement has used the Patriot Act for non-terrorist related surveillance routinely. The action by the DHS and U.S. Marshall's office was a clear case of state terrorism against this family, which resulted in a death of a family member. Individuals involved were never disciplined and in all likelihoods this act of domestic state terrorism had the blessings all the way to the top of DHS.

Not only is the United States guilty of state sponsored terrorism against its citizens; it has also been guilty of exporting state terrorism. Some examples of this was the Philippine-American War (1899-1902); the 1968 My Lai Massacre, and Cuba and Nicaragua. *The Republic of Nicaragua vs. The United States of America* was a case heard in 1986 by the International Court of Justice which ruled in Nicaragua's favor, and found that the United States had violated international law. The court stated that the United States had been involved in the "unlawful use of force", specifically that it was "in breach of its obligation under customary international law not to use force against another state" by direct acts of U.S. personnel and by supporting Contra guerrillas in their war against the Nicaraguan government and by mining Nicaragua's harbors. The ICJ ordered the U.S. to pay reparations.

The US was not imputable for possible human rights violations done by the Contras. The case led to considerable debate concerning the issue of the extent to which state support of terrorists implicates the state itself. Many history scholars claim that the United States committed state sponsored terrorism against the citizens of Japan by dropping atomic bombs on two Japanese cities when there were negotiations for Japan to surrender during World War II. Part of the reason those bombs were dropped on Japan was to get the Japanese government to surrender sooner and to also show to the Soviet Union, war capabilities of the United States.

The U.S. Congress needs to amend the Patriot Act to include criminal penalties when the government abuses this statue. A question will remain how one can prosecute those who prosecute U. S. citizens. I came across the same problem in my civil case against the United States, and the opposing counsel allegedly committed criminal acts through the Court. I had filed a complaint through the Justice Department Inspector General, and obviously they ignored that complaint. I never received a final disposition from the Department of Defense in my criminal allegations against DFAS. The problem is the Inspector Generals' in federal agencies are employed by that agency, and they report to the senior leadership for that agency. Inspector Generals' throughout the federal bureaucracy should report to an outside entity such as the Office of Special Counsel (OSC). That should be the most logical chain of command. However, when dealing with the federal government logic does not always prevail.

LA Homeland Security Examiner, Julia Davis, also writes for the Examiner. She wrote an article titled "Office of Special Counsel (OSC) – the dark legacy".

She writes where on April 27th, 2010, the former head of the Office of Special Counsel (OSC), Scott J. Bloch, pleaded guilty to criminal contempt of Congress. This article provided an abbreviated list of Scott Bloch's dubious "accomplishments while as the head of OSC:

Knowingly and willfully ignoring whistleblower disclosures;

Dismissing and closing hundreds of whistleblowing complaints without investigation;

Deleting hundreds of files pertaining to whistleblowing disclosures and complaints of retaliation and reprisal;

Rolling back protections for federal employees against discrimination based on sexual orientation;

Staffing key OSC positions with cronies who shared his discriminatory views;

Engaging in retaliatory activities against OSC staffers who opposed his wrongdoing;

Assigning interns to issue closure letters in hundreds of whistleblower complaints without investigation;

Intimidating OSC employees from cooperating with government investigators;

Misusing prosecutorial power for political purposes;

Reducing the backlog of cases pending at the OSC by 56% percent by closing cases without an investigation and destroying electronic files;

During the fiscal year of 2008, the OSC filed 0 corrective action petitions with the Merit Systems Protection Board (MSRB);

During the fiscal year of 2008, the OSC obtained 0 stays from the Merit Systems Protection Board (MSRB);

Bloch reassigned his perceived critics within the OSC to field offices across the country – giving them 10 days to accept, or else they'd be fired.

Bloch imposed retaliatory transfers upon staffers he perceived as having a "homosexual agenda";
OSC under Bloch rarely recognized legitimate whistleblowers, typically only when the whistleblower has already prevailed elsewhere.

Julia Davis later writes "The OSC has operated without permanent leadership since 2008, leaving federal employees in the dark ages and without recourse. Legal professionals are now advising federal employees against coming forward. "When people call me and ask about blowing the whistle, I always tell them, 'Don't do it, because your life will be destroyed,'" says William Weaver, a professor of political science at the University of Texas –El Paso and a senior advisor to the National Security Whistleblowers Coalition. "You'll lose your career, you're probably going to lose your family if you have one; you're probably going to lose all your friends because they're associated through work; you'll wind up squandering your life savings on attorneys; and you'll come out the other end of this process working at McDonald's.""

When government agencies commit Acts of Terror against the citizens, then it is imperative that Congress acts to withdraw funding for those agencies, regardless of their mission. ICE now wants to restrict the rights of free speech by sending to prison, people who forward You Tube™ videos to others. ICS claims it is because of possible copyright infringements but their actions are to diminish your rights to Free Speech and access to outside media.

The Immigrations and Customs Enforcement Agency has expanded its operations from securing the influx of illegal immigration to finding out what Americans read and view on the Internet. Writers, news organizations and film producers put a lot of their material on the Internet. If these producers do not want other people to share their copyrighted information with their friends and families, then do not put that material out on the Internet.

They (ICE) have been committing acts of terror against its own U.S. born citizens. The U.S. Congress needs to stop funding this organization. Employees who have engaged in unlawful practices should be prosecuted and their federal employment status terminated.

Corruption is like a vicious cancer. It needs eradication. Transferring corrupt employees to other agencies only spreads the cancerous cells further. ICE was established in 2003 under the Bush Administration.

Mr. President, shut down these corrupt agencies who commit criminal acts or acts of terror against its own citizens.

CHAPTER 19 – PRESIDENTIAL POLITICS

This book would be incomplete without a few words regarding the 2012 Presidential race. When Barrack Obama was sworn into office, on a cold wintry day, the world looked up to this distinguished man who had promised hope and a change for a better tomorrow. After eight long years under the Bush Administration, the people wanted a better vision for the world. The people in this country wanted the wars to end in Iraq and Afghanistan. The new president was promising the people he would bring the troops home, with honor. The new president had promised a more open and transparent government no longer hiding in secrecy. He promised to restore the loss in liberties under the Patriot Act. He promised to create new jobs and to hold Wall Street and the bankers accountable for the financial collapse of the economy that was threatening a start of a global depression. People believed in his vision.

Many people had worked tirelessly on his presidential campaign. I had knocked on doors for this new president in Ohio. My daughter who was in high school, spent her free time working on this campaign. Barrack Obama promised us a new tomorrow. People were very hopeful that things would get better after enduring eight long years under the corrupt Bush Administration. Even the heavenly Angels were singing and dancing among the crowd at his Inauguration. They believed in him as being the chosen one to lead America and the world to new heights of peace and prosperity. The new president was facing many new challenges but the vision that he held would overcome these obstacles.

The angels were there to assist him in overcoming these hurdles. President Obama was committed in his early days of fulfilling the wishes and dreams of many across the world. He was committed to God to work tirelessly with integrity and wisdom. He promised to call out those politicians who wanted to harm the country for their own self-interests and hidden agendas. People were hopeful that he would rid the federal bureaucracy of incompetence and corruption and to stop the growing trend towards fascism under the Bush Administration. The American people brought him into office and they gave him a vast majority in the House and Senate.

So what happened? Why did the new president forego his beliefs where he is now leading the nation down a dark road, the same road that George W. Bush had taken us? Was he overcome by the power of the office? Did he become addicted to this power? Historians will be trying to answer that question in the years that will follow. The people who supported him as well as probably the angels found that he turned his back to them. Americans are no longer hopeful. Many now feel cheated and betrayed. No doubt the Republican Party is quite hopeful that the nation has gone into a nose dive with their assistance. The first month that President Obama was in office, the Republicans were blaming the economy and loss of jobs on the new president. Many Americans feel they were betrayed by both political parties.

During the president's first 100 days in office he had an ambitious agenda. General Motors and Chrysler were bailed out involving over 40 billion dollars. How did that help the city of Detroit? That city is experiencing a 25% unemployment rate as a result of this bailout money. Where did the jobs go? It certainly didn't help the autoworkers that much. Many of them found themselves unemployed. Early in the Obama Administration the health care bill, after a bitter battle in Congress, was passed. This bill was over 9000 pages in length. Obviously, no member of Congress was able to read that bill. People still do not understand the totality of this health care bill and how it will help people obtain health insurance. This bill was passed concealing a tax increase. Another provision that most Americans do not know about The Affordable Care Act is a provision on page 1312 establishing a civilian Ready Reserve Corps. President Obama had stated that this civilian force will be stronger than the military. That brings up a question, what will be the mission? Probably no one but the president knows that.

Americans, we have much more surprises in store for us. In the event of a National Emergency, the following Executive Orders will be implemented by the President. These Executive Orders were first signed by President Kennedy shortly after he took office. The president will determine what constitutes a National Emergency. These Executive Orders are:

EO, 10990 - Allows the government to take over all modes of transportation and control of highways and seaports.
EO, 10995 – Allows the government to seize and control all communications, media (telecommunications, Internet, Radio, TV, etc.). Author note: If there is a National Emergency would you not want to be able to contact your family members and other loved ones to ensure they are safe?
EO, 10997 – Allows the government to take over all electrical power, gas, petroleum, fuels and minerals.

EO, 10998 – Allows the government to seize all means of transportation, including personal cars, trucks and vehicles of any kind.

EO, 10999 – Allows the government to take over all food resources and farms.

EO, 11000 – Allows the government to mobilize civilians into work brigades under government supervision.

EO, 11001 – Allows the government to take over health, education and welfare functions.

EO, 11002 – Designates the Postmaster General to operate a National Registration of all persons.

EO, 11003 – Allows the government to take over all airports and aircraft, including commercial aircraft.

EO, 11004 – Allows housing and finance authority to relocate communities, build new housing with public funds, designates areas to be abandoned.

EO, 11005 – Allows the government to take over railroads, inland waterways and public storage facilities.

EO, 11921 – Allows the Federal Emergency Preparedness Agency to take control of all financial institutions in the U.S. (In other words they will seize all your financial assets.)

Now some of you might argue that the Republicans will never allow this to happen. Think again! Senator John McCain introduced Senate Bill 3801. This bill would have allowed indefinite detention on people without legal representation if a person criticizes the government. They would be labeled as an Enemy Belligerent. Fortunately, this bill did not pass.

Another variation also did not pass. President Obama supported this bill. President Obama has spoken about creating a new legal regime in the United States. Apparently, the U.S. Constitution is too restrictive to his causes. On the outside our president is happy and friendly, on the inside he hates the freedoms and liberties that Americans still enjoy. He wants to be your President, indefinitely, and he has the support of the Democrats and the Republicans in supporting anti-American legislation. The only thing the President and the corrupt shadow government needs now is for an "event" to take place so that they will enjoy dictatorial powers over all of us. They will own the wealth in this country in seeking world domination. The civilian Reserve Corps, which was expanded in the health care bill, will be needed to supervise the work gangs (slave labor) while the military is engaged in foreign operations.

The civilian Reserve Corps is not nothing new. This civilian Reserve Corp is made up of medical officers. Now what has become disturbing, President Obama has spoken of his vision being that, this civilian force will be greater than the military. Released videos of new recruits to this civilian Reserve Corp are made up of young black males receiving combat training. There weren't any Caucasians, Hispanics, Asians or other nationalities as newer members. You can expect to see, as slave laborers, many Mexican nationals who have crossed the border illegally. Also as slave laborers will be those who are labeled 'enemy belligerents'. So for those of us who have ever been critical of the government or the president may find exciting new opportunities. Media groups outside of the U.S. have been writing stories about the FEMA camps in the U.S. Popular Mechanics, from the Hearst Corporation, strongly denies FEMA camps being built.

In June of 2011, under the War Powers Act, the president is required to seek permission from the U.S. Congress to continue operations when U.S. troops are engaged in "hostilities". In regards to the military intervention in Libya, some members of Congress are demanding the president comply with the law. The president has indicated that the U.S. is not engaged in "hostilities" in Libya.   The Libyans who have been on the receiving end of U.S. and NATO bombers may have a different viewpoint.   In response, Speaker of the House, John Boehner, stated "It is clear that the Obama administration's claim that targeted bombings, missile strikes and other military actions in Libya do not constitute 'hostilities' under the War Powers Resolution is not credible." There are four rebel forces that NATO and the U.S. are supporting against the Libyan government. Two of those rebel groups are the Muslim Brotherhood and Al Qaeda who are trying to install an Islamic regime.   A civil war is in full swing in Libya. Prior to the outbreak in violence, Libya was on a path towards a representative democracy in the region.   The Libya people were being given the opportunity to vote on Referendums at the ballot, much like the citizens of Ohio, California and other states allow the citizens to bring up Referendums for the people to vote upon.   If the rebels are successful, democracy will not rise but Sharia Law will emerge. U.S. Senator John McCain wants no discussions on rather Congress should support the rebels for fear of giving comfort to Gaddafi and his sons. He (McCain) has apparently forgotten that in a Republic, people; need to have discussions to choose best actions Americans and others across the world may have some other surprises in store for all of us. Now having just read what been written so far, the readers may think to themselves that they will vote Republican in the next election. Think again! Many Americans elected in the 2010 election more Republicans. House Armed Services Committee Chairman Rep. Howard McKeon (R., Calif) had revealed his version of the National Defense Authorization Act for fiscal 2012, and he has cleverly included a provision that "would affirm that the United States is engaged in an armed conflict with al-Qaeda, the Taliban, and associated forces." Perhaps al-Qaeda in Libya might be considered the good terrorists by Washington insiders and the shadow government. The American Civil Liberties Union (ACLU) and more than a dozen mostly left leaning groups wrote a letter to members of the House Armed Services Committee to oppose the "reaffirmation" saying that it essentially declares war and gives broad powers to the president that normally belong to Congress. Apparently, the liberals are just trying to stir up trouble by promoting civil liberties and freedoms. President Obama was Democrat when running for President who later became a Republican disguised as a Democrat. If this legislation passes, and it may have already passed as you are reading these words, gives the President absolute and dictatorial power over the military, including the authority to launch military strikes within the United States against U.S. citizens. Hostilities will never end is an endless war with no clearly defined enemies and no borders. The United States, if not already, is on the path to becoming a state terrorist nation while embracing fascism. Under this legislation, the ACLU is very much concerned because the President could authorize the military to attack the ACLU building because they have supported the "terrorists" by arguing for their civil rights.

Keep in mind many U.S. citizens are now categorized by the Justice Department as being "domestic terrorists; if they are anti-war and those demanding their Constitutional Rights. America is not far from seeing the day when the government will be willing to assassinate U.S. citizens who are innocent activists by exercising their first amendment rights with many of them now being placed on the terrorist watch list by the FBI and DHS. Senator John McCain, a former prisoner of war, has introduced legislation that would make it illegal for military prisoners in U.S. overseas torture prisons to be returned to U.S. facilities. There has not been a declaration of war by the United States since WWII. Since the Bush Administration captured enemy prisoners are not considered POW's subject to oversight by international inspectors that is allowed under the Geneva Convention. The path that law enforcement is partaking; the FBI, DHS and other intelligence services will be operated no differently than the Nazi Gestapo and the Soviet KGB. History repeats itself, over and over again.

America is now facing the most critical election in U.S. history. Who they elect in the 2012 Presidential race will determine if the U.S. falls to fascism and the end of the Republic. The General Election could end up being the last presidential election. No more will America elect its political leaders. Americans need to choose a true political leader that is measured not by how many laws they helped pass to restrict individual rights and freedoms but by how many laws were prevented or repealed that restricts individual rights and freedoms.

There are those within the government, that are political and government leaders, who are trying to take this nation further into the darkness of abyss by creating situations that will cause anarchy and chaos as a means to overthrow the Republic. The federal employees of the U.S. government are losing their rights as Whistleblowers in identifying fraud, waste and abuse and other criminal misconduct. The American citizen is not the enemy or a domestic terrorist. The real terrorists are wearing suits seeking world domination. These individuals are also seeking control of the health care system to poison its citizens. Employees of the Justice Department, FBI, NSA, DOD, and other agencies need to wake up to the realities to all of this corruption before this nation perishes. Do not look outward but look inward. Think of the future for yourself, your children and their children and what life will be like if the vicious cancer of corruption endures in swallowing up more victims. I wrote this book as an advocate for non-violence and peace. To do nothing on my part would be a sin. By writing this book, I could become a target and become imprisoned or murdered but that would be a fate or risk I assume so that others will have a chance to find freedom and liberty.

Our founding fathers were not infallible. They all had their human imperfections. They also did not agree on everything. But one thing they all had in common was the common desire as statesmen to work for the common long term interests of this new nation and its people. They did not answer to the special interest groups like today's politicians. Most of them were involved in metaphysics with a strong belief in a higher intelligence. They left us with a blueprint for a new nation to prosper.

CHAPTER 20 – SPIRITUAL JOURNEY

I will be amiss if I did not make a discussion of spirituality in reclaiming not only our own personal lives but also in reclaiming America. Now many say that politics and religion do not mix. That statement I agree wholeheartedly. However there is a major difference between religion and spirituality. Religion is a faith of dogma that one holds towards a particular manmade religion. Spirituality is an individual set of beliefs independent of dogma based on an individual's experiences and personal faith. I will set forth my own personal observations and the many spiritual experiences that I have been blessed to receive and enjoy. These are my truths where I want to lead the reader to discover their own personal truths. In writing these words I have total and complete respect for people's faiths and religious beliefs.

It is significant that I share with my readers a little bit about my lifelong spiritual journey with the hopes that many others will also embark on their own personal spiritual journey. Know that the heavenly angels, spirit masters and spirit guides stand ready to help those along in this journey. The world that we live in is under great turmoil. Many are asking the question "Why God is allowing this to happen? And God is responding "so that you all can open up your spiritual eye and find that I am the divinity in all of you. You have all agreed to be a part of this great divine plan. You are now living in a great historic time with massive changes ahead for the planet Earth. With this great turmoil come a great change and a great enlightenment for the coming Age. Know that you are all loved. " But I am getting ahead of myself here.

The late winter and early spring of 2006, was a time in my life where I renewed a fresh spiritual awareness. I needed some healing in my life to get over what I had recently endured. I had been in an extensive legal battle with the State of Ohio and the United States where I had been denied rights granted under the Uniformed Services Employment Reemployment Rights Act (USERRA). I was beating myself up inside the way my life was going. I knew I had to let go of all this anger and frustration. For Christmas, one of my sisters had bought me a book to read "Heaven and Earth" by James Van Praagh. I resumed a spiritual path that I had been on but somewhere had gotten lost along the way. I read that book twice seeking answers.

My spiritual quest in seeking answers and the truth on why we are here began in my early teens. I had a thirst for knowledge. I wanted answers at that early age on who is God. Is God a deity that should be feared? What happens to us when we die? Do some people go to heaven while some people go to hell? Alternatively, is it at the end of one's life they no longer exist? Is there more than one God? Under the Ten Commandments, one of the Commandments instructs us "Thou shall have no other gods but me"? Does that mean there are other gods? Do we come back as a plant or animal or as a human being in a new life commonly referred to as reincarnation? Who really is this Jesus figure? If a person is not a Christian will they go to hell? Why did God let Jesus die on the cross? If he was all powerful why didn't he intervene and save his son's life? I had many questions that needed answering.

One evening, I awoke to a strange sensation in my body. I felt light and was floating over my bed. I could see around the room, and then I felt scared and that sensation immediately ended. I was no longer floating in thin air. I had trouble going back to sleep after that experience. Did I die? What I had experienced was the first of many out-of-body experiences also known as Astral Projection. Astral Projection is where your astral body leaves the physical body connected to a silver lining cord. When in this astral state; people can will themselves to travel within their house or other places on this Earth or physical plane as well as a spiritual journey through the astral world.

From those early experiences, I learned by actual experiences that people do survive beyond their physical body when they die. The soul lives on. Many people have had similar experiences, sometimes from an accident, where they die and see loved ones that have passed on or translated. These people return because it isn't their time. They are never the same after those experiences. They begin to appreciate the little things in life they had taken for granted, and they know that they will live on after their earthly stay.

After studying the book by James Van Praagh, a world renowned psychic and medium, I visited his website. On his website, there were forum boards and a JVP chat room for people from around the globe to discuss their spiritual beliefs. Once a week that chat room had guest speakers. Some of the regulars in that chat room were from the United States, United Kingdom, Canada, Australia, and South America. I was able to forge a friendship with some of them that still continues today.

One particular friend, Michelle (not her real name), was developing her psychic skills. She had a lifelong gift in being able to reach out to the spiritual worlds. On many occasions, she could channel the Archangel Michael. She was truly blessed in her skills. I had always held the belief in guardian angels and spirit guides. All of us have spirit guides who help us to get by in this world and to teach us. Some of us are able to connect with our spirit guides. The teachings that we all receive are through many of life's lessons. Many of us choose to repeat those lessons repeatedly. Many people have closed themselves spiritually rather it be due to their prejudices, religious beliefs, materialism, and the seven deadly sins such as greed, gluttony, lust, envy, sloth, wrath, and pride.

Over the course of several weeks and months Michelle and me chatted online quite often as friends. Sometimes she gave me readings and on one occasion, she performed an energy healing called Reiki. The Wikipedia definition of Reiki "is a form of spiritual practice used as a complimentary therapy for the treatment of physical, emotional and mental diseases. Mikao Usui developed Reiki in the mid 20th century in Japan, where he said he received the ability of healing without energy depletion after three weeks of fasting and meditating on Mount Kurama.

Practitioners use a technique similar to the lying on of hands, which they say, will channel "healing energy". Practitioners state that energy flows through their palms to bring about healing and that the method can be used for self-treatment as well as treatment of others. Practitioners are also able to perform this type of energy healing from far away. Normally, in Reiki, the practitioner doesn't touch the person's body.

After this Reiki session, Michelle told me that she could feel the Archangel Michael using her hands in conducting this energy or spiritual healing. She told me *"she never experienced that before with anyone, and that I was truly blessed."* Until that evening I had never heard much about the Archangel Michael. This was also my first exposure to Reiki.

One day Michelle sent me an e-mail telling me that the Archangel Michael had a message for me that evening. That evening, Michelle, was able to channel the Archangel Michael for me to receive his message. Obviously, I was taken aback that an angel would even want to contact me. He told me that I will eventually write this book but in writing this book, I need to do so out of love. He told me that *"You are a writer, and you have much wisdom to share."* He told me that eventually I would return to Texas. He told me that I had a good heart and a kindred soul, which is why I had been deceived and betrayed many times in my life. He told me to trust my instincts and gut feelings. He also joked around with me. The angels do have a sense of humor as well as God.

I would later be living on the north side of San Antonio in a gated community. One summer day, the temperatures in San Antonio were well in the high 90s, and all day I had been thinking of hitting the pool right after work. Driving home I was thinking of just driving my truck into the pool because it was so hot outside. I pulled into the allotment and saw some people already at the pool. Upon a closer look where I usually sit I saw three beautiful women sunning themselves in their bikinis. I thought I would be in heaven very shortly.

I got home and quickly changed into my bathing suit. I drove back up to the neighborhood pool, five minutes later. I walked up the ramp all excited about seeing some hot babes; I turned the corner and Oh Lordy!! Where those fine looking ladies were sitting, now sitting in those same chairs was a middle-aged bald guy, with a beer gut that could house commercial aircraft, and his two bratty kids. In my head, I thought I heard some serious roaring laughter and chuckling. God likes to mess with me at times.

The Archangel Michael had conveyed to me through Michele *"if you send out love you will receive love."* Life is to be treasured and enjoyed. It is up to all of us to ask for abundance in our lives and expect to receive abundance. If you want to receive abundance from the universe, ask for it, believe you will receive it, and to know and express to God that you deserve to be happy and receive abundance from the universe. Each thought that we have goes out to the universe, and it is a Universal Law that those thoughts will eventually manifest. Sometimes those positive thoughts will cancel each other out when we begin to think negatively. The universal consciousness doesn't determine or ascertain what is good or bad. That is why many people attract negativity into their lives. We are what we think. We become what we think. We all have the ability to heal ourselves spiritually, mentally and physically. God loves us all. God doesn't judge us."

I later asked the Archangel Michael about my displeasure with what is happening in Iraq about our young men and women who are dying over there at the hands of the terrorists and the insurgents. He told me *"First off, your soldiers are under a 'contract'. God is very displeased with the terrorists and the suicide bombers with their brutal attacks against the civilian population not only in Iraq but their killings throughout the world. They will meet their 'judgment'."*

In this session, I had also asked the Archangel Michael in regard to the legal battles I've had with the National Guard Bureau (NGB) and the Ohio National Guard as well as the second legal case involving fraud and corruption at the Defense Finance and Accounting Services (DFAS). He told me *"There has been many fingers pointing where the individuals involved have been laying blame on others. But look how you have grown. You are a much stronger person now. Look at how much you have accomplished. You need to stop beating yourself up. God doesn't beat himself up."* So sometimes in life, there are silver linings in our problems and obstacles that we face. He then told me *"In divine timing your case will get resolved in your favor."* I told him "Thank-you."

One evening, my friend Michele, had told me "in the spiritual worlds the entities that reside there do not have genital organs. Our spiritual bodies do not reproduce. There is no need to go to the bathroom." This brings me to the conclusion that all those suicide bombers who have died will have a rude awakening when they cross over to the other side and the virgins they are expecting in paradise, well they are virgins with no sex organs. It will take those suicide bombers many lifetimes to pay off their karmic debts to all of those victims.

The old saying, what goes around comes around rings true. God has given us all "freewill". It is up to each of us in how we live our lives. None of us can escape Karma. God loves us all. He is forgiving. He blesses us, but we are still accountable and Karma doesn't wipe our slate clean when we ask for forgiveness. The Karma that we all occur goes on many lifetimes before that Karmic debt is totally paid off, sometimes with 'interest'. It is 'our choice and our free will' to earn good or bad Karma.

The textbook definition of Karma is – "The doctrine of fate as the inflexible result of cause and effect, especially the principle by which a person is rewarded or punished in a subsequent incarnation for deeds in the previous incarnation; the theory of inevitable consequence." There are many that do not believe in reincarnation where we will all spend many incarnations returning to the physical plane. It is understandable why many people do not want to believe in reincarnation as well as Karma. People do not like to be held accountable for their deeds.

Do not worry about those who have wronged you, forgive them, for they will reap what they sow. Leave it in God's hands and the universe will sort things out in the end. A person may be able to hide from the 'law' but not the universe or the supreme deity. However, God loves each one of us where he allows us to pay off our Karmic debts as well as receive rewards for our good deeds in our future incarnations. In one life a person could be born as a Palestine and the next life as an Israeli.

God wants us as souls to gather and gain many experiences as well as learning life's lessons. There are many blacks in this country that hold racist views against the white man because of what happened to their ancestors who were held as slaves. Many blacks are angry at the whites and at times in anger they lash out at the whites or even against their own race. The people whom they lash out at are innocent victims. They had nothing to do with what happened when there was slavery in America. When people act out in anger and hatred because of slavery many generations ago, they are no better than those slave-owners. Just remember there is justice in the universe and those slave traders, whom many were blacks themselves trying to earn a living, have had to pay off their crimes to humanity over many lifetimes. Many of those slave traders, in later incarnations, have had to walk in the shoes of the black man.

It has been said that we all choose the life and the family that we are born into. We are born with a divine mission to accomplish. In this lifetime, you could have been born a black man to learn and experience being one quite possibly because of racist attitudes you had held in a previous incarnation. If one should take a new racist viewpoint then one continues a vicious cycle of being the aggressor and victim over many more incarnations.

When a child is born, that child is a perfect spiritual being, knowing only love. It is when this child grows up, he or she may develop prejudices and racist views from their parents and their environment. A child is not born into hatred but develops hatred based on life experiences. In order to get off that cycle of being the victim and aggressor is to accept people the way they are no matter what their color, ethnic origin, or religious upbringing. When one does that they build positive karma.

A person becomes much stronger if they can learn to send out love versus sending out hatred towards others.
When a person hates, they are very weak emotionally and spiritually; it is when they learn to love that they begin their journey back to soul's origins, which is the Love of God.

People may ask of themselves "Why do bad things happen to good people?" I know I have asked that question numerous times. For starters, God gave mankind a gift of 'freewill'. With freewill, people can choose to do 'good deeds',' or they can choose to do 'bad deeds'. People can choose to do good deeds to one another and live their lives as a productive and responsible member of society. People can also choose to do harm to other people. God and the angels do on occasion steps in when good people are being harmed. But for the most part God allows all of us to make our mistakes and errors in judgment. The theme of karma will sort things out in the end.

Several years ago I was working at the Ohio Air National Guard. I was making a 145 mile round trip commute daily from Canton, Ohio to Mansfield, Ohio. One morning was to be my last long commute to work. My wife and I just rented a new apartment in Mansfield. While driving at the corner of my eye, I saw a full-size automobile barreling down the street coming at me running a stop sign. There was no time to react. I knew I was going to be killed in my sub-compact vehicle. My life flashed before me. I braced for impact. I heard the crushing sounds of metal against metal, bending and shattering. Everything was happening in slow motion. I then witnessed something unexpectedly and unexplainable before my eyes.

I knew I was meeting certain death. There was now a large blue pick-up truck right beside me. This truck came out of nowhere, crossed over the double yellow line, passed me and took the blunt of the charging vehicle coming my way that blew a stop sign. The crushing sound of metal against metal was not my car but that blue pick-up truck. My car and I was saved and no one received any injuries. I witnessed a heavenly miracle, one of many more to come. Apparently, God has other plans for me.

CHAPTER 21 – SPIRITUAL JOURNEY CONTINUES

The spring of 2006, my spiritual journeys in leaving my body that I enjoyed while in the dream-state were increasing quite often. One such journey was where I had the opportunity to meet my mother who had passed away in October 2004. She was radiant and very lovely wearing a light blue dress. She was very happy and contented no longer suffering the pains of her illness that took her life. She has a companion who now lives with her in heaven; my long lost friend and pet, Curly. He is waiting for me on the other side. My mother and my dog, Curly, visits me quite often. I can feel her presence when she rubs her hands through my hair. I can feel Curly's presence when he visits me on occasions by when he rubs his fur against my legs. My mother spends a lot of time in heaven working in her garden. She is joined by many of her friends and family members that have passed on or translated. She has guided me, as well as my angel entourage, since her death. Curly is still protective of me like I was of him when we were together.

From day one Curly and I bonded together, and it is a bond that will never end. This bond began when a woman from work was trying to find a good home for one of her pups. She convinced me that I needed a dog, and she had one that I could adopt. I went over to her house to discuss this matter with her. While talking about that pup, there was another pup that came up to me that was very friendly and without realizing it, I started to pet that dog. He was rubbing his fur against my legs. He was the runt of the liter. She didn't think I would be interested in that four month old pup. So I asked about taking him home instead of the other pup that I came to see. Taking that pup home proved to be a wise decision for me.

Curly was the friendliest dog I have ever come across. He loved people. His main job was to keep the backyard free of squirrels and any stray cats. There were two squirrels that used to daunt Curly. The closest Curly ever got to them when chasing them down was about five inches. I don't know what he would had done if he ever caught one of them. That was a full-time job, sometimes 24/7, for Curly. Curly also was not one that liked being restrained. Even though I had a fenced in yard he would always eventually find a work around in getting out of the yard, no matter what I did. He would sometimes leave the backyard and wait for me to come home from lunch, just sitting at the end of the driveway. But he was smart enough and always one step ahead of the dogcatcher. Curly knew he was safe inside his backyard where he would run too as a safe haven just too daunt the local dogcatcher in his escapades. The local dog catcher notes to me were getting harsher in words.

Curly was a mutt, part Basset Hound and Brittany spaniel. Some evenings he did howl at night knowing that I would relent to bring him back inside so as not to disturb the neighbors. Even though he stayed mostly indoors at night, those nights that he was out back, he was working, to keep the backyard safe. One night I tried putting a mussel on him. I figured that would stop his barking and howling. I didn't hear anymore barking that night, so I figured the mussel must have done the trick. The next morning I came across little fragments of what used to be a mussel. He made sure it was totally destroyed so that it would never be used again.

One morning I tied a long leash on him to a pole. A utility company was planning on doing some work in the backyard, and they requested that I restrain him. I came back home shortly and saw that Curly's chain was completely wrapped around the pole minus the dog. He found a way out.

Later when I was considering running for public office I told a friend of mine. He asked which office? I jokingly told him head dog catcher. But I know better. Curly would haunt me if I did that. Curly and I will be together again when my mission on this planet has been completed.

One evening in April of 2006 in the middle of the night, heavy rain and strong winds awakened me. A storm was coming through Canton, Ohio after causing a path of widespread destruction through Kentucky and Indiana. This storm had produced a series of tornadoes. Earlier in the evening I had paid a visit to the JVP Chat room and saw some regulars in that chat room. One of the regulars whom I usually chatted with, where we both had made a strong spiritual connection was a woman, named Marvida.

However, on this particular evening there was another woman in there talking about her spiritual travels. She was telling others in the room about a God deity called the Sugmad and of a spiritual teacher and traveler, who goes by the name of the Mahanta. She was also talking about a God-like entity known in that Astral Plane as the Kal, ruler of the astral and physical plane. While she was chatting no one knew what she was talking about. This is quite understandable and if a person starts spitting out those names in front of other people, those people will think that person is some kind of nut and should be institutionalized. I know I would have if I hadn't already known what she was talking about.

There is a worldwide religion, with many members across the globe, called Eckankar, Religion of the Light and Sound. The teachings from that religion are where they teach its members about the audible sound and the light and how one can experience and travel throughout the Kingdom of God with the assistance and protection of a spiritual traveler, the Mahanta. The Kal, a deity, encompasses the positive and negative energy flows in the astral and physical planes. He is a god-like figure that keeps the lower worlds in harmony and balance. Should a person stumble upon or make contact with the Kal, that person will think that he or she has met the heavenly father God. This woman was telling others in the chat room that she is aware of the Mahanta and the Sugmad, the God of gods over the higher planes. But she was emotionally connected with this Kal deity. The Kal can take on many shapes of being a god-like entity expressing love and kindness and compassion.

Those are the positive traits of this deity. Other times he may appear as a monstrous and hideous figure, a god that should be feared, and rightly so. The Kal had appeared to her showing the loving god and also as a hideous monster.   She did not fear him.   Think of the Kal as Mother Nature even though they are different.   Mother Nature brings the nourishing rains and is a loving co-creator of the planet Earth. However, Mother Nature can in a heartbeat become vicious and destructive almost like some of my ex-girlfriends.   Mother Nature can send hurricanes, tornadoes and floods destroying in her wicked path.

I was concerned about this woman and did not feel good about her. I didn't want to be in her presence in that chat room. But I felt I should try and talk to her.   I asked her if she was a current or former member of Eckankar. She told me she was neither but was aware of the Mahanta and how that spiritual being helps people explore the heavenly worlds. She told me she wants to stay in the presence of the Kal. I encouraged her to break away her ties and follow the Mahanta in seeking out the Sugmad, the God of gods, the Supreme Creator, who resides beyond the fifth dimension or Soul plane. I was defending the Mahanta and God. The reason I am bringing this out is because it relates directly to what befell me later in the evening on a spiritual adventure I had after I had gone to bed.

That evening I was 'taken' on a spiritual journey to a higher dimension to the God consciousness. All of us are spiritual beings, where our soul seeks to eventually return home. That evening I became to know the oneness with God. Apparently, I did a good deed earlier in the evening and was rewarded by performing that act. We reap what we sow. That thunderstorm interrupted my spiritual adventure where I was immediately returned to my physical body. I could still fill the power of the God consciousness upon my shoulders. It was a feeling of power and knowing I've never experienced before. My first thought was I wanted this thunderstorm to end. Instantaneously, the rains and the thunder stopped. The winds became calm.

I closed my eyes and I returned to the God consciousness, fully aware of my physical body where I wasn't sleeping or just dreaming all of this. There was a duality of being simultaneously in a spiritual world and the physical world. I was truly blessed in being within the presence of God and enjoying the oneness with God. I got to experience firsthand God's love for all of us. The spiritual law of silence prevents me from speaking in details with regards to this spiritual initiation while in the God consciousness. But all of this was very real, and it was an experience that I will always treasure and cherish. No one can ever take that away. No matter what happens in my physical life or incarnation, I know where my soul resides and belongs. That is what is more important. After my spiritual odyssey, I opened up my eyes, and a thought occurred to me. The farmers will need the spring rains for their crops. I still had the power of God on my shoulders and immediately after having that thought. I heard the splattering of raindrops upon the roof where a light rain started as I then slowly drifted back to sleep. God trusted me for a few moments with his powers.

I was baffled from that experience. Was this all just a dream in this spiritual journey where I had the experience of enjoying a oneness with God? Was it just a coincidence that when I willed the storm to stop it stopped immediately? Was it just a coincidence that when I willed for the rain to start back up it immediately started to rain? Would I have a new future as a weather forecaster? Those were baffling questions for me where I didn't have the answers. Shortly thereafter, I had more types of unexplained experiences, not in the heavenly worlds but here on earth, that defies those laws of physics and nature. These additional experiences had no earthly logical explanations. There were other people who had witnessed these other experiences or miracles.

One of my spiritual friends is a woman who lives in the San Francisco area, Marvida. We had shared many evenings chatting online, as well as writing numerous e-mails to one another. I shared with her many of my spiritual adventures. One such adventure was when I was given the opportunity to view the Ancient Secrets of the Universe. I found myself drifting down a tall wall several stories high with ancient writings. That was an awesome experience seeing all the secrets of the universe. It would have been great if I had brought along my camcorder to record what all I was reading. I shared with my friend my experiences with the Archangel Michael.

Not long after that she wrote me telling me of her recent experience where she was able to take a spiritual travel with this great Angel. He had held her with his hand while they flew through the universe at breath taking speeds. She told me about her experience when she was fitted with angel wings on another journey. Yes there is such a thing as human angels. She is truly blessed. There was an occasion where she stood before God, the Archangels and Goddesses, and Jesus. She told me they then became one with God and then they all separated again. God had told her "we are all one". To this day, Marvida, truly an angelic one has embarked on a new career at my urging in helping and healing others through massage therapy. Those who are fortunate to come to her for a healing are truly blessed. Those of you are living or visiting the San Francisco area. You need to look her up, make an appointment with her as she uses the power of the angels within her hands.

Because I had made tremendous growth in my spiritual enfoldment, that created many challenges in my relationships. Many times relationships end because two people grow at different speeds where they become opposites. In today's time the planet is undergoing a change in consciousness that started at the beginning of the new millennium. Everyone is going through this change together, while they realize it or not, in preparation of entering a new age of enlightenment. Some people have not awakened yet, spiritually, or are doing so slowly while many are making tremendous strides. These changes are causing some havoc in friendships and relationships. This is also why there are much chaos and conflict throughout the world.

I had returned briefly to Ohio while pursuing a federal court case against the Ohio National Guard and the Office of Personnel Management. I was staying with my father while this case was pending in federal court. My father was living alone after my mother had passed away. Being there I could spend some time with my elderly father. I had been away for a number of years while serving in the Air National Guard and the Air Force.

One day his automatic garage door opener stopped working. He tried unplugging it and plugging it back in with no results. It was inoperable. The wall switch wasn't working. Neither one of us could determine if there was a short in the wiring or if the motor had burned out or maybe there were some loose wires in the garage door opener. Over the course of several days, he would hit the wall switch, and nothing would happen. I had tried it, myself and nothing would happen.

One morning my father was in the garage and decided to maybe check out the wiring connections before calling a repairman. He was in the process of getting a step ladder when I came out to the garage. I was looking up at the automatic garage door unit, and I pointed to it telling my father maybe there was a connection problem to the wiring. As soon as I said that, a strong and very powerful thought came to me to just push the wall button one more time. I thought that thought was silly, but it was a very overwhelming thought. I had this strong feeling that it will work now after I had pointed to that unit and sure enough the garage door raised itself when the garage door opener kicked on.

My father immediately turned around carrying the step ladder, in amazement. He asked me what I had done, and I said "Well all I did was point to the opener and pushed the wall button." He raised and lowered the garage door several times, each time it worked fine. We both couldn't explain what happened. I jokingly told him I must have some miraculous powers in my fingers for when I pointed to it. We had a good laugh over that. That garage door opener is still working now, several years later, with no more problems.

One day while I was still in Ohio, I went to work at a part time job. When I had reported for work the building was extremely warm that hot and muggy summer day. The air conditioning had gone out during the previous shift. I turned on the AC and went out back and the compressor was blowing out cool air instead of hot air. It appeared the unit needed service work requiring a Freon recharge. As the day progressed; inside the building grew warmer and very uncomfortable. I needed to come back to work a few days later on Friday, and hopefully they would have it fixed by then. The weather forecasters were predicting hot and humid days with highs in the mid-90s. That Friday when I arrived at work it was stifling hot in the building. They had the doors open and the manager and the company had yet to send out a repairman. I knew this was going to be a long hot weekend to work. I was disappointed that the manager hadn't done more to get the air conditioning working. The previous day one of the employees had gotten sick at work from the heat. I was determined to do something that day.

I was living a very short distance from work. I went home to bring back a fan but all that did was blow around hot air. A customer came into the store and remarked that it was hot inside. I'm thinking to myself that 'it doesn't take a rocket scientist to figure that out'. However, he did say he has worked on air conditioners. Once he said that, I took him outside to the compressor unit. The air conditioner had been shut off since it wasn't working; only blowing out warm air. While outside a thought occurred to me while pointing to the outside compressor, there was a power shutoff box to the unit. I asked him to unplug it and then plug it in again. He did so knowing full well that wasn't the problem. Another thought occurred to me to go back inside and turn on the AC. Sure enough it started right up, and the outside air compressor immediately started spewing out hot air like it should. That customer was baffled into why the AC was now working. It was my 'intention' that when I started the shift, I was determined to get it working.

Later that evening, the assistant manager called into the store, and I told her I was able to get the AC working again. She was ecstatic. The remainder of the summer I enjoyed cool air while at work. I think it was a miracle that this all came about. Now for the readers out there, if your appliance or air conditioner does not work, please do not call me to fix it. Call a repairman. Every time that customer returned to the store, he was still baffled on what occurred that one afternoon. It was something that was unexplainable and to this day remains a mystery to me as well as this next story.

The summer of 2006 I had taken up fishing again. Previously, I could never catch anything. I would put a worm on the hook and after the worm screams had died down, I would drop the baited hook in the water. The fish would pull on the line letting me know to re-bait the hook. Sometimes by looking into the water, I would see fish all around my hook nibbling away. I fed a lot of fish that summer.

One day I accepted an invitation to go fishing with a buddy from work. He was living in a house along a small lake. It was great being out with nature enjoying the warm air. I finally caught a fish or maybe just snagged one by accident as the fish was swimming by the baited hook. I brought it in and it measured maybe three inches in length. It didn't matter I finally caught my first fish after many years of trying. But I had to throw it back in since it was too small to keep. About an hour later, my bobber went under. I pulled on the pole and this time I had a big one. After about ten minutes in what seemed like an eternity, as the fish was getting closer, I saw that it was a large catfish, fighting me, not wanting to be caught. As I was about to bring it out of the water, the fish somehow managed to get free. Which is just as well, I wasn't so sure if I wanted to remove that bad boy from the hook while it was thrashing around. It didn't really matter if I caught anything that day, I just enjoyed being at the lake.

My buddy from work and I had started talking about 911 on that fateful September day in 2001. He was telling me that he viewed a lot of photos on the Internet showing the destruction of the World Trade Center and how some pictures, in particular, were troubling to him. He said there were photos of the billowing clouds arising from that disaster that had the image of God in the smoke. He had thought that there was an image of an angry God. I told him "I thought it was a photo of the Devil." As soon as I said that, he motioned for me to turn around. My back was to the lake.

I turned around and was flabbergasted and speechless at what I saw. We both were stunned and didn't know what to make of what we were seeing. His girlfriend's son was also seeing the same thing, no more than seventy-five yards, across the lake from where we were standing. I don't know if others at that lake had seen what had just manifested, instantly. There in front of us was a small white puffy and billowing cloud, not fog that hot and dry afternoon, but a cloud just hovering three feet over the lake. Josh said he wished he had a camcorder or a camera to record what we were witnessing. Otherwise no one would believe us. But the three of us were all seeing the same thing in amazement. Was this just another coincidence where we were talking about the image of God in those flames and clouds of smoke from the terrorist attacks at the World Trade Center, where immediately we saw the manifestation of a cloud?

While watching this phenomenon, after a few moments, we stood there stunned by what we were viewing and witnessing, we saw that cloud was starting to be inhaled into the woods. Streams of cloud vapors were rushing over the lake, up to a bank and into woods, being vacuumed away. Three minutes later the cloud had dissipated. Neither of us could explain what we just saw. Since that day, every time my buddy goes to his fishing spot, he keeps looking for that cloud to reappear while trying to understand and comprehend what he witnessed on that summer day in July. This was an experience we will never forget. It defies the physical laws of nature.

I believe God had a message for us. I believe he was not happy about the events of September 11th with all of those who were involved in this plot to kill innocent people with no justifiable reason. But I truly believe that the higher spiritual court will sort things out in the end. One may escape the justice of mankind but no one escapes the justice of the heavens.

This spiritual court is where many enter for a full life review at the end of their earthly stay. This is where we are all judged. But we are not judged by God but by ourselves. You may wonder how that can be. See in this life review you will feel the emotions of all those that you have touched in your earthly incarnation. There is another type of judgment and I may walk alone in this concept but I believe that December 21st, 2012 is a very significant spiritual day. I believe that is the Judgment Day and this judgment will be made in the heavens without us being aware of it – but know that it will occur. The angels have been quite busy determining who the good souls are and who the bad souls are. Those with a good heart will move forward in their spiritual destiny and quest while the rest will be held back and accountable.

Those who have committed evil will face a most unbearable type of justice. They will get to experience not just the emotional harm but the physical harm and pain they caused others. The leaders in the world who have gone bad will experience a hell like no other where they will feel the emotional and physical pain they have caused to others; these numbers could well be in the millions. They will see themselves as others have seen them. Some will know they had lived a life of being a ghastly beast. They will tremble at themselves when they know what is about to occur by this beast. God will not judge – you will. God will show mercy and allow those to pay their debt and to redeem themselves by returning in more incarnations – some as an indigenous people. No one escapes karma. Your belief or non-belief in karma makes no difference to the outcome.

CHAPTER 22 – COMBATING TERRORISM

The message that we received by that manifestation was that God was angry that day by the atrocities that were committed against innocent men, women and children at the World Trade Center, the Pennsylvania air crash and the Pentagon at the hands of terrorists. I know deep in my heart those terrorists who committed those brutal attacks are not spending eternity in paradise. No doubt those terrorists had to meet their Day of Judgment. September 11th was also a bad day for Islam where radical Islamic extremists carried out acts of terror. These extremists have debased the teachings of the Prophet Mohamed because of their hatred to those who have different beliefs and faiths.

The Prophet Mohamed had walked the face of the earth to uplift and raise the consciousness of Muslims. Just like Mohamed, Jesus had also walked the face of the earth to awaken people to the love of God. Buddha, Krishna and other spiritual teachers have spread the word of God to uplift humanity spiritually. God had given mankind as a gift, freewill, but it is up to people to live their lives under the rules and laws of mankind and the Kingdom of God. Teachers and masters have been sent by God to the many races and ethnic origins of people. Many religions have sprung up as a result of these masters and teachers. Christianity was formed around the teachings of Jesus. Islam was formed around the teachings of Mohamed. So if God sent all these teachers to the various ethnic races why do people not respect other faiths and cultures? We are all children of God. We are all loved equally by God.

There are many nations that hold a deep hatred towards the United States. I'm not making claims that Americans are perfect. I'm not making claims that the United States government has never done harmful acts against the citizens of other nations. Many people around the globe have a deep mistrust to American foreign policies. That is understandable for most Americans hold a high degree of mistrust against the U.S. government. I say to the Islam world, America is not your enemy. America has been your protector and liberator during the past century. The people of Islam are not in chains or enslaved because of the blood that has been spilled by American men and women serving in the military.

With the rise of Nazi Germany, the world and mankind were in deep peril. Nazi Germany was on the war footing in establishing a New World Order. Their first phrase was to eradicate the Jewish population from the earth. Nazi Germany had their sites on the rich oil fields in the Middle East. If it was not for the intervention of the United States in defeating Nazi Germany, the Middle East would today be under the control of Nazi Germany or later during the Cold War the former Soviet Union. The people of Arab descent would be enslaved if not killed off by genocide. The people of Islam are free today because of America. The chains that now bind the people of Islam come not from America or Israel. Those chains are self-binding. Release those chains and be free. America is not your enemy. Your enemy was defeated. There are many that claim Adolph Hitler was the Anti-Christ. This Anti-Christ has been defeated by the heroic actions of many Americans.

I say to the people of Islam, your leaders, are the ones who are enslaving you by preaching hatred. When you look inside your heart, you will find the love of God. Ask God to release those chains, release those negative energies of hatred. Fill your heart with love and you will be free. America will welcome you with open hearts when you do so. American is a forgiving nation. Nazi Germany was the infidels. Your leaders have been preaching hatred to enslave and control you. America is the melting pot of the world. America is made up of every ethnic race and religion from around the globe. In the eyes of God, we are all brothers and sisters.

To the people of Palestine, your enemy is not Israel or America. The hatred towards Israel has been fueled by many extremist leaders to enslave you. These extremist leaders do not care if you are free. If they wanted you to be free they would have given you land and the financial resources to form your own nation instead they preach hatred to control you. Your destiny has always been in your own hands. Israel welcomes peace with you. Israel has supported your people. Free yourself from these extremists with radical viewpoints. America wants to welcome you to the world. America wants you to gain statehood. Statehood has always been possible when you choose the path of peace. Unfortunately, your leaders preach hatred to gain power and control over you.

Iran does not want the Palestine people to have peace and prosperity. Iran wants only one thing, and that is the destruction of Israel. The Palestinians are merely pawns in their grand scheme in developing nuclear weapons to obliterate Israel and possibly other nations. They do not care if many Palestinians lose their lives by doing so. If the oil-rich Arab nations had really cared about the Palestinian people do you not think they would help those people by providing a safe environment and building their economy. There are many in the Arab world that is serving their self-interests in perpetuating the Israeli/Palestinian conflict. If Iran was really concerned about the plight of the Palestinian people they would be sending food and supplies as well as efforts to create economic prosperity. Instead they send weapons to kill people. People need jobs not death and turmoil.

One of the barriers to the Palestine and Israeli conflict is the occupation of Arab and Palestinian land by Israel. The Arabs lost land to Israel in the 1967 war. Now had the Arab nations been successful by occupying Israeli territory, would they be willing to give up that land if there had been a different outcome? Perhaps if the Arab world wanted peace for the Palestine people, then they should provide homes and territory for Palestine. Should the United States return to Mexico, the states of Texas, New Mexico and Arizona? Should the United States return all land taken from the American Indian? Many people in America have lost their homes by bank foreclosures, should the banks be forced to return those homes back to the original owners? Likewise, Israel should not be clinging to the hope that they will return to the borders that once existed in the Biblical days. Things change, Israel should be satisfied that a wrong was righted by the United Nations in reestablishing an Israeli state.

Does not the robin co-exist peacefully with the blue jay? Does not the blackbird co-exist peacefully with the red cardinal? Do not the ducks and geese co-exist peacefully among each other? Robins and blue jays are different colors. So why cannot the Palestine's and Israelis co-exist peacefully?

The Palestines and Israelis are of God's creation. Are they not? So why would God, the creator, want people to kill one another because they have different beliefs and customs? Why would God, the creator, want Islamic extremists' kill non-believers of the Islam faith? Is God a Muslim? Is God a Christian? Is God a Jew? Of course not, the people of the Muslim, Jewish and Christian faiths are all of God's children. God wants to see all of his children co-exist peacefully. Those that speak of murder are not speaking the truth and love of God. The Prophet Mohammed was not doing battle with Judaism. The Prophet Mohammed was doing battle with other Arab tribes in the Arabian Peninsula. The people from Islam, Christianity, and Judaism are all children and descendents of Abraham.

There are some who want to die as martyrs. They want to die for a certain cause thinking that God will bless them. Hatred is a deadly sin. How can one win the love or admiration of God for a weakness of hatred? Anyone can hate. Loving one's neighbor who is an enemy is a character trait that spells of power and strength. There have been many suicide bombers who have died by blowing themselves up and taking many innocent civilians with them. They commit this act of murder and atrocity thinking they will die as a martyr. In five or ten years from that murder, how many people from the suicide bombers terrorist group will still remember that martyr? Most likely, no one will conversely remember. So what good was gained by this act other than serving the forces of evil? Is it not the desire of mankind to live in peace and harmony and to pursue happiness? How can one be truly happy when they serve the forces of evil? Would not the want-to-be

martyrs find peace and happiness in creating a family instead?

I say to the terrorists that if your most senior leaders want you to die for the cause. Why are they not fighting in the trenches and spilling their own blood for the cause? Why are they not donning suicide vests to die as a martyr? Could it be that the hatred they hold in their heart is really to satisfy their own ego by having you die instead? Perhaps your senior leaders are addicted to power and mastery over you. Without a cause of hatred, they would be nothing. But with this cause of hatred are they not really nothing? The deadly sin of hatred is really a strong overpowering weakness. It takes one great power to send out love to those who they do not agree with. What have the people of Islam gained, besides more death and destruction, at the hands of those who have ruled by hatred? Now there have been winners in this age of terrorism. American and other world-wide defense contractors are reaping huge benefits and profits by developing new weapon systems to fight terrorism.

Launching spy drones has become a big business. Developing new spy surveillance over Americans and international countries have become a big business and very profitable. The age of terrorism has added fuel and creditability to Big Brotherism. If the terror organizations and the insurgents around the world should ever lay down their arms, that will spell disaster to many American firms, which have reaped financial gains by the threats of terrorism.

Terrorism has enabled the American government to become more powerful. Terrorism has enabled further imperialism and influence into places like Iraq, Afghanistan and other Middle Eastern countries. That is what has been gained by the suicide bombers, while many of the Islam faith has died, not just by the American military but by their own brethren.

Why do you think that Osama Bin Laden was not killed or captured before May 1st 2011? It served the interest of many to keep Osama Bin Laden alive and in power. For they have gained further power as a direct result of Osama Bin Laden. Do you not think that America had the capability of capturing or killing earlier their former terrorist informant Osama Bin Laden? He has served the purpose of some within the American government. Once the age of terrorism is over, those who have held power and benefited by terrorism, they will crumble and then that is when the people of Islam will have a better future.

I say to the terrorists if you want to win your jihad over western influence and control. Lay down your arms and become productive members of your society. That is how you will win your jihad. You have the power to destroy the infidels that way for the infidels will no longer have a cause. Send the infidels "love" and the infidels "hatred" towards Islam will crumble. Your people will then be at peace. American troops will have to return home for they no longer would have a war mission. There are many who want to see this war on terror to continue indefinitely. For they have gained much power. I say to the terrorists sending our hatred is easy. The difficult task is sending out love to your enemies. That takes power and gumption. I say to the terrorists that you cannot win with your bombs and guns for America has many more. You cannot win by spilling your blood from your heart.

However, you can win your jihad by spilling out love from your heart. There can be a day when the West and the Middle East will co-exist peacefully as the robin and the blue jay birds. There will be a day when Palestine and Israel will co-exist peacefully, as independent states, as the red cardinal and the blackbird.

CHAPTER 23 – DIVINITY

Earlier I had written about some of my spiritual experiences from the spring and summer of 2006. Since that time, my spiritual as well as political evolvement had continued in leaps and bounds. I had become more concerned about the welfare of this planet. I have been able to tune into the consciousness of the Divinity in learning new truths. The Divinity or the God consciousness is making us all move forward. This change is happening worldwide. Change can be quite chaotic and unsettling to people. People always ask for "change" but when it appears, they sometimes have trouble coping with new changes in their lives. There are movements now across the planet for global peace and prosperity. This movement includes many who are from all walks of life and all of man's many religions.

People are starting to realize that we are interconnected in some way. People are realizing that everyone is a part of the Divine spark and every individual is unique and many of us desire a better world. No longer will people be dependent upon others to solve the problems in the world but they themselves can be a part of the solution and as a collective consciousness, they can move many mountains. Granted many people are spewing out negative energies through the universe. Nevertheless, many more are now spewing out positive energies of love, peace, happiness, and acceptance of others.

As I said earlier my spiritual growth has grown in leaps and bounds. In August of 2008 in one of my meditation sessions I asked that I be given the opportunity to meet God and the spiritual masters in person in my nightly travels. That night I was given that opportunity. In front of me stood God, several ascended masters, and prophets. My heart was filled with joy and abundance of love. Standing beside our heavenly father another individual stood out who was a spiritual master from another galaxy. His head and body was much larger than a human being. His clothing was what one would see in the famous TV series, Star Trek. Shortly afterwards I met a dear friend of mine who was also on a spiritual travel that evening. We both walked down a grassy knoll together. In front of us was a large group of inhabitants who were walking towards us, they all went by us one by one receiving a blessing from the two of us. Do not believe the U.S. Government in their denials that we are being visited by extraterrestrials. They have been watching us since man first appeared on the planet Earth.

The Christian Bible makes many references to these beings. Back in those days they were referred to as gods. Who do you think helped build the Egyptian pyramids? The world still does not have the technology to build pyramids of that magnitude. The Aliens had made contact with the U.S. government at Carswell shortly after the United States began their nuclear weapon program. The United States did not trust the Soviet Union, and they feared the Aliens. In exchange the Aliens were willing to provide mankind advanced technology. The United States said "no". The Soviets later acquired nuclear technology. We know how that all worked out. The nuclear arms' race with the Soviets began. Should there ever be a nuclear exchange between countries; the planet Earth could put things out of balance in the universe with the Earth on a different orbit and axis.

A month later I was distraught over a romantic relationship. I cried out to the heavens asking 'why?' In the early morning hours I was awakened by God. He briefly talked to me about that other person, and he told me what my future would hold. I told him that I could not go down that path. It would be too difficult. He said "Robert, who you are today, you will not be the same person five years henceforth." A few months later God would awaken me again asking for my permission on something. He said to me "Robert you take care of the day to day affairs and responsibilities in your life, and I will take care of the major events in your life." At first my thought was to try and negotiate. I received a quick mental thought from God saying "this is God you are talking too". So I decided it was for my highest good to make our agreement with no strings attached. I sold my soul to God.

Sometimes in casual conversation people will ask me what is my religion or what church do I attend? Usually I just say that I was raised an Episcopalian. For me to attend church services on a regular basis would take me many steps backwards. How can I go back to becoming a member of a manmade organized religion when I have traveled to the far reaches of the heavenly worlds? I have been to the Land of the Angels and to the Land of the Demons. I much prefer the former. Besides I am no longer welcomed at the Land of the Demons since my first and only visit. I had to do battle with many demons that were coming at me as black orbs. I stood my ground, as being One with God, and when it looked like I could be overwhelmed, I made a wise crack comment that they found humorous. The moment, through mental telepathy, when they found my remark humorous

I saw a spark of 'goodness' and sent a flash of light at them. The Land of the Demons lost quite a few members to the Light.

One of the first times I had reached a very high state of consciousness; I felt being pulled back to my body. I didn't want to leave. I had great wisdom and great clarity of mind. I knew all things. However, being pulled back, I felt my consciousness of KNOWING slipping away. The human mind is not capable of retaining this type of extreme higher consciousness. However, I am able in mediation call upon a higher power to seeking an answer to something. My intent in writing this book is to show others how to raise their spiritual consciousness.

Everyone has the spark of the divinity. It matters not to God what a person's religion or faith they hold. All religions are a path to God. Most of all religions claim to be the only right path. But a person's religion can only take one so far. It is up to the individual to seek a higher calling. When one does that, the person's angelic and spirit guides will be there to take them to the next level. Until one is given the opportunity to meet face to face with the Oneness, they will have many more lifetimes to accomplish that task. However, eventually everyone will get there. That is our destiny. It is in everyone's power and destiny to raise their spiritual consciousness and experience the Oneness.

I had always sought out the truth on my own. I never believed in having blind faith. I always sought out confirmation on my spiritual quest. Many ministers and priests want us all to have blind faith. In one of my previous incarnations, I was a bible thumping preacher. I thought I had the answers and expected my followers to have blind faith in the Christian religion. Obviously, I didn't have it all figured out in that life. For me, I am close to the Divinity around water rather it is a river, lake, and ocean or even just taking a shower. I am always much closer to the Divinity when writing. Spiritually, I have grown in leaps and bounds in writing this book. Much of what I have written just flows through me. I am not a psychic or a medium. Those practices are of the lower worlds. A friend of mine is a medium. She can see and speak to those who have passed on. I tried to raise her consciousness so that she could be connected to the angels. She told me she cannot do that because of her religion. She continues her readings through earthbound spirits. That was her choice and I respect her for that. And she will probably continue to have many more incarnations.

Many religions hold a belief that there is a battle between God and Satan. There is no battle. There is no Satan. Granted there are spirits which are very evil as well as demons, but there is no Satan as depicted by the Church. The Church conjured up Satan or the Devil to control the masses. Where there is light there is no darkness. There are places within the astral plane where the inhabitants feel they are in hell. Many of them are looking forward to incarnating back to Earth. There is filth in this place, but the inhabitants earned that place while living their lives here on Earth. They lived in filth during their life. Nobody no matter what their economic status should live in filth.

Unfortunately there are many who choose that existence. In my spiritual travels, I have visited that region in the astral plane. People raise your consciousness. Do not accept living in filth. Clean up your home. Paint your walls. Throw out your old decaying furniture. Get rid of the clutter in your lives. If you do so, that will attract positive energies into your life. Get rid of those negative energies that surround you. God wants to see all enjoy abundance in their lives.

Civic leaders need to get involved in beautifying their cities. Destroy the old decaying and abandoned homes. If you do so, a new rebirth will manifest in your city. Take a new and positive approach to urban renewal. Instead of filling your jail cells with non-violent offenders, employ them in urban renewal projects throughout your city or town.

CHAPTER 24 - ERADICATING WORLDWIDE TERRORISM

Mankind is faced with the plaque of worldwide terrorism. Islamic extremists have radicalized the Koran to justify their acts of violence. They are not targeting just people from the Jewish and Christian faiths but also many followers of Islam and the Prophet Mohammed. They do not care if they commit blasphemy against the Islam religion and the Prophet Mohammed. They just want to kill and bring as much misery and turmoil as possible. This needless violence against the human race has to be and will be eradicated.

It is important to understand the psychotic thinking and the hatred that goes behind all of these acts of violence. Their mindset is beyond rational thinking. A rational person would not commit indiscriminate violence and murder. They think nothing of corrupting the teachings of the Prophet Mohammed to further their cause, which is simply HATRED. The organized leaders of these hate groups against humanity have convinced their followers that they will find paradise in heaven if they commit hell on Earth. A rational person knows that to enter into the eternal Kingdom of God it has to be earned by righteous acts and not by committing heinous crimes. Terrorists do not comprehend that all people of the world, regardless of their faiths or skin color, is loved by all in the heavenly realm. The God who resides on the fifth plane does not have a chosen people for everyone is loved equally and unconditionally. Why would the Father/Mother God want to destroy one of their creations?

What makes a mind justify these indiscriminate acts of violence? How can a new child who is born with only love in their hearts turn to hatred as they grow older? The central culprit is the mind's ego. It is all about gaining control over others to feed their ego need for power. Terrorists use religion as their justification to recruit others in their hate campaign.

Terrorist leaders seize upon the need for people to belong to a group. That is why they have been successful in recruiting potential suicide bombers. People who are ego-centered have a need to belong. These suicide bombers think they are doing work for Allah in bringing death and destruction to others. However, in actuality they are doing the work for the darkness and the terrorist leader who wants to control others. Killing is a way to satisfy their 'ego'. Some terrorists become crazed and bloodthirsty with killing and dismembering people to satisfy their need and obsession with controlling others. The wrath of the people will eventually hunt down these vicious, bloodthirsty killers as a wild and savage animal.

Religion is sometimes the main culprit and recruiting tool in fueling hatred towards others the religious leaders need to stop inciting all this violence. No one religion has a direct path to finding God. Jesus was born as a Jew but his ministry was not of the Jewish faith. He was a spiritual teacher trying to uplift the spiritual consciousness of the people. The Islam church leaders need to uplift the spiritual consciousness of the people and preach brotherly love towards all. If the Islam church leaders are not able to speak of love towards all how do they expect to be a true spiritual leader? The true word of God is love and peace. The word of God is not hatred and turmoil.

When one speaks of hatred and turmoil that message is sent outwards to the universe and the universe not detecting what is good or evil returns hatred and turmoil as negative energies. All of our thoughts are like a boomerang. What we think eventually is what we receive. Speak of love and peace from your heart and you will receive and be surrounded by love and peace. Speak and think of war and a greater menace of destructions manifests. So speak and think of peace and a greater prosperity will evolve.

Until one reaches the state of God consciousness what we think, speak and act is like a mirror in front of us. We become what we think and speak. Speak of others as the 'infidel' then one becomes one reflected by the mirror. Under the Universal Law of Attraction, we attract like minded people in our lives. By judging others as the "infidel" we become one and attract other "infidels" into our lives. That path is one of self-destruction. Know that the corrupt organized terrorist organizations are and will self-destruct. They have become their own enemy. They have become what they hate. They have become the "infidel". They have called upon God to destroy the infidels and God has answered their prayers.

Speak of others as God's beloved creatures and the eyes of the soul opens up to the Divinity that resides in each living orgasm. People open up your spiritual eye and look beyond the mirrors of the mind, and there you will find our heavenly Father/Mother God surrounding you with love and blessings. *"Welcome home. We have been waiting and watching you over the ages. We have seen your many struggles and triumphs - Archangel Michael."*

It is paramount that the Islam faith, as well as other faiths, condemns acts of violence and terrorism for the Divinity resides in every single soul. The ultra-conservative Clerics in Iran, should, instead of spewing out anger and hatred from your hearts, shed those, and seek the higher ground towards a path to the Divinity. Raise the spiritual consciousness of your people and receive the abundant gifts of God.

CHAPTER 25 - RESOLVING THE ARAB/ISRAELI CONFLICT

This book would be incomplete without a discussion of the Arab/Israeli conflict. This conflict extends back to many centuries before the birth of Christ. Much has been written over the ages of the rights of Jews to exist. Looking back over the long history of these people one might come with a conclusion that "a whole lot of people do not like Jews". For countless centuries the Jewish people have been a group persecuted and put into exile, to scatter throughout the world. Many nations and races have over the centuries tried to eradicate the Jewish population.

The Jewish people trace their origin to Abraham. Whose birth name was Abram. Abraham (Abram) was the descendent of Noah's son, Shem. The Jewish people trace their ancestry back to Abraham's second son, Isacc. The Prophet Mohammed is an ancestor of Abraham's first born son, Ishmael. The Abrahamic religions of Christianity, Judaism, and Islam all trace their roots back to Abram. Jesus was a descendent of Abram, who was later named Abraham by Yahweh. Abram had two wives, Sarai and Hagar that bore offspring. Hagar had given birth to Ishmael, and Sarai had given birth to Isacc. Ishmael and Isacc were half-brothers.

A story is told in Genesis 15:12-18 where "Abram fell into a deep sleep where he encountered God again. God then prophesied to Abram that the nation born to him would be removed to another land where they must be trialed for four hundred years and afterward, they would be greatly blessed with many possessions and occupy their own land. This prophecy was that of the Israelites in subjection to Egyptian rule, for four hundred years, before returning back to Canaan to claim it as their own. Abram entered into a covenant with Yahweh who declared all of the regions of land that his offspring would claim under Genesis 15:18-21:

"To your descendants I give this land, from the river of Egypt to the great river, the Euphrates, the land of the Kenites, Kenizzites, Kadmonites, Hittites, Perizzites, Rephaites, Amorites, Canaanites, Girgashites and Jebusites."

Yahweh had told Abram that many nations will be born from his offspring.

Abraham, his son (Yitshak) Isacc and grandson Jacob (Israel) are referred to as the patriarchs of the Israelites. All three of them lived in the Land of Canaan, that later became known as the Land of Israel. They and their wives are buried in the Ma'arat HaMachpela, the Tomb of the Patriarchs in Hebron. King David (1010-970BCE) made Jerusalem the capital of Israel. His son Solomon (970-931BCE) built the first temple in Jerusalem.

In 587 BCE, the Babylonian Nebuchadnezzar's army captured Jerusalem, destroyed the Temple, and exiled the Jews to Babylon located in the present day Iraq. Eventually, the Persians (Iran) conquered Babylon. The Persians sent the Jews packing again to the Land of Israel. The Jewish built a second Temple in Jerusalem. From 587 BCE onward that region was ruled by a number of empires: Babylonian, Persian, Greek Hellenistic, Roman and Byzantine Empires, Islamic and Christian crusaders, Ottoman Empire and the British Empire.

When the Land of Israel was under Roman occupation God had mercy upon the people of Israel. For centuries the priests were proclaiming that the Messiah will deliver them out of exile and domination. Those prayers were answered and God sent his Son to deliver them a new life to free them of their chains. The priests were fearful of the Romans. The Romans tried to eliminate all traces of the Jewish faith and changed the name of Israel to Palestine. It was the divine destiny that Jesus would be their Messiah. He was gaining many followers. The priests were fearful of Jesus bringing the wrath of the Romans. The priests also did not want to give up any of their power to Jesus. Pontius Pilate was not interested in killing Jesus. He did so because of the demands coming from the Jewish priests. If the priests would have set aside their fears and thirst for power, Jesus would have filled his divine destiny as the Messiah. Instead, they chose the wrong path again and the nation of Israel did not rise until 1948. Today the leaders of Israel have not learned anything from their history. The Jews are still looking for their Messiah. Their Messiah came and gone. Would another one meet the same fate as Jesus?

In 1948, Great Britain ended colonial rule over the former Syrian province of Palestine. Palestine was divided into two nations, present day Jordan and Israel. The day after the declaration of independence from Great Britain, armies of five Arab countries, Egypt, Syria, Transjordan, Lebanon and Iraq, invaded the new nation of Israel. Israel later withdrew its army from captured land in that war. Again Israel was invaded in 1956 called the Sinai War. The Israeli army later withdrew. In the 1967 War, Israel did not withdrew its forces.

However, the occupied territory by Israel was home to many Palestinians. The Palestinians were cheerful that the Arab nations would occupy Israel. That didn't happen. The Palestinians like the rest of the Arab world did not like the Jewish people. The Arab world was not happy that Israel didn't withdraw its military forces this time around. Israel being surrounded by many enemies most likely wanted a buffer zone from future possible invasions. Egypt had sent two divisions to the Sinai. That wasn't sufficient to launch an offensive war. However, the Israeli's took a different viewpoint and attacked. The 1967 Six Day War was an avoidable war.

How does international law between civilized nations weigh in on military actions? Israel had signed an agreement under the Geneva Conventions. The Geneva Convention requires an occupying power to change the existing order as little as possible during its tenure. One provision from the Geneva Conventions is that "an occupying power must leave the territory to the people it finds there. It must not bring its own people to populate the territory." Article 49 states "The occupying Power shall not deport or transfer parts of its own civilian population into the territory it occupies."

In the (Intifada: The Palestinian Uprising Against Israeli Occupation, ed. Lockman and Beninan): "In violation of international law, Israel has confiscated over 52 percent of the land in the West Bank and 30 percent of the Gaza Strip for military use or for settlement by Jewish civilians... From 1967 to 1982, Israel's military government demolished 1,338 Palestinian homes on the West Bank. Over this period, more than 300,000 Palestinians were detained without trial for various periods by Israeli security forces."

There is a story about a Palestinian man who became a victim of this occupation through no fault of his own. "There is nothing quite like the misery one feels listening to a 35-year old {Palestinian} man who worked for fifteen years as an illegal day laborer in Israel in order to save up money to build a house for his family only to be shocked one day upon returning from work to find that the house and all that was in it had been flattened by an Israeli bulldozer. When I asked why this one done—the land, after all, was his—I was told that a paper given to him the next day by an Israeli soldier stated that he had built the structure without a license. Where else in the world are people required to have a license (always denied them) to build on their property? Jews can build, but never the Palestinians. This is apartheid." (Edward Said, in The Nation, May 4th, 1998) A side note to this story, in the United States, the government agency would first fine the individual without a valid permit and then charge that person demolition fees and charges.

The United States and other countries had offered numerous proposals in resolving this conflict. "Senator William Fulbright proposed in 1970 that America would guarantee Israel's security in a formal treaty, protecting her with armed forces if necessary. In return, Israel would retire to the borders of 1967. The UN Security Council would guarantee this arrangement, and thereby bring the Soviet Union—then a supplier of arms and political aid to the Arabs—into compliance. As Israeli troops were withdrawn from the Golan Heights, the Gaza Strip and the West Bank they would be replaced by a UN peacekeeping force. Israel would agree to accept a certain number of Palestinians, and the rest would be settled in a Palestinian state outside Israel.

The plan drew favorable editorial support in the United States. The proposal, however, was flatly rejected by Israel. 'The whole affair disgusted Fulbright,' writes his biographer Randall Woods. 'The Israelis were not even willing to act in their own self-interest." (Allen Brownfield in "Issues of the American Council for Judaism." Fall 1997.)

Israel made a grave mistake in not accepting this peace opportunity. This stalemate generated the beginning of the Palestine Liberation Organization (PLO) led by Yasser Arafat. The PLO grew in numbers with support of many Arab countries in resisting Israel. The hatred towards Israel was always present. This occupation of Arab land would grow and fuel more hatred towards Israel and then later against the United States. This began the beginnings of terrorism that grew worldwide. Thousands of people have died in Israel and the Palestine territories over hatred. Israel would later begin settlements on the occupied territories that fueled more worldwide hatred and anguish towards the Jewish people and all who supported them.

This hatred that has been festering manifested into a terrorist organization called Hamas to resist Israeli occupation. In 1970, Israel had the opportunity for a lasting peace after its people have been wandering in the deserts and throughout the world for hundreds of years. Because of greed and other factors, Israel lost that opportunity to exist and live in peace with its neighbors. The Jewish people have had to live in fear in an endless bloodbath. Israel has been in a state of war now for decades. Too many on both sides, war is employment.

I recently read something that I had found very disturbing that goes back many years, which gives a good explanation why this conflict has gone on for so long. I had always thought and I'm sure many Americans feel the same way that Israel was always the victim. "In Israeli Prime Minister Moshe Sharatt's personal diaries, there is an excerpt from May of 1955 in which he quotes Moshe Dayan as follows: 'Israel must see the sword as the main, if not the only, instrument with which to keep its morale high and to retain its moral tension. Toward this end it may, no—it must—invent dangers, and to do this it must adopt the methods of provocation-and-revenge... And above all—let us hope for a new war with the Arab countries, so that we may finally get rid of our troubles and acquire our space.' Quoted in Livia Rokach, (Israel's Sacred Terrorism)"

This region has experience horrific anguish and atrocities against both sides. Both sides have committed acts of terrorism against each other. Why has the United States allowed itself to get involved in all of this drama? Israel had nothing to lose. They were already hated over the centuries' way before Christopher Columbus discovered the West Indies. By bringing in the United States, they were able to allow much of that hatred to be levied against America. What has Israel ever done that has been good for America? We all know they despise all those who are not of the Jewish faith. The Palestinians' hate America and they have marched in their streets waving banners 'Death to America'! When America suffered a terrorist attack on September 11th, 2001, they were cheering in the streets.

This Arab/Israeli conflict has ushered in an era of Terrorism. The United States was brought into the middle of all of this. America has her sons and daughters dying in Iraq and Afghanistan.   The CIA had given birth to Al Qaeda.   The Palestinians are just pawns being manipulated by many in the Arab world. The Arab world could care less about the plight of the Palestinian people. They serve their (Arabs) purpose in prolonging this conflict. Iran supplies' arms to the Palestinians to fight the Israelis. Wouldn't the Palestinian people been better off with Arab investments for jobs and food and clothing for these people? What have the U.S. government leaders and politicians been thinking?   What would Abraham think of his children embroiled in all of this hatred? The people of Judaism and Islam are the children of Abraham.

Suppose a couple in America adopts two young infants, one of Arab and one of Israel's descent. Let's say this is a loving couple to their children. These children all then raised in a good home knowing only love. The Arab and the Israeli children would grow up loving each other. Why, because they weren't taught hatred by their parents. In another scenario, there is an Israeli couple who adopted that same Israeli child. Their neighbors are of Arab descent, and they adopt the Arab child. Both sets of parents hold hatred towards each other because of their descents. Both children would grow up hating one another. Hatred many times is taught by parents who express their own prejudices and judgments. These parents were taught hatred by their parents. That is what is happening, hatred is taught throughout the world. The United States instead of dropping bombs on people; they should be dropping educators (preferably with parachutes) to teach love, respect, understanding and tolerance.

The clocks of time cannot be turned back. Even if Israel would withdraw from the occupied territories, peace will take a long time to manifest, if ever, unless of course there could be a "wild card" in this equation. The path in this conflict, if continued, will lead to more misery and destruction and then finally the annihilation of many people in the region. There is a window that is approaching that could alter this destiny, if the people on both sides would grasp the opportunity.

The children of Abraham during the ages have been in battle with one another. Most of these battles have erupted over religious beliefs of hatred to one another. Religion is not God-made. Religion is man-made. Spiritualism takes one to a higher ground. There has been an era where the children or descendents of Abraham, have been fighting and murdering their brothers and sisters. The Israelis and Arabs are really one people that came from different tribes. Israelis are Arabs.

They just own a different perspective in their religious views. All the descendents of Abraham's share both the Arab and Israeli blood. You are all one. You are all half brothers and sisters with the same bloodline. You are both loved equally by the Father/Mother God. You are all loved equally by Jesus and Mohammed. Jesus was not a Christian. A whole man-made religion, Christianity, emerged to worship Jesus. Jesus and Mohammed walk hand-in-hand, in brotherly love, and so can the descendents of Abraham. This will not happen overnight. There is much healing that needs to be undertaken.

There is a wildcard. That wildcard is Iran. The elderly Iranian clerics are in their final days. The Iranian clerics have preached hatred. They do not preach about God's love only hate. The youth of Iran does not accept the beliefs of these clerics. The youth in Iran is wondering why they need to hate another people because of their religious beliefs or ethnic origin. They are not accepting the hatred that has been taught by their parents and clerics. The youth in Iran will be taking another path. They know they live under a corrupt political system. They see the corruption for what it is. They are not buying into it. They are awakening like the others in Egypt, Libya, Bahrain, Morocco, Tunisia, and other countries that will be following. The youth across the world are the crystal children. They will be making great strides in the technologies and political ideologies. All the corrupt political dynasties across the world will falter.

There is sacred ground to both the followers of Islam and Judaism near Jerusalem. This is where the descendents of Abraham will build two Temples on this high plateau. Both Temples will be separated but still joined together structurally. The people of both faiths will be welcomed to attend either Temple. The new Iran will provide needed funds for these two Temples. When these Temples are built that will be the dawn of a new era of peace and prosperity in the Middle East. These two Temples on this Mount will bring about a new healing to erase and cleanse the karmic dusts. This will be a proud moment for Abraham, Jesus and Mohammed joined by the many heavenly angels.

(Note: I have a gift of clairvision. The morning following this writing I was shown, by the angels, a rocky mountainous region. I didn't recognize where I was being shown. I asked mental telepathically if this was on the planet earth or another planet. I've seen other planets. I immediately was shown a ground level area that had tire tracks. So this was on this planet. It is also confirmation that this is where God wants the Temple built. There is a high plateau for the Temple overlooking a deep oval shaped crater.)

Some who read these words will scoff at what has been written. In 1940 would people believe that the United States would become great friends with Germany and Japan? Decades ago during the heat of the Cold War, would people believe that the United States and the former Soviet Union would be on friendly terms; working together on the International Space Station? Would people believe that the former Soviet Union, who was seeking a New World Order of One World Governance, crumbled without a shot being fired?

Nostradamus had predicted that the fire would rein down from the skies. What he was referring to was a nuclear confrontation between the two nations. That prophecy never came true. Could anyone have predicted that the Berlin War would come down? Much has been written in the Revelations. Do people think that God has not read those Revelations? Predictions and prophecies are in many times just probabilities. Miracles do happen.

We have the power to change our destiny for the better. For a long period of time, the United States has been a financial powerhouse throughout the world. Would anyone have predicted the financial collapse of Wall Street and the major banks? And would anyone have predicted that the Green Bay Packers would beat the Pittsburg Steelers in the 2011 Super Bowl? Never rule out the wildcard. Never rule out God's Master Plan.

Since Biblical times the Middle East has been conquered and occupied by many world empires. Many of the countries within the Middle East have warred with one another over border disputes. If you look at Europe their history is also filled with many empires and nations conquering one another. There have been many false religious prophets in the dark history of mankind which have advocated murder. What has been gained by all of these wars? Nothing!

Years ago the European nations saw that it was becoming very difficult to trade with one another over the fluctuating currencies. The nations of Europe joined together into an economic union. They have one monetary currency, and that is the Euro. This economic partnership and open borders have brought about a lasting peace and economic prosperity. The Middle East should consider the same type of economic union to include Afghanistan and Pakistan as well as Israel. Some may argue that Israel should not be included. Putting ethnic and religious differences aside, would not Israel be a favorable asset to a Middle Eastern Union?

Israel has the best minds in the Middle East for military strategies. The Jewish people have many individuals who are savvy experts in financial strategies. The oil will not last forever in the Middle East. The oil fields will begin to dry up. When that happens the economic prosperity a few of the nations have enjoyed will perish into economic ruin. You cannot have open borders when there are radical fundamentalists whose sole intention is to kill and steal. Those people need to be separated from society. By joining together now and developing long term economic strategies for the post-oil economy, the Middle East will prosper economically and politically with a centralized currency.

CHAPTER 26 - POLITICAL UNREST

Good people do not need laws to tell them to act responsibly,
while bad people will find a way around the laws. Plato

There is much turmoil on the African continent and throughout the entire Middle East. It is sad to see all these people dying. The world is moving closer to an Age of Enlightenment. In this coming shift, chaos is all around us. People are being awakened. This awakening is happening worldwide. Governments who are blocking the internet from their people cannot stop this Divine awakening from happening. Years henceforward there will not be any dictators or repressive governments.

The people of the African continent as well as the Middle East will be making hard decisions on the type of government that will best serve their nation and its citizens. Now is the time for those seeking a higher calling in defining their country's future. The choices and decisions will not be easy, but it is a task that will define their destiny for the betterment of generations to come.   There are many forms of government throughout the world, take the best benchmarks from the best forms of government that serve the people.

A passage is quoted here from "The American Ideal of 1776 – The Twelve Basic American Principles written by Hamilton Abert Long in 1976.   This passage discusses the differences between a Democracy and a Republic.

"An Important Distinction: Democracy versus Republic

It is important to keep in mind the difference between a Democracy and a Republic, as dissimilar forms of government. Understanding the difference is essential to comprehension of the fundamentals involved. It should be noted, in passing, that use of the word Democracy as meaning merely the popular type of government--that is, featuring genuinely free elections by the people periodically--is not helpful in discussing, as here, the difference between alternative and dissimilar forms of a popular government: a Democracy versus a Republic. This double meaning of Democracy--a popular-type government in general, as well as a specific form of popular government--needs to be made clear in any discussion, or writing, regarding this subject, for the sake of sound understanding.

These two forms of government: Democracy and Republic, are not only dissimilar but antithetical, reflecting the sharp contrast between (a) The Majority Unlimited, in a Democracy, lacking any legal safeguard of the rights of The Individual and The Minority, and (b) The Majority Limited, in a Republic under a written Constitution safeguarding the rights of The Individual and The Minority; as we shall now see.

A Democracy

The chief characteristic and distinguishing feature of a Democracy is: Rule by Omnipotent Majority. In a Democracy, The Individual, and any group of Individuals composing any Minority, has no protection against the unlimited power of The Majority. It is a case of Majority-over-Man.

This is true whether it be a Direct Democracy, or a Representative Democracy. In the direct type, applicable only to a small number of people as in the little city-states of ancient Greece, or in a New England town-meeting, all of the electorate assemble to debate and decide all government questions, and all decisions are reached by a majority vote (of at least half-plus-one). Decisions of The Majority in a New England town-meeting are, of course, subject to the Constitutions of the State and of the United States which protect The Individual's rights; so, in this case, The Majority is not omnipotent and such a town-meeting is, therefore, not an example of a true Direct Democracy. Under a Representative Democracy like Britain's parliamentary form of government, the people elect representatives to the national legislature--the elective body there being the House of Commons--and it functions by a similar vote of at least half-plus-one in making all legislative decisions.

In both the Direct type and the Representative type of Democracy, The Majority's power is absolute and unlimited; its decisions are un-appealable under the legal system established to give effect to this form of government. This opens the door to unlimited Tyranny-by-Majority. This was what The Framers of the United States Constitution meant in 1787, in debates in the Federal (framing) Convention, when they condemned the "excesses of democracy" and abuses under any Democracy of the unalienable rights of The Individual by The Majority. Examples were provided in the immediate post-1776 years by the legislatures of some of the States. In reaction against earlier royal tyranny, which had been exercised through oppressions by

141

royal governors and judges of the new State governments, while the
legislatures acted as if they were virtually omnipotent? There were no effective State Constitutions to limit the legislatures because most State governments were operating under mere Acts of their respective legislatures, which were mislabeled "Constitutions." Neither the governors not the courts of the offending States were able to exercise any substantial and effective restraining influence upon the legislatures in defense of The Individual's unalienable rights, when violated by legislative infringements. (Connecticut and Rhode Island continued under their old Charters for many years.) It was not until 1780 that the first genuine Republic through constitutionally limited government was adopted by Massachusetts--next New Hampshire in 1784, other States later.

It was in this connection that Jefferson, in his "Notes On The State of Virginia" written in 1781-1782, protected against such excesses by the Virginia Legislature in the years following the Declaration of Independence, saying: "An elective despotism was not the government we fought for . . ." (Emphasis Jefferson's.) He also denounced the despotic concentration of power in the Virginia Legislature, under the so-called "Constitution"--in reality, a mere Act of that body:

"All the powers of government, legislative, executive, judiciary, result to the legislative body. The concentrating these in the same hands is precisely the definition of despotic government. It will be no alleviation that these powers will be exercised by a plurality of hands, and not by a single one. 173 despots would surely be as oppressive as one. Let those who doubt it turn their eyes on the republic of Venice."

This topic--the danger to the people's liberties due to the turbulence of the democracies and omnipotent, legislative majority--is discussed in The Federalist, for example, in numbers 10 and 14 by Madison (in the latter noting Jefferson's above-quoted comments).

The Framing Convention's records prove that by decrying the "excesses of democracy" The Framers were, of course, not opposing a popular type of government for the United States; their whole aim and effort was to create a sound system of this type. To contend to the contrary is to falsify history. Such a falsification not only maligns the high purpose and good character of The Framers but belittles the spirit of the truly Free Man in America--the people at large of that period--who happily accepted and lived with gratification under the Constitution as their own fundamental law and under the Republic which it created, especially because they felt confident for the first time of the security of their liberties thereby protected against abuse by all possible violators, including The Majority momentarily in control of government. The truth is that The Framers, by their protests against the "excesses of democracy," were merely making clear their sound reasons for preferring a Republic as the proper form of government.

They well knew, in light of history, that nothing but a Republic can provide the best safeguards--in truth in the long run the only effective safeguards (if enforced in practice)--for the people's liberties which are inescapably victimized by Democracy's form and system of unlimited Government-over-Man featuring The Majority Omnipotent. They also knew that the American people would not consent to any form of government but that of a Republic. It is of special interest to note that Jefferson, who had been in Paris as the American Minister for several years, wrote Madison from there in March 1789 that:

"The tyranny of the legislatures is the most formidable dread at present, and will be for long years. That of the executive will come its turn, but it will be at a remote period." (Text per original.)

Somewhat earlier, Madison had written Jefferson about a violation of the Bill of Rights by State legislatures, stating:

"Repeated violations of those parchment barriers have been committed by overbearing majorities in every State. In Virginia, I have seen the bill of rights violated in every instance where it has been opposed to a popular current."

It is correct to say that in any Democracy--either a Direct or a Representative type--as a form of government, there can be no legal system, which protects The Individual or The Minority (any or all minorities) against unlimited tyranny by The Majority. The undependable sense of self-restraint of the persons making up The Majority at any particular time offers, of course, no protection whatever. Such a form of government is characterized by The Majority Omnipotent and Unlimited. This is true, for example, of the Representative Democracy of Great Britain; because unlimited government power is possessed by the House of Lords, under an Act of Parliament of 1949--indeed, it has power to abolish anything and everything governmental in Great Britain.

For a period of some centuries ago, some English judges did argue that their decisions could restrain Parliament; but this theory had to be abandoned because it was found to be untenable in the light of sound political theory and governmental realities in a Representative Democracy. Under this form of government, neither the courts not any other part of the government can effectively challenge, much less block, any action by The Majority in the legislative body, no matter how arbitrary, tyrannous, or totalitarian they might become in practice. The parliamentary system of Great Britain is a perfect example of Representative Democracy and of the potential tyranny inherent in its system of Unlimited Rule by Omnipotent Majority. This pertains only to the potential, to the theory, involved; governmental practices there are irrelevant to this discussion.

Madison's observations in The Federalist number 10 are noteworthy at this point because they highlight a grave error made through the centuries regarding Democracy as a form of government. He commented as follows:

"Theoretic politicians, who have patronized this species of government, have erroneously supposed that by reducing mankind to a perfect equality in their political rights, they would, at the same time, be perfectly equalized and assimilated in their possessions, their opinions, and their passions."

Democracy, as a form of government, is utterly repugnant to--is the very antithesis of--the traditional American system: that of a Republic, and its underlying philosophy, as expressed, in essence, in the Declaration of Independence with primary emphasis upon the people's forming their government so as to permit them to possess only "just powers" (limited powers) in order to make and keep secure the God-given, unalienable rights of each and every Individual and therefore, of all groups of Individuals.

A Republic

A Republic, on the other hand, has a very different purpose and an entirely different form, or system, of government. Its purpose is to control The Majority strictly, as well as all others among the people, primarily to protect The Individual's God-given, unalienable rights and therefore, for the protection of the rights of The Minority, of all minorities, and the liberties of people in general. The definition of a Republic is: a constitutionally limited government of the representative type, created by a written Constitution--adopted by the people and

144

changeable (from its original meaning) by them only by its amendment--with its powers divided between three separate Branches: Executive, Legislative and Judicial. Here the term "the people" means, of course, the electorate.

The people adopt the Constitution as their fundamental law by utilizing a Constitutional Convention--especially chosen by them for this express and sole purpose--to frame it for consideration and approval by them either directly or by their representatives in a Ratifying Convention, similarly chosen. Such a Constitutional Convention, for either framing or ratification, is one of America's greatest contributions, if not her greatest contribution, to the mechanics of government--of self-government through constitutionally limited government, comparable in importance to America's greatest contribution to the science of government: the formation and adoption by the sovereign people of a written Constitution as the basis for self-government. One of the earliest, if not the first, specific discussions of this new American development (a Constitutional Convention) in the historical records is an entry in June 1775 in John Adams' "Autobiography" commenting on the framing by a convention and ratification by the people as follows:

"By conventions of representatives, freely, fairly, and proportionately chosen . . . the convention may send out their project of a constitution, to the people in their several towns, counties, or districts, and the people may make the acceptance of it their own act."

Yet the first proposal in 1778 of a Constitution for Massachusetts was rejected for the reason, in part, as stated in the "Essex Result" (the result, or report, of the Convention of towns of Essex County), that it had been framed and proposed not by a specially chosen convention but by members of the legislature who were involved in general legislative duties, including those pertaining to the conduct of the war.

The first genuine and soundly founded Republic in all history was the one created by the first genuine Constitution, which was adopted by the people of Massachusetts in 1780 after being framed for their consideration by a specially chosen Constitutional Convention. (As previously noted, the so-called "Constitutions" adopted by some States in 1776 were mere Acts of Legislatures, not genuine Constitutions.) That Constitutional Convention of Massachusetts was the first successful one ever held in the world; although New Hampshire had earlier held one unsuccessfully - it took several years and several successive conventions to produce the New Hampshire Constitution of 1784.

Next, in 1787-1788, the United States Constitution was framed by the Federal Convention for the people's consideration and then ratified by the people of the several States through a Ratifying Convention in each State specially chosen by them for this sole purpose. Thereafter the other States gradually followed in general the Massachusetts pattern of Constitution-making in adoption of genuine Constitutions; but there was a delay of a number of years in this regard as to some of them, several decades as to a few.

This system of Constitution-making, for the purpose of establishing constitutionally limited government, is designed to put into practice the principle of the Declaration of Independence: that the people form their governments and grant to them only "just powers," limited powers, in order primarily to secure (to make and keep secure) their God-given, unalienable rights. The American philosophy and system of government thus bar equally the "snob-rule" of a governing Elite and the "mob-rule" of an Omnipotent Majority. This is designed, above all else, to preclude the existence in America of any governmental power capable of being misused so as to violate The Individual's rights-- to endanger the people's liberties.

With regard to the republican form of government (that of a republic), Madison made an observation in The Federalist (no. 55) which merits quoting here--as follows:

"As there is a degree of depravity in mankind which requires a certain degree of circumspection and distrust: So there are other qualities in human nature, which justify a certain portion of esteem and confidence. REPUBLICAN GOVERNMENT (that of a Republic) PRESUPPOSES THE EXISTENCE OF THESE QUALITIES IN A HIGHER DEGREE THAN ANY OTHER FORM. Were the pictures which have been drawn by the political jealousy of some among us, faithful likenesses of the human character, the inference would be that there is not sufficient virtue among men for self government; and that nothing less than the chains of despotism can restrain them from destroying and devouring one another." (Emphasis added.)

It is noteworthy here that the above discussion, though brief, is sufficient to indicate the reasons why the label "Republic" has been misapplied in other countries to other and different forms of government throughout history. It has been greatly misunderstood and widely misused--for example, as long ago as the time of Plato, when he wrote his celebrated volume, The Republic; in which he did not discuss anything governmental *even remotely resembling--having essential characteristics of--a genuine Republic. Frequent reference is to be found, in the writings of the period of the framing of the Constitution, for instance, to "the ancient republics," but in any such connection the term was used loosely--by way of contrast to a monarchy or to a Direct Democracy--often using the term in the sense merely of a system of Rule-by-Law featuring Representative government; as indicated, for example, by John Adams in his "Thoughts on Government" and by Madison in The Federalist numbers 10 and 39. But this is an incomplete definition because it can include a Representative Democracy, lacking a written Constitution limiting The Majority.""*

A Democracy can be repressive to the people. The United States has made countless mistakes in installing Democracy in Iraq and Afghanistan. There was no effort made to determine the best type of government for the people in these countries. Problems arise when the Majority rules. Problems also arise in the formation of political parties based on ethnic and racial groupings, which is a primary factor in causing a widespread insurgency in both countries. The United States has become a Totalitarian Democracy. The two major political parties have become opposing powers in an obsession of gaining political control and power over the other party.

Partisan politics will divide a nation. Non-partisan politics will unite a nation. Bi-partisan politics is really a compromise of partisan politics, and the result is a combination of two extreme points of view; neither one good for the country as a whole. Having Absolute Powers corrupt. The world has seen many leaders such as Lenin, Stalin, Napoleon, Hitler and many others which wanted to control regions and territories outside of their country. They were seeking domination over others to include world domination. There has been much talk about One World Government and a New World Order. This New World Order what the leaders do not want people to know is that for it to work, will require a depopulation of eighty percent of the world population.

The United States is on a dangerous path of knowing everything there is about an individual. They use the auspices, of "we want to protect you" so that people will give up their rights and freedoms. Many U.S. presidents as well as other world leaders have bought into a New World Order. The revolts across the world are of great concern to many leaders where they fear losing their powers to the people who are demanding liberty and freedom.

With the new Era of Enlightenment fast approaching people will begin to awaken, and the light will be shining on those in power. There will be a day that individuals as they progress spiritually will be able to tell when the politicians, government and religious leaders are lying to them. The problem now in America most people know that the government and politicians lie, but sometimes they do tell the truth. The U.S. government uses misinformation to further their objectives. They are using the same methods that the former Soviet Empire used on their people. The difference is that the U.S. government is becoming increasingly sophisticated in these domestic spy programs that the former Soviets could only dream about.

Since the Taliban has started their own jihad against the Islam faith, NATO needs to withdraw and allow the Arab nations to fill the vacuum and diplomatically integrate all ethnic groups to form their own government that is not repressive to the people of Afghanistan. Democracy or any other form of government has to be chosen, not forced upon. The United States cannot allow itself to be the 911 of the world. The nations of the world need to either close down the UN or reestablish a broader charter that will promote tolerance, peace and prosperity. Genocide or tyranny in any country throughout the globe is unacceptable.

Could there be a secondary purpose in having a large military contingency in Afghanistan or Iraq to extract precious metals or fossil fuels for commercial profit? We live in a civilized world. Are there leaders who are trying to revert back to the Dark Ages? There needs to be integrity at all levels of government. Those who are profiting from these wars should be ashamed of themselves. The world body needs to ensure governments not have a license to behave badly.

CHAPTER 27 - UNLOCKING THE SECRETS OF THE UNIVERSE

We are not human beings having a spiritual experience.
We are spiritual beings having a human experience.
Pierre Teilhard de Chardin

When discussing the universe one has to understand how this universe did begin. What triggered that event? There are many theories as to the creation of the universe. What existed prior to this creation? There has been much discussion of the two most common theories was it Evolution as explained by Charles Darwin or was it God's Creation? Evolution and Creation are two opposite viewpoints. For Evolution to occur there has to be a power behind that. A question also arises who is this God? Furthermore, is there more than one God? The major religions have their own beliefs, and they all believe that their beliefs are correct and have everlasting truths and all the other major religions and faiths have it all wrong. Many religious wars have been fought over the centuries which continue through today to change people's beliefs.

Maybe there is some truth in both theories as well as possibly the Big Bang theory. Students in the public education system should be exposed to both theories. I'm going to do the best I can to explain what I feel is the truth. It's up to the readers to do their own interpretation and discover their own "truths" which I have done in a lifelong journey in seeking the truth which prompted the writing of this book.

It has been said that the universe was once an empty matter-less void. Then a catalytic event occurred where matter was formed by that energy. The universe is made up of waves of energies. There is speculation if one were to travel faster than the speed of light matter will form. There have been many thoughts where God or a supreme deity had traveled throughout the universe at those breathtaking speeds and in his wake matter was created. This supreme deity or cosmic intelligence was both the omega, and the alpha made up of both positive and negative energies. This cosmic intelligence doesn't differentiate between what is good just like Mother Nature. Mother Nature or Gaia as she is sometimes referred too creates and nourishes life and also destroys life. Her rains provide water for plant and protein forms of life but Mother Nature also has a destructive power when its energies create tornadoes, hurricanes and typhoons.

The Kingdom of God is made up of several worlds, with us living here in the physical world. Many have heard of the Fifth Dimension or Soul Plane where one is a pure soul. The worlds below are parts of the negative worlds. The negative worlds are kept in balance by both the positive and the negative. Many people refer to God in the Holy Bible as the Old Testament God and the New Testament God. Many people claim to be God fearing individuals. One should not fear God. God is pure love or at least the God that I pray too who resides on the Soul Plane that wants us all to receive abundance and love and enjoy the fruits of our labors in our lives.

It may be hard for some people to grasp the concept that there is more than one deity or ruler. However, there are many worlds above us and with that come many rulers over those planes. When a spiritual traveler comes across one of these deities or rulers they think they have met the one and only God. There is a God, who is a pure soul and that is the Father/Mother God. I strongly believe that God wants us to seek out the truth of why we are here in this physical universe and for our souls to evolve and raise our energy vibrations or consciousness to a much higher level. God wants us to have faith in our convictions and our own personal truths that we have learned in our lifetime. I read a church billboard which stated "God doesn't need you be successful just faithful". I read and thought the pastor of that church was way off. God wants us all to be successful and lead an abundant life and to have faith in ourselves. God doesn't need to be worshiped as an idol; God wants us all to worship ourselves and to take care of our bodies and health; to love ourselves and to send out love to others.

Jesus was sent to this world to raise the consciousness of the masses so that they can find their God, who resides on the fifth Soul Plane. There are many paths to God and there is no one religion that has a monopoly on God. We all need to find the path that suits our spiritual needs as we constantly raise our conscious levels as we evolve as individuals. Now there are many people throughout the world who have lost faith in God or doesn't believe he/she exists. Many people live their lives, as though there is no heaven or hell, and that they are accountable to no one but themselves. When biting into a black or red raspberry or a strawberry or even munching on a watermelon, how can one think there isn't a God or Creator of life? Those tasty fruits and vegetables didn't just happen by chance or accident but were planned by a much higher intelligent power.

But now in the scheme of things, why were snakes created? Myself, that is one reptile that our world could do without or at least in my world. Sure they have a function in making sure the field mice and rats are controlled in nature, but then again, we could also do without field mice and rats. Why does Mother Nature with her gentle rains that later turn into sunny skies where Mother Nature on another day will create havoc and loss of life with horrendous storms?

There have been many summers where there has been an extraordinary amount of hurricane activity that was created by the negative energies of this planet. People's thoughts actually send out either negative or positive energies. There are many spiritual organizations that hold worldwide prayers and those prayers or affirmations send out positive energies throughout the world and universe. These spiritual organizations conduct worldwide prayer groups in ending the violence in the Middle East. It's crucial that many people get involved in these worldwide prayer groups. Sometimes all it takes is just one more person praying to cause a change.

Many religions share a fantasy, whereas when we all pass on, we will enjoy everlasting life and peace. Once a person is 'saved' they will escape what the Christians call 'hell'. The laws of the universe doesn't make it that easy where once we are saved all of our sins are absolved, and then we can once again sin all we want. As soul we incarnate on this planet Earth to gain experience and to experience all aspects of life. God has given us the "free will" to make our own choices in life.

Rather we want to believe in the laws of Karma that is an individual option to hold our own beliefs. However, no one escapes the wheels of Karma. Karma can be said to be 'what goes around comes around', or 'we reap what we sow'. God in most cases will allow a person to sin all they want because in the end of life, comes Judgment Day. This is where we are judged by how we lead our life. Some are moved forward on their spiritual journey and destiny while many others eventually have to return to Earth again to resolve those problems they had in their past life. This is called Reincarnation.

There are many out there that do not want to believe in reincarnation. That is understandable. Many people do not want to be held to account for their prior sins and trespasses. God loves us all and that is why he gives us opportunities to become better people and souls. He knows that we all will eventually find our way back home to the Kingdom of God. He is patient and is willing to wait many ages for our return home. Our salvation will come after; we pay off our karmic debts that we all incur over many lifetimes. Once a person reaches a state of God Consciousness, a person does not need to incarnate again. That path is not easy and only happens to the spiritual warrior who sheds the ropes and Maya that confines them to the lower worlds.

An example of karma may be where a person would steal money to take something from another person that does not belong to them. When one does that, they incur a karmic debt to that other person. That debt eventually has to be repaid no matter how many lifetimes it takes. Every action, every thought is recorded in our many lives or incarnations in the 'akashic records'; much like the National Security Agency (NSA) here in America. Until one attains the Soul Plane, the Fifth Dimension, that person will keep returning. In most instances immediate reincarnation does not take place when one enters the Heavenly gates. There we will all spend some time with our loved ones who have preceded us and then when we do return, we choose the family we want to incarnate with for our highest good. For me my earliest memory that has stayed with me all these years was before I was born where I was standing beside my mother watching my father work. We all have our own reasons why we have chosen to reincarnate and to learn specific lessons or to pay off a karmic debt. We have all been given a choice or another chance when we entered this life. You may have chosen to be born as a Jew or a Palestine or a black man or an Asian. All of us on this planet are interconnected to everyone else on the planet.

Now many of you have wanted to be with your soul mate. We all want that and many people have been fortunate to come across such a person who fits their description of a soul mate; and many of us are still searching. God wants us all to be happy. He wants us all to find that special someone to be in our life. He gave the human race the pleasures of sex as a gift to men and women. The bible teaches us that we were created in the image of God. Our heavenly father depicts the masculine. So what depicts the feminine side? Is God a single entity? Shouldn't he also be happy with a soul mate? Are there also in the heavenly realms, goddesses? The answer is yes. God is joined with his twin soul mate, our heavenly Mother God, or Goddess. The both of them make up the Father/Mother God. Eventually, we will all meet up with our twin soul as one.

There are many barriers to finding our true home within the Kingdom of God. The spiritual path is not an easy road. There are jagged edges and many roadblocks. One has to be a spiritual warrior to find the Oneness. However, do know that those barriers are tumbling to make it easier for those who follow the path to God. Just like there have been many barriers to global peace and prosperity, but eventually we will get there. It will not happen by blind faith, but by people believing in themselves. They can make a difference. The angels welcome, one soul at a time.

CHAPTER 28 - HOLY TRINITY OF MEDICINE

After editing the section regarding health care in the back of my mind, I felt this topic needed more discussion. I just didn't at first know where I wanted to go. We all know that Americans as well as the global population needs affordable health care and affordable health insurance. Nevertheless, what is most important is that we all receive quality health care. What good is low-cost health care and low-priced health insurance if it doesn't make us well when we are sick or injured?

I was born and raised into a medical family. My father, a World War II veteran, was a Chiropractor where he had his practice in Canton, Ohio. I was raised growing up on the importance of the natural healing. If you catch a cold you take Vitamin C. If you over exert yourself in exercising you take Vitamin C. My father was a pioneer in the Chiropractic profession. The American Medical Association (AMA) back in those days didn't recognize Chiropractic as a legitimate health care practice. They were both opposing forces; much like conservatives and liberals. One medical viewpoint was that medicine was the cure all for all illnesses and diseases and the other viewpoint was that one didn't need to introduce harsh chemicals into the body.

When I was in the Air Force developing a new computer system, many times when we fixed one problem, we created a host of other computer bugs. The same thing applies to medicine; a person would take a prescription to treat one condition but the side effects of that drug would create a host of other medical problems. Many times the side effects are worse than the original condition being treated. We all know this. We alsoknow that we need to see a physician if we have a bone sticking out of our bodies.

Over fifteen years ago I was involved in my first major traffic accident. A lady pulled out in front of me, and I hit her car broadside coming to an immediate stop. I didn't know it at the time that my chest crushed the steering column. The next morning my former spouse and I were in extreme pain. We went to the Emergency Room and were released with no broken bones. After a few days, I was having severe chest pains. The ER contacted my family doctor and he prescribed Nitroglycerin. I didn't feel comfortable with that diagnosis, and so I didn't fill that prescription.

Later it will turn out that by crushing the steering column my chest pains were from a myocardial contusion (bruised heart); an often fatal injury. I was lucky. Up to this time, I had been leery of accepting full faith in the medical profession. In my early years in the Air Force, I was diagnosed with shingles; a rare outbreak for people in their 20s. The doctor prescribed a medication with what I thought initially was a high dosage amount. I asked him about that, and he told me it was the correct dosage. I saw him again after I was released from the ER where I received emergency treatment for being unable to breath and extremely high blood pressure. A friend of mine, a pharmacist, told me that the Air Force doctor prescribed a dosage five times the recommended amount. I decided to let the shingles run its course naturally where I made a complete recovery.

This is why it is important for everyone to make informed medical decisions in regard to your well being. Doctors do make mistakes. Prescription drugs can be highly fatal. It never hurts to get a second opinion. If I had complete faith in the medical profession you would not be reading this book. There are three types of healing theories. The first is modern medicine, which relies heavily on prescriptive drugs. The second is the natural healing professions such as chiropractic, massage therapy, and naturopathic professions. The third are the holistic healers or also called divine healers. I had discussed earlier where Reiki uses natural or spiritual healing energies. So there are alternative avenues for healing one's body, mind, and soul.

With all the wonderful marvels of modern medicine why are people increasingly dying from heart disease, cancers, aids, liver disorders and so forth? A growing problem is obesity in people. The world is seeing highly educated doctors and others in the medical profession. Hospitals have state of the art medical equipment. It just doesn't make sense. What is causing all these diseases? What can the individual do to prevent these crippling and devastating diseases? Does modern day medicine have all the answers? Do the Food and Drug Administration (FDA) as well as the pharmaceutical companies have our best interests at heart? Do the major corporate food producers have our best interests at heart?

For starters I would like to emphasize that I am not a medical or a legal professional. This book is not about providing any type of medical or legal advice. If you need medical attention call 911. If you need legal assistance, after you call 911 for medical assistance, a lawyer will be right behind the ambulance. Since we are on the subject of disclaimers; please read the following disclaimer.

LEGAL DISCLAIMER: Please do not read this book while driving a motorized vehicle. Do not read this book while chewing gum; walking up and down stairs; or climbing up on a step ladder; do not chew on the pages of this book, to include the cover; as a matter of fact – Do Not Read This Book. After you purchase this book, take it straight home, being careful to obey all traffic laws and yielding the right-of-way on the roads. Place the book on your book shelve ensuring it is out of reach of young children. If you are thinking of suing the author for anything he has written then "This is a work of fiction. Names, characters, places and incidents are either the product of the author's vivid and insane imagination or are used fictitiously, and any resemblance to actual persons, living or dead, business establishments, events or locales are entirely coincidental."

Several years ago I began my study on energy fields. Every living creature and every living tree and plant life sends out energy fields. Energy is all around us. Energy is present in the sub-atomic particles to the Sun. Want to increase the positive energies in your home or office, add plants. Those who practice Reiki manipulates a person's energy fields to release negative energies. Earlier I had discussed how a friend of mine performed Reiki from a distance. Some people may scoff at Reiki healing because it is something that they cannot see, feel or hear. One morning, I was awakened by angel friends. I heard them talking in a low voice. They were performing Reiki on me to balance my chakras. An angel was down at my feet discussing with another angel where I had some pain in my feet. This was true that pain had persisted since I had bunion surgery. The angel was releasing the negative energies from my feet.

I was in awe that they would be giving me all this attention. Of course I was very grateful. Even in my darkest hours, I have never blamed God or anyone else. All I asked was that I complete my divine vision. No matter what befell me, the angels were always by my side cheering me on. My father had been diagnosed with stage three lung cancer. The doctors had scheduled him to receive chemotherapy and radiation therapy. Shortly, after my sister notified me of his cancer, I felt a feeling inside that all would be well. I imagined that his cancer was being surrounded by light particles. Two days later my sister called me and told me my father was experiencing some difficulties, and he was in the emergency room. Again a feeling of calm came over me. A few hours later she called me from the hospital. The hospital had performed some x-rays on my father. They could not find any more traces of cancer in his body. He hadn't even started chemotherapy and only had two radiation treatments. They canceled his chemotherapy. My father would later pass away from old age. He lived his life. It was time for him to go home and join my mother. Miracles do happen!

Something I want to interject here. When it comes to the dramas that people create, the Father/Mother God does not interfere. God does not take sides over issues that befall people. He only sees people as their higher self and does not judge. Listen to your higher self and your spirit guides. Doing so will eliminate many of the problems one incurs in their lives. Sometimes we just have a lesson that needs to be learned. Sometimes it is karma. What goes around comes around. The human body is a very complex machine. Some people still believe that pursuant to some cosmic accident, without intelligent design, life was formed. They think we are here as an accident or a mutation in evolution, which is what is being taught in our schools. There is intelligent design. The Old Testament tells how many of the people who lived during that period of time lived to be several hundred years old. What has changed? Why cannot people live to be several hundred years old? We have modern medicine and all those marvels that surgeons can perform. Back in the biblical day's mankind did not ingest all the harmful chemicals and preservatives found in today's food. The water was clean. The air that they breathed was not polluted. The fruits and vegetables did not contain harmful pesticides. The people did not have modern medicine with all its harsh drugs. People in those times took a holistic approach to their health. They knew of the healing properties in herbs and other plant life. Furthermore, during that time, the Star people from other galaxies assisted people in those times.

People are now just waking up. I had recently interviewed someone who is involved in energy healing. She calls herself an Energist. I was interested in learning more about this to share in this chapter.

I asked her if she practiced Reiki?

She said *"I do not do Reiki but it does have to do with the Chakras. In short, I was born with the ability or abilities that as a child I quite didn't know what to do with them. Knowing certain things and voicing them as I got older scared my mother. I would go into another type of "vision" and could see dark energies penetrating a person and parts of their bodies, organs... I knew or could sense if a person's leg hurt, for example. Early on*
I could feel quite a bit of a person's pain and later I learned how to guard myself against it and now I only feel a little. That's so when I treat a person and my pain is gone I know their pain is gone...I later found this out after many, many years...As I got older I didn't want to keep scaring my mother and I wanted to be "normal".

Little did I know that my journey would take me to discovering all that I am and that my calling would be of help to others learn that they are not "normal" and that there is nothing normal about us but that we are incredible beings. I went through a very difficult dark period in my life which contains tragedies that lasted a year, one right after the other. Before this I had pretty much denied my gifts and did not use them. But when I had to pull myself out of this darkness is when I began to try and figure out what and how to go about it. I took an Angel Healing class and later took a Metaphysical course for three years with a man that left the legal field just like me.

He was an attorney in Mexico and he too made his practice his calling, these tools came to him and he has a school in Monterey. I had always had an interest in the human body and how it worked. Taking these classes allowed me to really learn the energy within our bodies...With the angel healing/energy techniques the client lays on the table and they (the chakras) are aligned. It's a wonderful practice but you have to lie down and it takes the practitioner literally about an hour to align the client.

When my guides told me that I would be advising many high profile people and I would soon be named, there came a day when I was told to go into meditation. I did so and then my phone rang, the phone that my clients have to call me, text me with questions. If I am in meditation I do not answer and don't actually have my phone in the meditation room but that particular day my guides were like, we are going to give your name out and you need to meditate. So I did so on the spot... the phone rang and I was told, answer it because she's going to be instrumental in your practice. I was to ask her what she felt when I worked on her and all she kept saying was...'energy, just energy'.

Every time I am asked about the topic of energy and how it pertains to us, it's such an important topic because it affects every aspect of our lives. We are comprised of energy, everything is and so I believe people need to wake up to the realization of what they surround themselves with, not just the people, the music they listen to, the television programs, the books that they read and also what they bring into their homes. I truly believe that the reason we are in the state that we are in is related to the entertainment industry. How much healthy stuff is out there? It's out there if you look for it but most people just want to be spoon-fed to them so they settle for the talk and reality shows that feed on drama. People grow up with their parent's philosophies and if they are lucky grow up to be curious and question what they have learned from their parents and actually search for what is truly inside us all and what we can do with that energy."

There are many gaps in modern medicine and much of those gaps have been perpetrated by the pharmaceutical industry. The pharmaceutical industry is major contributors as a special interest groups to political campaigns. They influence legislation pertaining to the medical field. It is in their interest if healthy people get sick from those medicines. Doctors do not advise their patients on the benefits of natural herbs and vitamins. People have to seek out that information.

The chapter title is the Holy Trinity of Medicine. The ideal solution for people to live a longer and healthier lifestyle is combining Eastern and Western medicine with angelic/holistic healings. Clinics and hospitals on staff should have the Chiropractors, Osteopaths, the Naturopathic Physicians, Massage Therapists, Energists and Holistic/Spiritual Healers. God created the human species, so why legislate God out of the healing process?

The human body is made up of DNA cells. Ninety-five percent of the DNA cells carry information. Someday medical science will figure out to reprogram those DNA cells on diseased organs. But as humans we can also heal ourselves. Many of our ailments are caused by what we eat and also by what we think. If you continuously send out negative energies those energies will be returned which can impair a person's health. As people start progressing on a more spiritual path, they will find ways to heal themselves. As mentioned earlier ninety-five percent of the

DNA cell holds information. For example a patient with a bad heart could call upon their higher self, to search a previous incarnation when they had a healthy heart. That person could then call upon his higher self and the angels to transfer the DNA from that previous incarnation where they had a healthy heart. The same thing could apply to regenerating lost limbs.

People the government wants to take complete control over your health and well being. Do not succumb to that. Trust yourself and your instincts. Take control of your life. Trust your angel and spirit guides. Allow the God Source to make you well. By allowing the God Source in becoming a partner with your doctors and other medical professionals you will live a vibrant life.

Recently, the Feds raided an Amish farm that was selling raw milk to its customers. Amazingly the Amish have survived for centuries in the foods that they eat and drinking raw milk. Your government will prefer that people eat processed foods and non-organic fruits and vegetables. Living a long and healthy lifestyle is bad for the drug companies and bad for Social Security. This is why we need government managed health care. It is for our own best interests. You the reader may not agree but the government believes this. Can things get any crazier?

CHAPTER 29 - NEW WORLD ORDER

This book would be incomplete without a more thorough discussion of the New World Order. This name has been talked about quite often. Many people believe that this New World Order will be a world governed by Elite rulers who will own the wealth at the detriment of the masses. There are those from the New World Order group who have called upon the extinction of 90 percent of the world population. This will be done by poisoning the water and food supplies; engaging in endless wars; and Hitler style FEMA camps. This sounds like total madness and insanity. It is a satanic cult. Some of you might want to ask who is included in this New World Order clique. Surely no one of any statue would want to be a part of this satanic culture. This New World Order cult has in its membership many prominent groups. Some of these groups are the Bohemian Grove, Illuminati, Bilderberg Group, Freemasons, Council on Foreign Relations and a host of many more. Many of these are secret societies with very guarded lists. Adolph Hitler was a member of a secret society. These are the men who decide on wars for profit. It is estimated that over 160 million people were killed in wars during the 20th century. The 21st century is off to a good start.

The Bohemian Grove has the reputation of being a place where the rich and powerful go to misbehave. The term 'misbehave' is too good of a name for it. All who want to aspire to the height of being President of the United States must enter through these gates. Presidents Nixon, Reagan, Bush Sr., George W, and many other presidents have crossed the gates inside the Bohemian Grove. These men engage in the annual two weeks of drunken follies and many times drunken gay sex. It is not just about some old white guys having fun. The Bohemian Grove has 2500 members of the Elite in the world. The Bohemian Grove is located in a 2700 acre campground in Monte Rio, California.

In this drunken festival are many rituals that are performed. Now some people will wonder why the national media isn't reporting on these activities. In 1983 there were 50 media corporations. Today there are only six corporate media outlets. The corporate media has become a select group of corporations that form a monopoly. These CEOs are members of these secret societies. Eyes have been closed to the development of this monopoly. This group of elite around the world is part of an evil fraternity – the darkness among men at its worst.

Let's take a look at their rituals that are performed. In these rituals and keep in mind the very elite from Banking, Government, Media, Politicians and others engage in these rituals that worship an owl. The name of this owl is called Moloch. The worship of Moloch goes back to the biblical days. The U.S. $1 bill has a picture of this owl cleverly hidden on the upper right side of the bill. It is visible to the naked eye but better seen through a magnifying glass. In one of the Bohemian Grove's ceremonies is called the Cremation of the Care. During this ceremony the members wear costumes and cremate a coffin effigy called "Care" before a 40-foot-owl. Let us hope there is no one, living or dead, in those coffins at this secret retreat. Perhaps that is why it is secret.

Gustave Flaubert's *Salammbô*, a semi-historical novel about Carthage published in 1862, included a version of the Carthaginian religion, including the god Moloch, whom he characterized as a god to whom the Carthaginians offered children. Flaubert described this Moloch mostly according to the Rabbinic descriptions. In this book Flaubert describes a human sacrifice:

"The brazen arms were working more quickly. They paused no longer. Every time that a child was placed in them the priests of Moloch spread out their hands upon him to burden him with the crimes of the people, vociferating: "They are not men but oxen!" and the multitude round about repeated: "Oxen! Oxen!" The devout exclaimed: "Lord! Eat!" and the priests of Proserpine, complying through terror with the needs of Carthage, muttered the Eleusinian formula: "Pour out rain! Bring forth!" The victims, when scarcely at the edge of the opening, disappeared like a drop of water on a red-hot plate, and white smoke rose amid the great scarlet colour. Nevertheless, the appetite of the god was not appeased. He ever wished for more. In order to furnish him with a larger supply, the victims were piled up on his hands with a big chain above them which kept them in their place. Some devout persons had at the beginning wished to count them, to see whether their number corresponded with the days of the solar year; but others were brought, and it was impossible to distinguish them in the giddy motion of the horrible arms. This lasted for a long, indefinite time until the evening. Then the partitions inside assumed a darker glow and burning flesh could be seen. Some even believed that they could descry hair, limbs, and whole bodies. Night fell; clouds accumulated above the Baal. The funeral-pile, which was flameless now, formed a pyramid of coals up to his knees; completely red like a giant covered with blood, he looked, with his head thrown back, as though he were staggering beneath the weight of his intoxication."

Moloch was a worthless worship encompassing black magic as its worst. This is what is called the Satan, Devil, Lucifer, Mammom, Baal, Demonism, Black Mass, and Witchcraft. People do not realize that many of the Occult practices involve interacting with the dark forces.

There are several Molech/Moloch references from the Christian Bible:

Leviticus

18:21 You must not give any of your children as an offering to Molech, 29 so that you do not profane 30 the name of your God. I am the Lord!

20:1 The Lord spoke to Moses: 20:2 "You are to say to the Israelites, 'Any man from the Israelites or from the foreigners who reside in Israel who gives any of his children to Molech must be put to death; the people of the land must pelt him with stones. 20:3 I myself will set my face against that man and cut him off from the midst of his people, because he has given some of his children to Molech and thereby defiled my sanctuary and profaned my holy name. 20:4 If, however, the people of the land shut their eyes to that man when he gives some of his children to Molech so that they do not put him to death, 20:5 I myself will set my face against that man and his clan. I will cut off from the midst of their people both him and all who follow after him in prostitution, to commit prostitution by going after Molech.

Kings

23:10 The king ruined Topheth in the Valley of Ben Hinnom so that no one could pass his son or his daughter through the fire to Molech

Jeremiah

32:35 And they built the high places of Baal, which [are] in the valley of the son of Hinnom, to cause their sons and their daughters to pass through [the fire] unto Molech; which I commanded them not, neither came it into my mind, that they should do this abomination, to cause Judah to sin.

These are some very sick individuals who are engaged in these satanic practices. It is nothing but pure evil and an affront to God. People, these are our world leaders in business and government who engage in these dark occult practices. The members from the United States government and political offices dominate these secret societies. Is it no wonder America is on the decline and close to falling to a military/civilian dictatorship? America, we need to wake up. Our Republic has fallen and the Constitution has been shredded by all this evil and wickedness.

Recently the United States Congress has passed the 2012 National Defense Authorization Act that now allows Indefinite Detention by the military with no trial or legal counsel of any U.S. Citizen; for any reason. President Obama had threatened to veto this legislation but instead, reneged on his promise and signed it into law. The President had condemned this language, using Hollywood theatrics, and used a worthless Presidential signing statement. He has called upon Americans to vote him a better Congress. America, we not only need a new Congress but a new president. In 2009, President Obama gave a speech in front of the United States Constitution announcing his initiative for "Prolonged Detention and Indefinite Detention" of U.S. citizens. This is not the change that I voted for in 2008.

Unless our President pulls an October surprise and cancels this Election, you can expect the 2012 Presidential Election will be the last free election in the United States. His friends on Wall Street and the Elite will contribute up to a $1 billion for his reelection. That money will purchase much propaganda and disinformation. They are banking on the ignorance and continued apathy of the voters. 59% of Americans do not vote. There are now some groups frustrated with the corruption that want to boycott the elections. Sometimes like our U.S. Congress; when people get hold of a really bad idea they run with it. Unfortunately, the Republican presidential candidates are not much better.

In getting back to the Bohemian Grove, most of all our presidents have attended these functions. It is almost like a necessity if one wants to become president. Presidents who have attended these functions are Richard Nixon, Ronald Reagan, both President Bush's and it has been speculated that Barrack Obama and John McCain attended while campaigning from president. The Bilderberg Group also hosts the world elite to include many U.S. government and political leaders. Even though these secret groups and societies are frequented by many Republicans; the Democrats also participate.

If one would do a search on the Internet in regards to these secret societies or satanic cults you could discover there is a secret hand signal. This secret hand signal is where the 3rd and 4th digit of the hand is folded inside; which is a hand sign of Satan. There are many prominent individuals throughout the world who are using these satanic hand signals as being something very popular. These people are playing with the dark forces. President Obama and former President Bush routinely use these hand signs. This brings me to the question of the Moloch god, signified by the owl. When our presidents for instance at the conclusion in giving a national address; they ask God to bless the American people and the United States; so what God are they seeking the blessings from – Father Almighty or Moloch?? (No wonder the world has gone crazy.)

(A satanic ritual using the hand signal to signify the darkness)

This has become a very popular fad among many people. What these people do though is to give up their 'free will' to the darkness. In the Appendix are spiritual exercises, one can use, to free themselves from these dark forces.

Some of you might be thinking, why the U.S. media isn't reporting on some of these findings; that I've brought out in this book. In 1987, there were 50 media corporations reporting on the news. The national media was allowed to become monopolized, where there are now only six media giants. The happenings on what has been going on behind closed doors in Washington DC as well as these secret societies is because the executives from some of these media giants are also members of the Bohemian Grove and other societies. It is no longer the national media but the corporate media. Is it not easier for the government to control six media outlets versus fifty media outlets? Americans are no longer receiving the 'real' news but 'censored' and politicized news. The media is controlled. Now some of you might think we still have a free press. Think again.

In June 2011 the United States was experiencing some horrendous storms that left many people flooded out of their homes when the Missouri River flooded. Also under water was the Fort Calhoun nuclear power plant. The FAA restricted the airspace over this nuclear disaster. Not wanting people to know what was going on; the Obama administration instituted a total news blackout in the United States. We may never know how much radiation was leaked or the dangers this disaster poses to American citizens. In nuclear disasters, the immediate dangers do not come out till years later. I had written in another chapter about the dangers of nuclear power plants and the dangers they pose to the world. There are much safer and more reliable sources of alternative and renewable sources of energy.

Americans cannot get the 'real' news from the controlled corporate media. Much of the news is filtered and politicized. The widespread corruption among government agencies goes unreported. This only encourages more corruption to fester and breed with no accountability. Former President Nixon was nearly impeached which forced him to resign over a break-in at Watergate, not committed by him but by his subordinates. Today, such an event would be mere peanuts and not worthy of media or Congressional attention. So who now really owns and pulls the strings in Washington DC?

The Fourth Reich

Many Americans today are losing their jobs and their homes. Many have become homeless because of the economic conditions in the United States. In 2008, the world witnessed the economic meltdown. Many banks and some corporations were bailed out just prior to President George W. Bush in leaving office. High interest mortgages were packaged into bundles and sold as derivatives. Congress and the new president-elect promised banking reform. Today, many loans are still being packaged as derivatives and homeowners cannot refinance their mortgages. President Obama sought legislation to help homeowners. However, that is only good if the person has excellent credit and has not been late with their mortgage payments. So the massive foreclosures still continue. Banks have now instituted tighter standards in granting loans. Many banks are pursuing other investment avenues to earn income instead of providing loan services. Let us take a trip back in time.

America has become a police state under the Bush and Obama administrations. Many people are claiming that America has entered a dangerous political period where fascism in support of this police state has flourished. In the 20th century millions of people perished under the Nazi government of Hitler. So why would America even want to go there. Makes absolutely no sense. Have we learned nothing about history and the evils of humankind? Apparently not! Greed and a lust for power have dominated American politics.

During the conclusion of World War II, the Nazi German industrialists had mapped out a new strategy. They could no longer dominate the world by being a military power. They embarked on a plan to dominate the world through the financial sectors. The Nazi's ordered the German industrialists in 1944 to develop a plan for post-war Germany. They wanted to return to power as a strong German empire; the Fourth Reich. When the conditions were ripe they would take over Germany again. This secret August 10th, 1944 meeting was documented in the Red House Report.

The Third Reich was defeated on the battleground. Germany exported massive amounts of money through neutral countries. The very powerful Nazi-era bankers, industrialists and civil service employees became champions of democracy. They soon prospered after the war in the reconstruction efforts. They worked to develop a new cause to integrate European economic and political integration. SS Obergruppenfuhrer Dr. Scheid told a group of industrialists "German industry must realize that the war cannot be won. It must take steps in preparation for a post-war commercial campaign." He ordered the industrialists and bankers to make contacts and alliances with foreign firms, but down individually and not as a group so as to not attract attention or suspicion.

During the war years the Germans had built up a gigantic economic empire by looting and murdering. Those assets were later secretly transferred into Swiss banks. This post-war plot required German industry to expand its reach across the war torn European continent. They accomplished this through super nationalism, a voluntary surrender of national sovereignty to an international body. France and Germany were the primary drivers behind the European Coal and Steel Community (ECSC), which laid the groundwork to a European Union. The ECSC was the first super nationalist organization, which was established in April 1951 by several European countries. Some of the leading figures in the Nazi economy became leading figures in the European Union.

Slave labor was an integral part of the Nazi war machine. Krupp and Flick, Hermann Abs, post-war Germany's most powerful banker, had prospered in the Third Reich. Abs joined the board of Deutsche Bank, Germany's biggest bank, in 1937. As the Nazi empire grew so did Deutsche who had 'Aryanised' the banks and corporations of conquered nations. Many of these 'Aryanised' companies used slaver labor and by 1943 Deutsche Bank's wealth had quadrupled. This bank was deeply interconnected with the SS and the Nazis' where it ran its own slave labor camp at Auschwitz, known as Auschwitz III, where tens of thousands of Jews and other prisoners died producing artificial rubber. The Deutsche Bank, is also a principle in the ownership of a private, international bank; the Federal Reserve Bank. The German economic miracle that provided an economic boom to the post-war reconstruction was built on mass murder. The number of slave and forced laborers who died while employed by German companies in the Nazi era was 2,700,000. Numerous other well-known corporations were also involved in slave and forced labor such as BMW, Siemans, and Volkswagon; that produced munitions and the V1 rocket.

Europe has enjoyed peace and stability under the European Union. Joseph Goebbels, Hitler's propaganda chief, once said: "In 50 years' time nobody will think of nation states." So today's drive within the European Union towards a European

Union towards a European federal state is tied up in the plans for the *Fourth Reich.*

The Federal Reserve Bank

Since the inception of the Federal Reserve in 1913 it has been shrouded in secrecy. The Federal Reserve Bank is a private bank with its ownership spread among several mega banks and corporations; here in the United States and across the globe. The Federal Reserve with its global foreign partners determines U.S. economic and monetary policy. There is very little oversight from the U.S. Congress. German industrialists from the Hitler era have a controlling interest in the Federal Reserve. There is an excellent article that was written by Dean Henderson for the Centre for Research on Globalization titled "The Federal Reserve Cartel: The Eight Families." More information on this bank and other global issues can be found at www.globalresearch.ca . This article in its entirety is provided.

In order to build a New America we must travel back in time to see where our problems began. Once we do so, finding common sense solutions can be found. The Federal Reserve is the entity that provides funding when the United States runs a deficit budget. The Federal Reserve in the computer agency has the capability of creating 'money' from nothing. In a recent audit of the Federal Reserve, there were findings that this bank made secret loans to U.S. and foreign banks and corporations totaling nearly $25 Trillion. There have been substantiated allegations made where the Federal Reserve Bank is unable to account for $9 Trillion dollars; that has come up missing. That is an amount equal to three years of the yearly budget of the United States government.

THE FOUR HORSEMEN OF BANKING (BANK OF AMERICA, JP MORGAN CHASE, CITIGROUP AND WELLS FARGO) OWN THE FOUR HORSEMEN OF OIL (EXXON MOBIL, ROYAL DUTCH/SHELL, BP AND CHEVRON TEXACO); IN TANDEM WITH DEUTSCHE BANK, BNP, BARCLAYS AND OTHER EUROPEAN OLD MONEY BEHEMOTHS. BUT THEIR MONOPOLY OVER THE GLOBAL ECONOMY DOES NOT END AT THE EDGE OF THE OIL PATCH.

According to company 10K filings to the SEC, the Four Horsemen of Banking are among the top ten stock holders of virtually every Fortune 500 corporation.

So who then are the stockholders in these money center banks?

This information is guarded much more closely. My queries to bank regulatory agencies regarding stock ownership in the top 25 US bank holding companies were given Freedom of Information Act status, before being denied on "national security" grounds. This is rather ironic, since many of the bank's stockholders reside in Europe.

One important repository for the wealth of the global oligarchy that owns these bank holding companies is US Trust Corporation - founded in 1853 and now owned by Bank of America. A recent US Trust Corporate Director and Honorary Trustee was Walter Rothschild. Other directors included Daniel Davison of JP Morgan Chase, Richard Tucker of Exxon Mobil, Daniel Roberts of Citigroup and Marshall Schwartz of Morgan Stanley.

J. W. McCallister, an oil industry insider with House of Saud connections, wrote in The Grim Reaper that information he acquired from Saudi bankers cited 80% ownership of the New York Federal Reserve Bank- by far the most powerful Fed branch- by just eight families, four of which reside in the US. They are the Goldman Sachs, Rockefellers, Lehmans and Kuhn Loebs of New York; the Rothschilds of Paris and London; the Warburgs of Hamburg; the Lazards of Paris; and the Israel Moses Seifs of Rome.

CPA Thomas D. Schauf corroborates McCallister's claims, adding that ten banks control all twelve Federal Reserve Bank branches. He names N.M. Rothschild of London, Rothschild Bank of Berlin, Warburg Bank of Hamburg, Warburg Bank of Amsterdam, Lehman Brothers of New York, Lazard Brothers of Paris, Kuhn Loeb Bank of New York, Israel Moses Seif Bank of Italy, Goldman Sachs of New York and JP Morgan Chase Bank of New York. Schauf lists William Rockefeller, Paul Warburg, Jacob Schiff and James Stillman as individuals who own large shares of the Fed. The Schiffs are insiders at Kuhn Loeb. The Stillmans are Citigroup insiders, who married into the Rockefeller clan at the turn of the century.

Eustace Mullins came to the same conclusions in his book The Secrets of the Federal Reserve, in which he displays charts connecting the Fed and its member banks to the families of Rothschild, Warburg, Rockefeller and the others.

The control that these banking families exert over the global economy cannot be overstated and is quite intentionally shrouded in secrecy. Their corporate media arm is quick to discredit any information exposing this private central banking cartel as "conspiracy theory". Yet the facts remain.

The House of Morgan

The Federal Reserve Bank was born in 1913, the same year US banking scion J. Pierpont Morgan died and the Rockefeller Foundation was formed. The House of Morgan presided over American finance from the corner of Wall Street and Broad, acting as quasi-US central bank since 1838, when George Peabody founded it in London.

Peabody was a business associate of the Rothschilds. In 1952 Fed researcher Eustace Mullins put forth the supposition that the Morgans were nothing more than Rothschild agents. Mullins wrote that the Rothschilds, "...preferred to operate anonymously in the US behind the facade of J.P. Morgan & Company".

Author Gabriel Kolko stated, "Morgan's activities in 1895-1896 in selling US gold bonds in Europe were based on an alliance with the House of Rothschild."

The Morgan financial octopus wrapped its tentacles quickly around the globe. Morgan Grenfell operated in London. Morgan et Ce ruled Paris. The Rothschild's Lambert cousins set up Drexel & Company in Philadelphia.

The House of Morgan catered to the Astors, DuPonts, Guggenheims, Vanderbilts and Rockefellers. It financed the launch of AT&T, General Motors, General Electric and DuPont. Like the London-based Rothschild and Barings banks, Morgan became part of the power structure in many countries.

By 1890 the House of Morgan was lending to Egypt's central bank, financing Russian railroads, floating Brazilian provincial government bonds and funding Argentine public works projects. A recession in 1893 enhanced Morgan's power. That year Morgan saved the US government from a bank panic, forming a syndicate to prop up government reserves with a shipment of $62 million worth of Rothschild gold.

Morgan was the driving force behind Western expansion in the US, financing and controlling West-bound railroads through voting trusts. In 1879 Cornelius Vanderbilt's Morgan-financed New York Central Railroad gave preferential shipping rates to John D. Rockefeller's budding Standard Oil monopoly, cementing the Rockefeller/Morgan relationship.

The House of Morgan now fell under Rothschild and Rockefeller family control. A New York Herald headline read, "Railroad Kings Form Gigantic Trust". J. Pierpont Morgan, who once stated, "Competition is a sin", now opined gleefully, "Think of it. All competing railroad traffic west of St. Louis placed in the control of about thirty men."

Morgan and Edward Harriman's banker Kuhn Loeb held a monopoly over the railroads, while banking dynasties Lehman, Goldman Sachs and Lazard joined the Rockefellers in controlling the US industrial base.

In 1903 Banker's Trust was set up by the Eight Families. Benjamin Strong of Banker's Trust was the first Governor of the New York Federal Reserve Bank. The 1913 creation of the Fed fused the power of the Eight Families to the military and diplomatic might of the US government. If their overseas loans went unpaid, the oligarchs could now deploy US Marines to collect the debts. Morgan, Chase and Citibank formed an international lending syndicate.

The House of Morgan was cozy with the British House of Windsor and the Italian House of Savoy. The Kuhn Loebs, Warburgs, Lehmans, Lazards, Israel Moses Seifs and Goldman Sachs also had close ties to European royalty. By 1895 Morgan controlled the flow of gold in and out of the US. The first American wave of mergers was in its infancy and was being promoted by the bankers. In 1897 there were sixty-nine industrial mergers. By 1899 there were twelve-hundred. In 1904 John Moody - founder of Moody's Investor Services - said it was impossible to talk of Rockefeller and Morgan interests as separate.

Public distrust of the combine spread. Many considered them traitors working for European old money. Rockefeller's Standard Oil, Andrew Carnegie's US Steel and Edward Harriman's railroads were all financed by banker Jacob Schiff at Kuhn Loeb, who worked closely with the European Rothschilds.

Several Western states banned the bankers. Populist preacher William Jennings Bryan was thrice the Democratic nominee for President from 1896 -1908. The central theme of his *anti-imperialist campaign was that America was falling into a trap of "financial servitude to British capital". Teddy Roosevelt defeated Bryan in 1908, but was forced by this spreading populist wildfire to enact the Sherman Anti-Trust Act. He then went after the Standard Oil Trust.*

In 1912 the Pujo hearings were held, addressing concentration of power on Wall Street. That same year Mrs. Edward Harriman sold her substantial shares in New York's Guaranty Trust Bank to J.P. Morgan, creating Morgan Guaranty Trust. Judge Louis Brandeis convinced President Woodrow Wilson to call for an end to interlocking board directorates. In 1914 the Clayton Anti-Trust Act was passed.

Jack Morgan - J. Pierpont's son and successor - responded by calling on Morgan clients Remington and Winchester to increase arms production. He argued that the US needed to enter WWI. Goaded by the Carnegie Foundation and other oligarchy fronts, Wilson accommodated. As Charles Tansill wrote in America Goes to War, "Even before the clash of arms, the French firm of Rothschild Freres cabled to Morgan & Company in New York suggesting the flotation of a loan of $100 million, a substantial part of which was to be left in the US to pay for French purchases of American goods."

The House of Morgan financed half the US war effort, while receiving commissions for lining up contractors like GE, Du Pont, US Steel, Kennecott and ASARCO. All were Morgan clients. Morgan also financed the British Boer War in South Africa and the Franco-Prussian War. The 1919 Paris Peace Conference was presided over by Morgan, which led both German and Allied reconstruction efforts.

In the 1930's populism resurfaced in America after Goldman Sachs, Lehman Bank and others profited from the Crash of 1929. House Banking Committee Chairman Louis McFadden (D-NY) said of the Great Depression, "It was no accident. It was a carefully contrived occurrence...The international bankers sought to bring about a condition of despair here so they might emerge as rulers of us all".

Sen. Gerald Nye (D-ND) chaired a munitions investigation in 1936. Nye concluded that the House of Morgan had plunged the US into WWI to protect loans and create a booming arms industry. Nye later produced a document titled The Next War, which cynically referred to "the old goddess of democracy trick", through which Japan could be used to lure the US into WWII.

In 1937 Interior Secretary Harold Ickes warned of the influence of "America's 60 Families". Historian Ferdinand Lundberg later penned a book of the exact same title. Supreme Court Justice William O. Douglas decried, "Morgan influence...the most pernicious one in industry and finance today."

Jack Morgan responded by nudging the US towards WWII. Morgan had close relations with the Iwasaki and Dan families - Japan's two wealthiest clans - who have owned Mitsubishi and Mitsui, respectively, since the companies emerged from 17th Century shogunates. When Japan invaded Manchuria, slaughtering Chinese peasants at Nanking, Morgan downplayed the incident. Morgan also had close relations with Italian fascist Benito Mussolini, while German Nazi Dr. Hjalmer Schacht was a Morgan Bank liaison during WWII. After the war Morgan representatives met with Schacht at the Bank of International Settlements (BIS) in Basel, Switzerland.

The House of Rockefeller

BIS is the most powerful bank in the world, a global central bank for the Eight Families who control the private central banks of almost all Western and developing nations. The first President of BIS was Rockefeller banker Gates McGarrah- an official at Chase Manhattan and the Federal Reserve. McGarrah was the grandfather of former CIA director Richard Helms. The Rockefellers- like the Morgans- had close ties to London. David Icke writes in Children of the Matrix, that the Rockefellers and Morgans were just "gofers" for the European Rothschilds.

BIS is owned by the Federal Reserve, Bank of England, Bank of Italy, Bank of Canada, Swiss National Bank, Nederlandsche Bank, Bundesbank and Bank of France.

Historian Carroll Quigley wrote in his epic book Tragedy and Hope that BIS was part of a plan, "to create a world system of financial control in private hands able to dominate the political system of each country and the economy of the world as a whole...to be controlled in a feudalistic fashion by the central banks of the world acting in concert by secret agreements."

The US government had a historical distrust of BIS, lobbying unsuccessfully for its demise at the 1944 post-WWII Bretton Woods Conference. Instead the Eight Families' power was exacerbated, with the BrettonWoodscreation of the IMF and the

World Bank. The US Federal Reserve only took shares in BIS in September 1994.

BIS holds at least 10% of monetary reserves for at least 80 of the world's central banks, the IMF and other multilateral institutions. It serves as financial agent for international agreements, collects information on the global economy and serves as lender of last resort to prevent global financial collapse.

BIS promotes an agenda of monopoly capitalist fascism. It gave a bridge loan to Hungary in the 1990's to ensure privatization of that country's economy. It served as conduit for Eight Families funding of Adolf Hitler- led by the Warburg's J. Henry Schroeder and Mendelsohn Bank of Amsterdam. Many researchers assert that BIS is at the nadir of global drug money laundering.

It is no coincidence that BIS is headquartered in Switzerland, favorite hiding place for the wealth of the global aristocracy and headquarters for the P-2 Italian Freemason's Alpina Lodge and Nazi International. Other institutions which the Eight Families control include the World Economic Forum, the International Monetary Conference and the World Trade Organization.

Bretton Woods was a boon to the Eight Families. The IMF and World Bank were central to this "new world order". In 1944 the first World Bank bonds were floated by Morgan Stanley and First Boston. The French Lazard family became more involved in House of Morgan interests. Lazard Freres- France's biggest investment bank- is owned by the Lazard and David-Weill families- old Genoese banking scions represented by Michelle Davive. A recent Chairman and CEO of Citigroup was Sanford Weill.

In 1968 Morgan Guaranty launched Euro-Clear, a Brussels-based bank clearing system for Eurodollar securities. It was the first such automated endeavor. Some took to calling Euro-Clear "The Beast". Brussels serves as headquarters for the new European Central Bank and for NATO. In 1973 Morgan officials met secretly in Bermuda to illegally resurrect the old House of Morgan, twenty years before Glass Steagal Act was repealed. Morgan and the Rockefellers provided the financial backing for Merrill Lynch, boosting it into the Big 5 of US investment banking. Merrill is now part of Bank of America.

John D. Rockefeller used his oil wealth to acquire Equitable Trust, which had gobbled up several large banks and corporations by the 1920's. The Great Depression helped consolidate Rockefeller's power. His Chase Bank merged with Kuhn Loeb's Manhattan Bank to form Chase Manhattan, cementing a long-time family relationship. The Kuhn-Loeb's had financed - along with Rothschilds - Rockefeller's quest to become king of the oil patch. National City Bank of Cleveland provided John D. with the money needed to embark upon his monopolization of the US oil industry. The bank was identified in Congressional hearings as being one of three Rothschild-owned banks in the US during the 1870's, when Rockefeller first incorporated as Standard Oil of Ohio.

One Rockefeller Standard Oil partner was Edward Harkness, whose family came to control Chemical Bank. Another was James Stillman, whose family controlled Manufacturers Hanover Trust. Both banks have merged under the JP Morgan Chase umbrella. Two of James Stillman's daughters married two of William Rockefeller's sons. The two families control a big chunk of Citigroup as well.

In the insurance business, the Rockefellers control Metropolitan Life, Equitable Life, Prudential and New York Life. Rockefeller banks control 25% of all assets of the 50 largest US commercial banks and 30% of all assets of the 50 largest insurance companies. Insurance companies- the first in the US was launched by Freemasons through their Woodman's of America- play a key role in the Bermuda drug money shuffle.

Companies under Rockefeller control include Exxon Mobil, Chevron Texaco, BP Amoco, Marathon Oil, Freeport McMoran, Quaker Oats, ASARCO, United, Delta, Northwest, ITT, International Harvester, Xerox, Boeing, Westinghouse, Hewlett-Packard, Honeywell, International Paper, Pfizer, Motorola, Monsanto, Union Carbide and General Foods.

The Rockefeller Foundation has close financial ties to both Ford and Carnegie Foundations. Other family philanthropic endeavors include Rockefeller Brothers Fund, Rockefeller Institute for Medical Research, General Education Board, Rockefeller University and the University of Chicago- which churns out a steady stream of far right economists as apologists for international capital, including Milton Friedman.

The family owns 30 Rockefeller Plaza, where the national Christmas tree is lighted every year, and Rockefeller Center. David Rockefeller was instrumental in the construction of the World Trade Center towers. The main Rockefeller family home is a hulking complex in upstate New York known as Pocantico Hills. They also own a 32-room 5th Avenue duplex in Manhattan, a mansion in Washington, DC, Monte Sacro Ranch in Venezuela, coffee plantations in Ecuador, several farms in Brazil, an estate at Seal Harbor, Maine and resorts in the Caribbean, Hawaii and Puerto Rico.

The Dulles and Rockefeller families are cousins. Allen Dulles created the CIA, assisted the Nazis, covered up the Kennedy hit from his Warren Commission perch and struck a deal with the Muslim Brotherhood to create mind-controlled assassins.

Brother John Foster Dulles presided over the phony Goldman Sachs trusts before the 1929 stock market crash and helped his brother overthrow governments in Iran and Guatemala. Both were Skull & Bones, Council on Foreign Relations (CFR) insiders and 33rd Degree Masons.

The Rockefellers were instrumental in forming the depopulation-oriented Club of Rome at their family estate in Bellagio, Italy. Their Pocantico Hills estate gave birth to the Trilateral Commission. The family is a major funder of the eugenics movement which spawned Hitler, human cloning and the current DNA obsession in US scientific circles.

John Rockefeller Jr. headed the Population Council until his death. His namesake son is a Senator from West Virginia. Brother Winthrop Rockefeller was Lieutenant Governor of Arkansas and remains the most powerful man in that state. In an October 1975 interview with Playboy magazine, Vice-President Nelson Rockefeller- who was also Governor of New York- articulated his family's patronizing worldview, "I am a great believer in planning- economic, social, political, military, total world planning."

But of all the Rockefeller brothers, it is Trilateral Commission (TC) founder and Chase Manhattan Chairman David who has spearheaded the family's fascist agenda on a global scale. He defended the Shah of Iran, the South African apartheid regime and the Chilean Pinochet junta. He was the biggest financier of the CFR, the TC and (during the Vietnam War) the

Committee for an Effective and Durable Peace in Asia- a contract bonanza for those who made their living off the conflict.

Nixon asked him to be Secretary of Treasury, but Rockefeller declined the job, knowing his power was much greater at the helm of the Chase. Author Gary Allen writes in The Rockefeller File that in 1973, "David Rockefeller met with twenty-seven heads of state, including the rulers of Russia and Red China."

Following the 1975 Nugan Hand Bank/CIA coup against Australian Prime Minister Gough Whitlam, his British Crown-appointed successor Malcolm Fraser sped to the US, where he met with President Gerald Ford after conferring with David Rockefeller.

CHAPTER 30 – IF I WERE PRESIDENT

As I write these words Americans will be selecting their new president in the 2012 General Elections. I could address the usual issues where politicians develop their usual plans to fix such as Social Security, the Economy, Unemployment, Gun Control, Abortion, Health Care, Taxes, and Terrorism; well you know what I am talking about. These have been issues that have been debated for decades and nothing ever gets done to fix those problems. Most likely those unresolved issues will continue for many more decades. The politicians discuss these problems because it is 'safe' to do so. Many of the Presidential candidates in this election cycle do not want to discuss the 'real' issues facing all Americans. The Ruling Elite in the world do not want the real issues debated.

America is controlled by many special interest groups from around the world. There is much foreign influence on what happens in Washington, DC. For one, you have the very powerful Jewish lobby that spends millions to influence the political climate so that the legislatures will support Israeli government interests and to fight Israeli enemies. The Saudis' are a very influential group that spends millions on political campaigns to support their causes and to continue America's addiction to foreign oil. The U.S. military is their 'hired guns'. Of course, American taxpayers are the one who will eventually foot the bill for both Israel and Saudi Arabia. In Washington, one does not say anything derogatory against either group. Too much money is involved. It is all about greed for money and power.

America, we need to change this. With the ruling of Citizens United v. Federal Election Commission the influence from powerful lobbyists are going unchecked. It is a free for all. Money corrupts. With this corruption each year Americans are losing their rights and freedoms. The majority of Americans do not complain because of ignorance, voter apathy, or they feel they cannot do anything. Then there are other voices who want an armed revolution. Those calling for violence, many of them did not participate in voting – they want their guns to vote. From the ashes and rubble of greed and corruption we must build a New America. Americans must take back their country. America was established as a Republic. The remaining shreds of this Republic were extinguished when 87 U.S. Senators voted under the 2012 National Defense Authorization Act for "Indefinite Detention by the military for any reason with no charges, court trial or access to a lawyer". The government has numerous FEMA camps that will be run by the military and the Halliburton Corporation. It is obvious they have something planned for all of us. There are those that claim these camps already have U.S. citizens as prisoners. If so, the media will never report or investigate those allegations. The Free Press has gone by the wayside here in America. Being a journalist in today's era is one of report on safe topics only. Do not be too critical of the government. Allowing the national media become monopolized into the controlled corporate media comes with a heavy price – the elimination of the free press. They were willing to sell out freedom of speech and reporting the real news to be rewarded with corporate expansion into the six mega-media groups. If these media groups were dominate during the Nixon Administration – no one outside of the Beltway would have ever heard of the Watergate complex. Besides what the White House plumbers did back then is miniscule to what is happening inside the government, Congress and today's White House.

America, we need a president who is willing to take a new path in the pursuit of life, liberty and happiness. We need a president who is not willing to be bought and paid for by special interest groups and the global Ruling Elite. The only way for a president to be free of this influence is one who is willing to serve one term. Why would anyone want to be in the federal custody longer than four years? The White House is the granddaddy of the federal penal system. None of the Republican candidates would be willing to serve only one-term. President Obama wants to become your king.

If I Were Your President, this is what I would want to do to build a NEW America. Together we can make dreams come true. We need to create Community Support Centers throughout America. The United States has the highest prison population in the world. The United States executes more prisoners in the world. I believe the focus should be on how we can save those before they pursue a path of crime. To do so we need to focus on educating our young people on self-responsibility, self-esteem, self-confidence and ethics. We need community support centers that people can go to for assistance when their life turns into shambles. We need to offer help for the hopeless. No one should go to bed hungry or homeless. This is not socialism but taking care of our own and showing love and compassion.

We need to give people hope. Sure many times a person's lot in life was caused by their own actions. But sometimes events that happen in one's life can easily spin out of control and cause despair and hopelessness.

Our lawmakers at the state and federal levels are finding more things to criminalize. The Congress has just passed legislation (Mar 2012) – aka Anti-Protest Law. This bill passed by Congress makes it a felony—a serious criminal offense punishable by lengthy terms of incarceration—to participate in many forms of protest. The growing prison population is Big Business. There are many behind bars that should not be there. I believe that many of the prisoners behind bars who have committed non-violent crimes can be rehabilitated. Community Support centers can be used to prevent people from entering a life of crime. If I was your president I would shut down these FEMA camps meant to imprison Americans and use them instead for rehabilitative programs in early-release of prisoners. Conduct anger management classes. Create job training classes so that the released prisoners will have new job skills. Provide on-site career fairs for prospective employers to interview. These FEMA camps can provide temporary housing for those who are job seeking.

Social Security

If I was your president I would be committed to fixing Social Security with many new proposals. The problems in Social Security exist because while taxpayers were contributing into Social Security than what was being paid out in benefits; your elected representatives in Washington were too busy spending the surplus. They kept issuing IOUs against Social Security. Now that they have exhausted the surplus Social Security is no longer a cash cow for them. The Republicans are now calling this socialism which is bad. Corporate Socialism for Bank and Corporate bailouts is good with them. We know who butters their toast.

Former presidential candidate Hermain Cain had been talking about his 999 tax plan. Now I didn't agree with his 999 tax plan that made me think of something else. Something better! It could possibly be great for America.

In piggybacking on Hermain Cain's National Sales Tax plan let us look at it a different way. Instead of a new National Sales Tax -- why not a new National Lottery System? Now I am not calling for a Lottery System that will compete against the state lotteries which has horrible odds and very little winners.

Many politicians have sold the Lotteries as a way to raise revenue for education which means they will not fund education. Why not as a method to generate new revenue to pay out future social security claims set up a new education lottery; a small business lottery; home ownership lottery -- where instead of a few winners there could be, based on a percentage of ticket sales --- thousands of education winners where they could win a 2 or 4 year degree voucher. A small business lottery; where winners could win a small business grant for an existing or new business grant with many winners. A Home Ownership Lottery -- Win your foreclosed home back or a voucher to purchase a new home. There could be lottery for a relief in income taxes or student loans.

Reserves need to be setup for Social Security and those monies kept separate from the General Treasury. Since Congress for decades have been issuing IOUs those funds need to be paid back into Social Security. A proposed income tax need to be established -- but not against you. All revenues received by the Treasury Department should be levied a 1 - 3% income tax and those tax revenues set outside for Social Security. It is time for Congress to pay back all those IOU's and not the American worker. Any decreases in Social Security benefits should be tied to decreases in benefits that members of Congress enjoy.

Green Energy

Energy is what drives the global economy. Over a century now our economy is based on a fossil fuel economy. Scientists expect that the world will have consumed all of the fossil fuels this century. How long this supply of fossil fuels last will depend upon our abilities to conserve our dwindling supplies of oil, natural gas, and coal. The growing economies around the world are consuming fast quantities of fossil fuels. It is not sustainable. When we run out we will have to wait a billion years. We must in order to survive and to prevent major wars over oil go to a green energy economy. We cannot allow the short term corporate coals of the energy companies shut down our industries for short term profits. We must start now to build a sustainable green/free energy culture. Time is not on our side. There are those who believe energy should be paid for. I believe in a future where energy is free.

Look all around, the world is teeming with free energy that has not been tapped. If one would view the earth from outer space what will you see? You will see a planet spinning around on its axis in a perfect orbit around the sun. That is pure energy – free energy that you see. We can do the same on this planet. The largest and most densely populated cities are located along the coastal areas of the seven seas. If one would walk along the sandy beaches and see the water washing upon the sands in a back and forth motion, what do you see. You see the lunar tides come in and go out – back and forth, like clockwork. People! That is energy that you see working. Mankind has built dams to fill up a water basin and then catch the energy of the water flowing. We can build hydroelectric plants out to see to catch the massive forces of the water go back and forth, back and forth, this energy is forever.

We must stop the oil wars and build the free and green energy for the benefit of our nation and the world. For several years I have personally been involved in green energy research. I did not get far with industry and the Obama Administration in making a totally green electric hybrids vehicle that does not consume fossil fuels. Electric cars are not green energy when they have to be recharged. They are more expensive and you only exchange one fossil fuel for another... the natural gas and coal that is burned in the power plants. But we can build a car that can go from one coast to the next without incurring a dime in fuel charges. The future is here for us to take. If I was president we will go to a free energy economy. We must build a New America.

There is a natural resource that is sustainable for a growing world population and economy. This natural resource does not need to be drilled or stripped mined. This natural resource can be used in building a totally green energy vehicle. It can be used as a petroleum product. It can be used to create bricks and as well as building new homes. This natural resource can also be used as a fuel in generating electricity. This natural resource can be available worldwide. However, it is not legal here in the United States. It was banned because it was competing against the lumber yards. This natural resource was banned because it was a plant of the cannabis family. It cannot be smoked but it does provide natural benefits to mankind. This plant is hemp. It grows very tall, as a very dense crop. This plant provides needed nutrients to the soil. Farmers will reap more plentiful and nourishing crops when rotating this plant as a crop. We must legalize the growing of hemp in the United States.

In this book I have made mention of other available green energy sources. Going to a green energy economy will create many employment opportunities at the risk of America becoming a super economic power. America is a super military power but we are a debtor nation. We can change all of this for a New America, but there are barriers and road blocks. We do not have a free market economy. We must break down those barriers from the special interest groups operating in Washington.

In order to take this nation to a free/green energy economy we must take advantage of our resources available to free us from foreign oil and their tentacle claws that they exert in U.S. foreign and domestic policies. There has been a recent large oil reserve finding in North Dakota. If we develop this oil reserve it will supplement part of the needs of the United States. The oil reserves are sufficient to meet the entire needs of America for one year. This would be a great resource should there be an emergency oil crisis. There are environment and other groups that are blocking this oil resource. If we do so it will end the need of the United States in engaging in wars for oil. Wars are more damaging to the environment as well as the human species.

The Federal Reserve

In the previous chapter on the New World Order I had mentioned the connection of the Federal Reserve in engaging in secret societies. Former President John F. Kennedy stated regarding these secret societies "For we are opposed, around the world, by a monolithic and ruthless conspiracy." We must end the control these secret societies have over our nation. They worship as a religion the dark forces such as the Moloch owl at Bohemian Grove in California. This is where the elite of the world to include our political and presidents engage in these satanic rituals. Their influence permeates throughout America to include our currency. They say "Money is the root of all evil'. If one would pull out a dollar bill from their wallet you will see through a magnifying glass a 'cute and charming' owl. You are looking at the darkness of this Moloch god, also known as Lucifer, the devil and Satan.

We must go back to the U.S. greenbacks and remove all satanic symbols. Then perhaps money can become the root of all that is good.

Ron Paul has talked much about ending the Federal Reserve. He is not getting much support from the media and even the GOP. He is making those who are involved in these monolithic secret societies because they have ruled over America the past century. We must and will be free of these Illuminati dark symbols. We must have the Federal Reserve under the direct control of the Executive, Legislative and Judicial branches of our government; free of foreign intervention into U.S. monetary and economic policies.

The United States Central Bank

If I was president I would propose the creation of a United States Central Bank. I believe we must lift barriers for a free market economy. We need to push for home ownership. Wall Street has pushed mortgage derivatives. These derivatives had pushed the country into an economic collapse in 2008. Since then it has become increasing difficult for many homeowners to purchase new homes. Banks consider many people the scourge of the earth while they themselves were the beneficiaries of a bail out by the American people. The high gasoline prices at the pumps led to economic slowdowns which cause America to go into a downward spiral. Without jobs people cannot afford new homes. We need to create a long lasting economic policy for a revival. This United States Central Bank will put the trust of the American people. We must invest in America. This Central Bank will need to have the authority in granting home mortgage, car, and small business loans directly to Americans at a simple 10% interest rate not compounded annually. A $180 thousand dollar loan at 10% would generate a mortgage payment of $1100 per month; with full ownership of the home paid off in fifteen years. This bank will offer ten and fifteen year mortgage loans. Doing so will create a housing market surge. The government will not make money on this program but it will benefit many Americans. With a lower monthly house payment it will generate more disposable income for people. They will have the ability to purchase more goods and services. This will lead to an economic boom. Uncle Sam will prosper with increased tax revenue by more Americans working.

I mentioned earlier that the media no longer provides the real news. Americans never hear about the corruption and rampant thieving in Washington. No longer can America be dependent upon the media giants to be the Forth Tier of our Republic in ensuring the balance of power within the government. The politicians are more concerned about lining their pockets and trying to keep their elected jobs. We need a new Forth Tier and that needs to be the American people.

Fair Election Amendment

If I were president I would propose to Congress a Constitutional Amendment to restore the Republic and restore lost rights and freedoms. We need to end the corrupt money in Washington. We need a Fair Election Amendment. This amendment will read:

"FAIR ELECTION AMENDMENT

1. All political elections will be publicly funded. The Federal Election Commission with the approval of the President will determine the dollar amounts allocated for the Presidential, U.S. Representative, U.S. Senate, and Federal Court Judge seats. Congress cannot impose a dollar limitation of raised funds to be eligible for public financing; candidate raised funds cannot exceed per election $1500 Individual/$2500 Corporate/$5000 Political Organizations.

2. U.S. Federal Judges will be elected for a term of 6 years in the General Election. Political parties may run their candidates in Primary Elections. The U.S. Court of Federal Claims will determine and announce federal bench vacancies.

3. All voting machines must have a paper back-up, to assure validity and integrity of Elections, when utilizing electronic voting machines.

4. The right of the people to present National Referendums for General Election votes will not be infringed upon by Congress or any government body. National Referendums can repeal any law, Executive Order, or Supreme Court ruling (that impacts the people outside of the court case)."

This amendment will create integrity within our government institutions and political processes. The American people will be the primary special interest group from sea to shining sea. The American people will have full oversight; no longer the oppressed or the governed for they themselves will hold to account and govern over the political and government leaders. This is the Divine right for all citizens.

America, we have already lost the Republic when the 2012 NDAA became law where the military has the authority to detain and torture anyone for any reason. The Secretary of Defense is supportive of citizen assassinations. This bill made it now legal to murder American citizens. They have been doing so for quite some time.

We must begin to build a New America. Let us make dreams come true. Let us build a nation that captures a new American Spirit for Peace.

WHEN WE END THE SUPPRESSION OF HUMAN RIGHTS BY THE UNITED STATES, CHINA, AND OTHER NATIONS; A WHOLE NEW UNIVERSE WILL OPEN UP. THEN MANKIND'S DIVINE PURSUIT OF GLOBAL PEACE AND PROSPERITY WILL BE FULL-FILLED.

CHAPTER 31 - 2012 COUNTDOWN

Two thousand years ago, there were many who were proclaiming that this was THE END OF TIMES. The Jewish people were seeking a Messiah. The Jewish people were seeking a new King to do battle with the Roman soldiers who were occupying their territory. The Jewish people were seeking their own state. Many people were proclaiming that John the Baptist was their new Messiah. The people were proclaiming that John the Baptist would be their new leader, their new King. Fearing that either John the Baptist or Jesus could be their new Messiah, both men were executed. The people were proclaiming that the Anti-Christ will soon appear. Today there are many who think that December 21st, 2012 will be THE END OF TIMES. There are many who think that the Anti-Christ is among us. There are many who believe in the second coming of Christ. The Mayan calendar ends on December 21st, 2012. That is also the day when the Sun and Earth will be lined up in the middle of the Milky Way. Is this all merely a coincidence?

God and the angels are working to bring about a new spiritual consciousness. Many people's consciousness today is of the lower worlds. Greed and the lust for power have taken over many across the spectrum in business and government. The United States has been on the path of a police state. America is no longer free. The government wants to control the population because they fear the population. President Obama had the opportunity to bring about a positive change not only to America but to the rest of the world. He is a decent and honest person, but now he has drifted towards this mindset that the people need to be watched. He had an ambitious agenda when he first took office but the Democrats in Congress dropped the ball. The Republicans in Congress chose the path of being the Grand Obstructionist Party. President Obama campaigned heavily in wanting to restore the loss in rights of the American people under the Patriot Act. Nevertheless, he has given up on that. He wanted to restore 'habeas corpus' a right granted under the Constitution. But that has fallen to the wayside. He is now leading the country on the same path as former President George W. Bush. Even former Vice President Cheney is now a big supporter of President Obama's agenda.

Many of you know by now that I am not religious but a very spiritualistic person. I'm of the same faith as the Divine Father and Divine Mother God. Jesus during his ministry on earth was also of the same faith as the Father/Mother God. At times when I talk or come across people I usually pick up on their thoughts. I see many of our leaders who are basically good people, but they have their heads buried in the sand. Many of them are well educated but their mind is cloudy.

In this book, I have spoken many times of the Father/Mother God. Our ministers and our priests have all referred to God as being of the male gender and this all dates back to biblical days where women were oppressed and took a back seat to man. If man was created in the image of God, then it should also be that woman was created in the image of God. The two are inseparable. You have all heard that we all have a twin soul which is true. It so is truthful that God has a twin soul, the Father/Mother God.

December 2012, will usher in a new age that is dawning upon us where the people whose mind is clouded and buried in the sand will begin to wake up. They will see life in a new perspective and begin shedding old ideas and embrace fresh idealistic viewpoints for the higher good of all. During this time, a new economy will emerge across the globe. Government socialism, communism and even capitalism will fade away into a new economy that will bring much abundance to the people of the world. Eventually, many countries and regions will have to follow the same path that the European Union had undertaken by joining together into an economic partnership.

The Europeans had seen that America became a world power by being united in a union of the states. When there is a union for economic trade, there are no wars between each other because they are dependent upon one another to prosper. South America is an emerging continent, and they will be the next major economic center when they go to a continent without borders with one central currency. At the moment, there is one nation that is an obstacle for economic growth, and it is the only country left with a dictator in South America. That dictator will be going by the wayside.

Cuba is still a communist country, and the United States is at the same time adamant about continuing the economic embargo because it is a communist country. The United States has traded a long time with China. China is now a major economic world leader. There is no reason to continue the Cuban embargo. Cuba has removed those nukes. Congress and the

U.S. President needs to open the door to Cuba so that the people will prosper and become a peaceful nation.

Mexico is suffering economically. People every day are crossing the border into the United States. If Mexico prospers so will the United States. A prosperous Mexico will bring huge dividends in commerce to the United States and Canada. .There will be a day soon for economic prosperity on the North American continent to go to a new currency to replace the dollar. The dollar subsequently will not be able to compete against the Euro and other world currencies.

There is one continent where 50 to 60 years henceforth will surpass China in economic growth. This continent has a lot of healing to go through and the world needs to step in and assist those people. This continent will need major investments in hospitals and other infrastructure. This continent over the years will be seeing an influx of migrants who will lead the continent into economic prosperity and peace. The Union of Africa is on the horizon. It will manifest itself into a major economic superpower. It will not happen overnight, and it might take two generations but they will emerge victoriously. The Union of Africa will also be a land without borders. The days of dictators will vanish. That is the Divine Will of God. It is God's Divine Will in ushering in a new era of peace, love and prosperity. There are those who want to stand in the way of the Divinity, but they will not be successful. God has given the human race—free will. But God's—Divine Will, takes precedence.

Leading up to December 21st 2012, the world will be faced with many challenges and some possible catastrophic events that have the probability of unfolding. No matter what happens the planet will survive. The sun will come up every day. The planet earth will still revolve around the sun. Mankind will survive. There will be no anti-Christ that will emerge. Do not believe everything you read on the internet from the doomsayers. There are some people claiming that President Obama is the anti-Christ. These claims are all politically motivated to create fear and doubt. Know that the angels among us are walking with us side by side. Do not fear the future. We are all living in historic times. Everything is as it should be according to God's Master plan. Forget the past, live in the Now. What we do in the Now creates our future. You are all co-creators of your universe.

You can choose to be happy or sad. You can choose to be frightful or enjoying life. The future is yours to co-create with your angelic and spirit guides. In the Universe, there is no Time only the NOW. Yesterday, God created the Universe. Tomorrow, God will destroy the Universe. We only have NOW. Can you change your past? Yes, you can. Yesterday, you might have been known as one who might have been greedy, selfish or dishonest. Today, you can change that past by becoming one who is honest and giving.

In writing this book I called upon my angelic guides. They answered by connecting me to the God Source in writing this book. For this chapter I asked a dear friend to ask her angel guides what will 2012 usher to the planet. In italics is a complete transcript on what she channeled. The future has several probabilities. Predictions are just that, and not etched in stone. What happens will be the direct outcome of the decisions made by the human race and the outcome of the 2012 Elections that will impact the rest of the world.

"On March 11th, 2007 the angels have started dividing up the souls on earth of good and bad and will continue until 2012. There are different outcomes for that day depending on the next president you vote in but neither comes to total destruction. One pathway is good, one is totally messed up, and one is about what we have now. You also need to prepare for the option of no sun to the earth for almost two years time. So you need to build more windmills for electricity. The reason for dividing up the good and bad souls is that the earth is being returned to Jesus. It is being prepared. Negative souls were allowed to control and influence for a period of time. You are headed for the changeover. Change of the guards. The people of the planet spend many years actually going back and forth between the two; good/bad' 'positive/negative'.

We are entering the next charka for our planet, which is the third eye. Those who hear the call will be ready to change their body make up from carbon 7. The veil should open even more and more allowing more humans to see and hear the angels that are present. But there are other things flying around that are negative. Those are found in law cases where someone claims not to know what they did but 'just did it'. They (spirits) can enter a body in sleep so always ask for protection before sleep as they will come around those easiest to enter; drinkers, drug users, beaters – those types of personalities.

It is as it should be.

You need to be aware that some DNA is being taken from people. There is another planet. Some are already being moved there. Your body is just a car, a pair of shoes as an example. Your soul advancement must be open to this change or fear will set in. Those who are firm in their beliefs will have an easy transition into this new stage of development. You have the crystal children now. They will help the adults. This planet will only last 87 more earth time years, give or take, on choices currently being made to your environment. However, in the end the souls who advance will not be affected. Those who choose to stay will not advance. They will be trapped here during this time as the veil thins.

You will see more and more 'ghosts' as you call them. They are you, just not in the body. When a body is ready, they come back in. We are trying to show you how to switch bodies as you do your shoes or car. It is just a soul. What you believe is what it is. So watch your thought processes. Create positive not negative. Walk with the knowledge that your requests on earth are of little importance. We, the angels, do not care of your choices. Those who choose of their own freewill to be toward the light over the darkness will be transferred out before this planet is no longer. DNA is being taken from them. We are creating children to save your race. But we are only taking from those who have chosen to bring peace. We come in peace but there are side effects.

We do not want to save those who destroy. 2012 the veil will open. The people of the earth WILL SEE the heavens. Some will become afraid causing issues to deal with. Some will welcome it and praise the name of God once again. Some will go into hiding thinking the world will be destroyed. This is silly. Do not allow such behavior. Stand firm in this message. Your world is in your hands. You have the power to save it yourself. We are only here to watch over you. To prevent your earth body from passing before it was time. Your soul will stay trapped without a body until a new one is available.

If you stop having children, then there will be no new bodies. There will come a time where no new children will be born for a period of time. That will be the final separation of positive/negative souls. When this time frame is over only those that enter will be of carbon 7. They will hear/see/feel all the same. With what is surrounding your skies you will see what you call your ET's. You have many things on your planet you are not aware of. Most are not good. We are taking water from your oceans. We are currently finishing the creation of the next planet with what is from here to go there for life support. You already have proof of this. Our ships have been recorded doing this very procedure. Do not think that what is shown is by accident.

We show little by little to prepare the less advanced. The more advanced will think nothing of this. There are more than us angels. You have the fallen angels. They do not carry staffs. They do not carry wands. They are not of gold. They are not of white. They are not the 'grays'. Do not allow them to surround your life in any manner. They are of those who have chosen to leave Heaven. They will lure you. They will deceive you. They will jump in bodies and cause harm to others to the reputation of the body. Their eyes will appear black then when the spirit leaves, they will not know. It will seem like a movie they watched over an action they did but will be left to deal with the consequences. If you cross its path tell it OUT or GO. They must obey as you are from God. There are also many other types of ET's you currently call 'gray'. They are here to help. They fly in your skies. They obey the angels. They are protecting the children, for the most part. They are collecting DNA or filling with golden liquid".

Mankind has suffered much over the ages. Mankind has suffered slavery, genocide and numerous other tragedies and atrocities. There is a strong probability that the Earth will experience a nuclear holocaust. It is up to the U.S. president and the United Nations to prevent such an occurrence. Do not believe that Iran is becoming a nuclear nation for peaceful purposes. Should this occur; there will be a manmade energy crisis. Continuing on the path in not stopping Iran will bring dire consequences to the people of the world. Iran and North Korea could have been stopped years ago but the previous and current administrations have been more focused on Iraq and Afghanistan.

We on this planet are all interconnected with each and the Divinity. This universal connection will further transcend all races, colors and ethnic origins. Embrace the future for the dawn of a new era. The Divinity within all of us is seeking peace, love and prosperity.

CHAPTER 32 - DAWN OF A NEW ERA

*"Beloveds do not falter and do not allow the predictions of doom
and gloom to diminish your vision for the future."*
Archangel Michael

America has many challenges ahead to fix the problems in this country as well as restoring America's brilliance in the world. Some of the problems facing this country are Global Warming, Safeguarding its Borders, Illegal Immigration, Ending the War in Iraq, and bringing Peace to the Middle East. It will take the synergy of all Americans to come together for the good of all. It will take the synergy of our friends and allies around the world to make this world a better place for everyone to pursue Life, Liberty and Happiness. Our next President will have his or her hands full over the next few years.

The Democrats and Republicans in Congress will have to work together. America faces too many threats from within and around the world for them not wanting to work together for the good of the country and the people in the world. The people need to elect into political offices those candidates who seek a higher calling. Elected officials will need to hold government bureaucrats who have their own corrupt agenda accountable to the people. Government bureaucrats work for the people, and they answer to the people. America needs to be strong again, not just militarily but strong in its values and desire for world peace and harmony.

Global warming is a condition that many nations are facing. The rising sea level may eventually flood numerous cities along the coastline of the United States as well as over the globe. Some scientists are predicting that global warming could give rise to a mini-ice age with the melting glaciers. This mini-ice age has started in 2011 with a record number of wintry blizzards. The ice caps will continue to melt but the earth is beginning a cooling down as a natural cycle not man-made. Global warming was not man-made. The polar caps have melted and froze back up again many times. Scientists know that. Scientists have discovered frozen tropical plants on the poles. The economic losses felt around the globe could be horrendous. Now the good news is that it will not happen overnight. We can still save the planet with the cooperation of the worldwide body. The nations of the world need to come together for solutions in combating this worldwide problem. Already many areas of the United States are experiencing serious drought situations due to global warming. There are many rivers and lakes drying up. These lakes and rivers have been a water source for millions of people. With the expected flooding along the coastlines and the expected continued drought inland something needs to be done.

There needs to be a way to bring the water that will be flooding numerous cities across America, inland. One way could be to start building water pipelines from the coasts and pump that water inland to the arid and dry regions much like the Alaskan Oil Pipeline. Investments in the infrastructure of building desalination plants are necessary. Plans need to be made to build levies around the major coastal cities to prevent widespread flooding along the coastlines. No doubt global warming will be changing the landscapes not only of America but also across the globe.

Now is the time for other nations to cooperate in assisting poorer nations to prepare for the future. Global warming will impact everyone across the globe. Scientists claim that global warming is caused by the gas emissions from the heavy industrialized nations. New alternative and renewable sources of energy need to be developed and funded to reduce the gas emissions. We do know that pollution is causing the breakdown of the ozone layer. Global warming is just a cycle that the planet is going through. It will be followed by Global Cooling. The winter of 2011 has been the hardest winter impacting the entire country.

Maybe God is giving us a worldwide problem so that mankind will have no other option but to put aside differences; to protect the Mother Earth for generations to come. The regional conflicts around the world that are engaged in land grabbing may become a moot point in less than 100 years when this planet becomes inhabitable. The people of the world need to unite for a common cause of saving mankind and protecting the earth as long as possible. Conserve the world's natural and fossil fuel resources to extend civilization as long as possible. The cost to fund all of this could be staggering.

However, doing nothing will eventually prove to be more costly. The United States can no longer continue the occupation and nation building of Iraq. This war in Iraq has costs the taxpayers in America hundreds of billions of dollars. The Iraqis and Afghans need to stand up for themselves. They are in a civil war. If they want to squabble among themselves and kill one another, then America needs to step aside. They need to be willing to to help themselves. With the occupation of American troops in Iraq, our presence in that country has become a recruiting ground for terrorist organizations. It is in the long-term interests of our national security interests to bring our troops home. Let the oil rich Arab nations stand-up to the plate to bring peace to that region.

America has to be more focused in securing our borders. Securing America is more important than securing Iraq and Afghanistan. The Bush Administration was more focused and obsessed with Saddum Hussein than what is happening in this country. The next president, in 2012, needs to focus on what is good for America. The world continues to need a strong America. Mexican nationals have been fleeing Mexico in record numbers by crossing over the border into the United States. This is where the government of Mexico needs to recognize the sovereignty of the United States and stop providing assistance to Mexicans fleeing their country. Illegal immigrants or refuges from Mexico are flocking to America because of the economic and political conditions ERin Mexico. Along with the refugees from Mexico are the illegal drugs coming into this country. While illicit drugs are being imported, assault weapons are being exported into Mexico illegally. Gangs are controlling the border towns in Mexico with these assault weapons.

The United States government needs to aggressively build a wall to curb the flow of illegal drug trafficking and the flow of refugees from Mexico. This wall will also prevent the flow of heavy assault weapons into Mexico. This onslaught of illegal immigrants is creating a serious refugee problem within the south-western states. When the U.S. Customs and Border Patrol Agents do catch illegal refuges coming into the country they are returned and those people come right back again. The illegal immigrants have no deterrent from entering this country. The United States needs to realize this is a serious refugee problem and consider building refugee camps to provide food and shelter. Able-bodied refugees can be used as labor in building a border wall. Giving amnesty to those who enter this country illegally is not the answer that only aggravates the problem. A better solution is for the United States government ease up on unnecessary immigration bureaucratic paperwork to allow more Mexicans to enter the country legally on work visas, provided they have a sponsor in this country.

The Mexican government needs to take an aggressive stance in combating corruption among government officials.

They need to do this in order to attract business and investments from the United States. Invest in Mexico. Currently, Mexico is experiencing a housing boom with record growth far exceeding other Latin America countries. Investment by U.S. banks in the housing market in Mexico could generate millions of new jobs for Mexican citizens, which would curtail the emigration from Mexico. Is it not better to invest in a country that does not pose a military threat than a country such as China that has nuclear weapons pointed along the western coast of the United States?

If America invests heavily in Mexico creating new jobs and personal savings for the Mexican citizens, that will create a thriving economy. With a thriving economy in Mexico, that will be an opportunity for increased trade in exporting products and services from the United States. Investing in Mexico will make America economically stronger.

With a strong and healthy economy in America the world will be a safer place when America seeks the cooperation of other nations and focuses on bringing about a peaceful settlement in the Middle East. Of the many citizens from Mexico who desire to enter the United States; then maybe you (Mexicans) ought to petition your government to become a U.S. Territory. You can become a U.S. citizen and an American and learn to speak the English language; instead of Americans being forced to speak the Spanish dialects.

Here is a quote from the late President Teddy Roosevelt in regards to immigration.

"In the first place, we should insist that if an immigrant who comes here in good faith becomes an American and assimilates himself to us, he should be treated on an exact equality with everyone else, for it is an outrage to discriminate against any such man because of creed, or birthplace, or origin. But this is predicated upon the person's becoming every facet an American, and nothing but an American. There can be no divided allegiance here. Any man who says he is an American, but something else also, isn't an American at all. We have room for but one flag. We have room for but one language here, and that is the English language. And we have room for but one sole loyalty and that is the loyalty to the American people. "

Major corporations love the many illegal aliens entering the United States. Why is that? Illegals are consumers. They may have to steal from others to purchase goods and services. They may be willing to work for much lower wages. The influx of illegal aliens entering the United States is helping the major corporations reduce the wages they have to pay out. In the border states along Mexico, many employers' in the United States require of their applicants to be bilingual. The state of Arizona had passed some tougher enforcement laws to give the local police more effective tools in combating illegal immigration into the United States. They felt Washington was not doing enough. The citizens of Arizona were being subjected to higher incidences of crime.

Phoenix is the capital of kidnapping crimes in the United States. The state of Arizona wanted more power to enforce U.S. federal laws pertaining to immigration. One would think the U.S. Justice Department would welcome the efforts being made by the state of Arizona to enforce federal statutes. Big business determines who gets elected and who stays in public office. For political reasons the state of Arizona was sued by the U.S. Justice Department in U.S. Federal Court. And we all know that the Justice Department normally always wins in federal court. The Justice Dept was able to get those state laws overturned.

The almighty dollar comes first and foremost to Big Business and the 'super elite' before God and country. The 'super elite' is the people who control the media, the politicians and We The People. They control us all and tell us what we can think and say. They will use fear to control us. The U.S. Supreme Court recently ruled, Jan 21st 2010 in Citizens United v. Federal Election Commission that corporations have free speech rights, and that they can pour unlimited amount of money into political campaigns.

This victory for Big Business and the 'super elite' will now give major corporations the absolute ability to determine political outcomes to further their cause to control your everyday lives. They now have the power to control the state and federal legislatures as well as future presidents. They now have the power over all of us. They do not care about us or our country or the world.

Initially after the ruling by the Supreme Court was heard, there were politicians who voiced their condemnation at this Court ruling. The president in the State of the Union speech expressed his regret in front of the Supreme Court Justices. The politicians were claiming "By golly we are going to do something about this." Even a draft Constitutional Amendment was made in the U.S. Congress. There were groups forming on Facebook, in protest. The politicians were not going to let this ruling stand.

In the 2010 Election, over $300 million in campaign contributions were received from the corporations. The massive influx of money quieted the politicians in both major parties. The politicians are now owned and bought by Big Business. They will now be determining the outcomes of future elections. They will be determining your health care choices and the foods that you eat; just about anything they desire. As individuals what you can you do? Not a darn thing! How can you as an individual compete now against corporate America? You can't!! You can vote but Big Business will now determine and select the candidates.

I had been running as an Independent candidate but I couldn't compete against Big Business or the two major political parties. I had to face reality and not waste my time and money in this race. The reason I had chosen to run as an independent was because both major parties do not truly represent the American people, just the special interest groups. So what can we do? We cannot just sit back and let corruption destroy all of us. We cannot let the lawyers and politicians dictate our lives and the lives of our children. As Americans we need to come together setting aside political ideologies and religious viewpoints else we all perish on this Titanic.

Many of you believe that we are heading into the direction of socialism, and that is partially true. However, the socialism that is being bestowed upon the American people is not a form of welfare to the poor but a form of Corporate Socialism. This Corporate Socialism began under the Bush Administration and has been gathering steam under the Obama Administration. People you need to be concerned when former Vice President Cheney is now giving high marks and kudos to President Obama. With the recent Supreme Court ruling, We The People will serve, We The Corporation and We The Government. It is in their special interests to maintain the large political divide in America and other nations across the globe. Many of you have read all the internet bloggers in their writings who bash the liberals and conservatives while unknowingly, do the work, for the 'super elite' and many politicians. The 'super elite' does the work of the 'darkness'. The 'darkness' wants to maintain the status quo of regional conflicts, war, poverty, economic collapse, and indiscriminate killing throughout the world. The 'darkness' gains its power by all this chaos.

Can We The People overcome the darkness that has transformed America and the world? The answer is Yes We Can! Not as individuals but as a synergy group. Making the decision of Yes We Can is the first step to the road to recovery. Many politicians who have been elected are basically good people, and they want to perform good deeds but they do not know how too. They become focused on political rhetoric and outdated ideology in their efforts to keep their jobs. They become wrapped up in party loyalty instead of loyalty to, We The People. Politicians spend most of their time and efforts in raising money to stay in office. They answer to Big Business, the 'super elite' and their party bosses.

God and the angels amongst us do not need to do battle with the 'darkness'. For where there is Light, there is no darkness. We The People need to turn on the light switch at the state and federal capitals. As a former candidate for the U.S. Congress I knew what it would have taken to get myself elected. However, I wasn't willing to pay that price. I failed miserably as a politician. I wasn't willing to sacrifice my basic beliefs and principles. But to get elected and to keep your elected job it all has to do with money. That money comes from special interest groups.

Most of our elected officials are hard working Americans, but they have their blinders on. They do not see the long term harm they are causing. Each year they give away more and more freedoms and liberties to the federal and state bureaucrats. As these bureaucrats are getting more powerful they see the state and federal legislatures as a necessary evil until the day will come when there will be no legislatures. This day is fast approaching. People we need to stop that from happening. Get involved!

In order for America to see a new breed of people in political office, people who would be willing to serve their constituents, people who are problem solvers, we need to change the campaign laws. We The People need new campaign laws in providing public financing of all campaigns.

Some of you might ask "How will the taxpayer fund this?" As many of you know the politicians in Washington serve the special interest groups. Pork barrel projects costing the taxpayers' money is put in all legislation expecting to pass. Our U.S. Representatives and Senators fund these projects that have no value to the people to stay elected. Not providing public funding for political campaigns have cost us all dearly. Let's stop this money pit for taxpayers and get back to the simple basics our Founding Fathers fought and died for.

What the people will gain by public financing of political campaigns will be fewer lawyers and politicians and more doctors, engineers, construction workers, nurses, computer operators, teachers, and many more from all walks of life serving one special interest group and that will be the American people. Fire the politicians and bring in the problem solvers. America needs idealists and visionaries who have the ability to see things in a way that others cannot.

Federal judges are appointed by the President and confirmed by Congress. The U.S. Dept of Justice makes recommendations to the President on who to appoint and which federal judges to retain. The judges in actuality work for the Dept of Justice. Justice Dept lawyers, invariably, always win in federal court. They control the judges' judicial career. We The People need to bring justice back to the people by electing those federal judges.

Citizens United really is Corporations United. They do not speak for the American people unless it is in their self-interests to do so. As individuals rather they are Democrats, Republicans or one of many of the hundreds small political parties are not going to have their voices heard. But there is another way. Never forget about the wild card. Public financing of political campaigns will weed out the hidden agendas of the politicians and will attract the problem solvers who answer to a higher calling; and that calling is the American people. Problem solvers dedicated to the future of America by promoting world peace and prosperity.

What needs to emerge is a for-profit-corporation who has a non-partisan open agenda of "public financing of political campaigns". The members can be the shareholders for this corporation. This corporation could raise taxable revenues in producing goods and services such as, a publishing magazine, etc. This corporation will monitor all the incumbents and challengers who support public financing of campaigns. This corporation, with a large voting bloc, could provide monetary contributions to the candidates, the problem solvers, dedicated to working for the American people. Fire the Politicians! Hire the Problem Solvers!

The extremists from the left and the right, who are in the minority, may scream and holler if they see they might be losing their power over your lives. The corrupt bureaucrats might be dismayed but the synergy of the people will prevail.

Today our legislatures at all levels think "there ought to be a law against this".

Tomorrow our legislatures at all levels will think "there ought to be a law to allow this".

Republican or Democrat?

A woman in a hot air balloon realized she was lost. She lowered her altitude and spotted a man in a boat below. She shouted to him, "Excuse me, can you help me? I promised a friend, I would meet him an hour ago, but I don't know where I am." The man consulted his portable GPS and replied, "You're in a hot air balloon, approximately 30 feet above a ground elevation of 2346 feet above sea level. You are at 31 degrees, 14.97 minutes north latitude and 100 degrees, 49.09 minutes west longitude.

She rolled her eyes and said, "You must be a Democrat." "I am," replied the man. "How did you know?" "Well," answered the balloonist, everything you told me is technically correct, but I have no idea what to do with your information, and I'm still lost. Frankly, you've not been much help to me."

The man smiled and responded, "You must be a Republican." "I am," replied the balloonist. "How did you know?" "Well," said the man, "you don't know where you are or where you're going. You've risen to where you are, due to a large quantity of hot air. You made a promise that you have no idea how to keep, and you expect me to solve your problem. You're in exactly the same position you were in before we met but, somehow, now it's my fault."

CHAPTER 33 - A NEW PATH TO PEACE

What the world desires immediately is a new voice in the United Nations to end poverty, famines, diseases, and wars. The United Nations needs a new World Ambassador to end conflicts before they turn into bloody and needless wars. The most critical part of any conflict or war is the events leading up to when shots and bombs are dropped. Once the hostilities begin it is very difficult to end the violence.

A new World Ambassador who carries the qualities of a statesman could intervene in the early hours to resolve problems and begin serious communications between the potential warring parties. We've seen this in Libya where now as of the publication of this book, U.S. officials are claiming it will take months. Had a World Ambassador been present in the early hours there could have been a chance to prevent further bloodshed.

Christianity, Judaism, and the Islam religions came from the biblical House of Abraham. These warring religions have battled one another over the centuries creating hated and distrust. God is love. The religious and spiritual leaders need to take the higher road and path of respect and tolerance toward other religious beliefs. In life, it is sometimes much easier to hate someone than to love someone. Those faiths or religions that do not speak of brotherly love are not a true religion or faith. Christians, Jews, and Muslims need to build cooperation and trust by talking in seeking peace and spiritual love. All three religions have roots in the Holy City of Jerusalem. Peace can come to that region if the religious and political leaders set aside their differences for the betterment of humanity.

Moderates of each religion need to try to convince the extremists to lay down their arms and suicide bomb vests. As stated in an earlier chapter one way is to build a holy temple near Jerusalem that would house the faiths and beliefs of the Islam and Judaism religion. From there another descendent would be added, Christianity, to make a Holy Trinity. Later surrounding these temples the other major religions will build a Temple. From there hotels and restaurants would emerge. People from around the world of all origins would build new homes. The United Nations with a change in their worldwide mission will relocate to this new area. Out of all of this a new city will emerge, an international city of brotherly love, the New Jerusalem. The way for this to happen is for the spiritual leaders of the largest religions in the world from Islam, Christianity, Judaism, Hindu and the Buddhist faiths and others to come together. They can come together in a spirit of brotherly love. In the middle of this geometric structure will be an open area of numerous waterfalls and gardens. The lush green grounds surrounding this World Temple of Peace can be a replica of the Garden of EDON.

This world temple will be a bright shining star reflecting the light of God and his love to all of us. Building this World Temple will manifest into becoming an epic center for peace. In the eyes of God, we are all equal. Our spiritual leaders of the past such as Mohammed, Jesus, Buddha, Krishna and many others are they not walking together within the Kingdom of God?

Mankind to survive needs to replace the seven deadly sins of greed, gluttony, lust, envy, sloth, wrath and pride; with the heavenly traits of faith, hope, charity, fortitude, justice, temperance and prudence. By doing this, the world will manifest into a happier place to pursue Life, Liberty and Happiness. If people can come together to do that, that will be the start of a lasting peace within the region. When peace comes to that region, the synergy created by love and trust for one another will spread to the far corners of the earth and the planet earth will move further into a new age, a Golden Age. A new spiritual age, where the people of the Earth can enjoy two thousand years of tolerance and acceptance. A new age where people will live in harmony and peace with one another. In those first golden ages of ancient history, mankind used wondrous spiritual tools and techniques to manifest unlimited energy and facilitated the creation of everything necessary to live in comfort and abundance. In those wondrous times, the Earth was a true paradise called the Garden of EDON.

Our heavenly mother and father will continue to watch over all of us. They are patiently waiting the day our consciousness evolves into a higher state of being while we all pursue our own life, liberty and happiness. Together in world prayers, someday, if enough people pray for world peace and that choice is strictly up to the inhabitants of this planet, we can all return to Planet EDON. It just might cause a change for that one extra person to pray for world peace and harmony.

There are some voices who want to end civilization as we know it or destroy America, both domestic and foreign but those voices will be defeated. The planet is entering into a new golden age, an Age of Enlightenment, a new peaceful and loving World Union, not a New World Order of the darkness with the skull and crossbones. Embrace this new change of consciousness that is now happening. Together and united, the world can create a new international holy city of worship and peace called New Jerusalem.   The other side of the veil is opening up to the Light.

Behold for the Dawn of a New World is shining brighter each day.

CHAPTER 34 - LOVE CONCURS ALL

The key ingredient for Peace and Prosperity is Love

Love for your fellow human beings

Loves means forgiveness, to self and others

Love means happiness

Love means love thy self first

Love means be kind to the animals

Love means be kind to your neighbours

Love means respect to one another

Love means be kind to the planet

Love means being a true friend to others

Love means show someone you care

Love means understanding

Society is better served with just a few laws and those laws are strictly adhered to and enforced. The basic Universal Law is the Golden Rule; "treat others the way you would like to be treated." Do not steal or take what is not yours and do not cause harm to another person or their property. In a society when one is intentionally causing harm to another person or their property, they should be forced to pay a price to society. They need to be held accountable and to compensate those that they harm. Those that pose a grave threat to society need to be incarcerated. Those people who can be rehabilitated can be released back into society after they have been rehabilitated. The people that can't be rehabilitated need to be kept away from causing harm to others. There is no free ride in life. Life doesn't always give us second chances. People do need to think of the potential consequences before they commit acts of crime against society. In the end, the Universe will hold all those accountable.

Political and religious extremism has caused much sorrow and armed regional conflicts throughout the world. Religious extremism has been an overbearing barrier to peace. The moderates in the churches need to come together with those of the other faiths and work together to bring a better world. President George Washington firmly believed in moderation in politics. The road to worldwide recovery starts with a moderate view in both religion and politics. The political divide in the United States caused by extremists from both the right, and the left do not represent mainstream America. Their voices have been the loudest. Most Americans view the two major political parties, Democrat and Republican, with disdain. President Thomas Jefferson believed that a curse for America would be when there are only two political parties. The time is ripe for a moderate far-seeing political party, to join forces with the many independent political interest groups. A visionary and idealistic view without the hype of political ideology from the past; a non-partisan viewpoint will once again bring hope to many in America and across the globe.

Is this book about a Call to arms? It most certainly is! Wrap your loving arms around your neighbor. Let's get started now. God and the Angels are waiting.

CHAPTER 35 – SPECIAL MESSAGE FROM THE FATHER/MOTHER GOD

People of the world rejoice in these words. Beloveds know that God and the heavenly angels are watching steadfastly over your planet. Your planet is undergoing many changes. You are all born into a historic time for your planet. The days of devastating and destructive wars will soon be behind you. You are witnessing the emergence of a new Economy to replace your current and corrupt economy. You will be seeing the end of many repressive government regimes across the globe. Many of you have had your eyes closed. It is time to open your eyes. It is time to reclaim your lives. It is time to reclaim your planet. It is time to reclaim your Divinity that has always been there. For each person is a part of the Divine Spirit.

Your planet needs to be healed. It has been abused for a long time. Your planet gives you your nourishing meals. Your planet provides the needed air that you breathe. Your planet provides the fossil fuels for your cars and homes. There have been many who have abused the soil that you all walk upon. Stop your wasteful ways. Conserve your precious natural resources. Safeguard and protect the forests and the wildlife that resides.

Know that those who harbor to control each and every aspect of your life will not succeed. Know that the light is not in a battle with the dark. For when there is Light there is no darkness. Do not listen to the doomsayers about the end of the world. Though you have the power to destroy mankind, mankind cannot destroy the planet. We have watched for many ages, the abuses and the harms that mankind has done to each other. You have all lived many lives on this planet. Why do many of you want to destroy your planet? For many of you will continue to return to the planet Earth many more times. Should you not desire to leave the planet in better shape than when you found it? For many of you will incarnate. Many of you will also be rewarded eternal life within the Kingdom of God after completing your divine mission on earth. Instead of being the aggressor you may end up being the victim in your next incarnation. You are all brothers and sisters of this planet. Be the blackbird and the robin.

In many ways mankind's religions have wrought much suffering among you over the ages. The Divinity is not found in the Church. The Divinity is found in ALL of you inside. When you hear the moaning dove and the birds chirp, they are singing God's words of love. Do not judge others harshly when you live inside glass houses. Do not look down on people's occupations when they are working to serve your needs. In the eyes of God the custodian is just as important as your corporate president. Blessed are those who thank those people who serve you daily.

Your fears have brought much destruction and suffering to mankind. Many of you purchase guns and other weapons to kill others. Many of you also purchase guns and other weapons to protect yourselves. When you harm someone you owe them a karmic debt. You will meet your victim again. Lead your lives by following the Golden Rule of treating others as you would like them to treat you. Do not steal that is not yours and do not harm another person. If mankind would only live by those golden laws, you all will live in peace and prosper more than you could ever realize. Teach your children wisely for they are the future of this planet. Encourage them to excel and that nothing is impossible.

All of you have been assigned guardian angels and guides. Call upon them. They are there to lead you wisely. Many of you are awaiting the second coming of Christ. You have already been sent many messengers and teachers. The religious priests had Jesus crucified. Jesus was your savior. If we send another messiah will you not also crucify that person? Do you think that the second Jesus will glide gently down amongst the clouds to save you all from your Armageddon? That is impossible in this physical dimension. However, many of you are 'Light workers" doing the work of the Divinity. You will succeed.

We give out unconditional love to all. Do not worship us. Worship yourselves dear god-people. May you all enjoy a lasting peace and happiness. The heavenly realms are here for you. Call upon us. Open your eyes and you will prosper. Live in harmony with one another. The shift in consciousness is coming. Your new world is unfolding. So it is.

"War should never be entered upon until every agency of peace has failed."
President William McKinley

CHAPTER 36 – FINAL WORDS

In writing this book there were at times when I was sensitive to the opinions of others, especially if they were on the path of far-right or far-left extremism as well as extreme religious viewpoints. One has to respect others viewpoints because we are all individuals. Each and every one of us has different opinions when it comes to politics or religion or even spirituality issues. There were many times I was concerned by what people would think of me especially in discussions of my spiritual expansion. It was more important to speak the truth and not censure any truths for fear of offending anyone or worry about ridicule against me.

Those of you who hold an extreme radical viewpoint or have hate and anger issues, this might not be the book for you to read. This book would be too troubling for you. This book was written for the majority of American citizens and other people around the world who are frustrated with politics in general and who are upset with political parties or tyrannical governments. This book was intended for those who desire or seek a higher path. You are the ones who are "awakening". The others may not ever awaken or at least not in their current lifetime. The "others" in many instances are the ones who have been trying to convert the rest of us to their "thinking"; even by lethal force if necessary.

Some I would have lost in the first chapter in the discussions of the U.S. Constitution where America is a One Nation under God. People across the globe need to have religious freedom and freedom from religion. Some people do not understand the broad differences between religion and spirituality. Most of us have been exposed to two and three dimensional concepts. Fifth dimensional concepts are beyond many people. The light-workers know what I speak of. The following Appendixes in this book are for those who want an introduction to fifth dimensional concepts and to learn a little more about the angelic ones and the Star people or extraterrestrial life, ET for short.

The physical universe is vast and it is still expanding. Scientists have increased their knowledge where just in our Galaxy alone, there are 50 billion planets. Of those, 500 million planets are revolving around their suns that are in the climate for life forms. The likelihood that the planet earth is the only planet in the entire universe that supports life is very minuscule. For those of you who wondering how the ancient pyramids were built out of the second hardest stone on the planet, you might want to read Appendix 2 about how to change the weight of mass.

I wrote this book out of unconditional love for mankind. Not all these words are mine or anyone else but by the divinity. Seek out your truths. I do not hold a belief or a faith in God for I know God. Scientists and physicists will never be able to disprove the divinity. The divinity and spark of God is in every molecule and atom. The best they can do is marvel at these wonders. In the coming years the human species will be witnessed to many marvels and events that will be unfolding, to some it may appear too frightful. Have love in your hearts for that is a contagious tranquility.

APPENDIX 1 – MEDITATIONS FOR INNER PEACE, LOVE AND PROSPERITY

I would like to share with the reader here a reading from the Archangel Michael as was transcribed by Ronna Herman from her website in a February 2008 message from this Angel, Following the Way of the Sacred Heart. Take what you can from this message. Believe what you want to believe. Many of us are on a spiritual journey in seeking Truth. Many others do not seek the truth, which is also fine. God gives us all free will. Those of you who practice meditation will find this message from the Archangel Michael very rewarding and refreshing and an excellent spiritual exercise to try. Michael is commonly referred to as "One who is like God". Remember when we pray, we talk to God. When we meditate, God talks to us. God and the Angels are always willing to talk to us and to show us the way, one soul at a time. Men you may also call upon these Divine Goddesses and Angels.

"Beloved Masters, as more and more of your old reality fades away and you move deeper into uncharted territory, you must learn to trust and have faith that the future is unfolding perfectly no matter how chaotic and disruptive it may seem at times. First, you must learn to trust yourself and this can be the most difficult step, for you have been taught that others are wiser than you, and they know what is best for you. This may have been true when you were a child; however, you are now adults with a golden opportunity before you: the wisdom of the cosmos is now available, and we of the higher realms are here in great force to assist you to attain Self-Mastery and to reclaim your rightful state as a spiritual human-Being. All of you have given your power away in some form in most of your incarnations on the Earth. You became conditioned and accustomed to what has been called the 'herd-state,' whereby others in positions of authority set the rules, told you what to do and, like or not, you followed, for it felt safer than to resist and try to chart your own course. We have often said that moving out of your comfort zone and the collective conscious belief structure is a very courageous thing to do. Bravely going forth to seek and live your own truth is the first step in taking back your personal power. As you release the shackles of the past and come to the understanding that you are in control of your future, you begin the process of awakening to your potential as a master co-

creator. As you gain wisdom and begin to enjoy the positive results of your endeavors, you begin to trust yourself and your judgment. Your multisensory perception expands and becomes stronger, and you learn to view both the positive and negative results of the choices from a higher vantage point, thereby gradually learning to make decisions from a heart-centered point of view. Faith is an intrinsic facet of trust: faith in yourself and your judgment, faith in those around you who have proven themselves trustworthy and honorable, faith in the Father/Mother God, the universal laws, and the Divine Blueprint for the future of humanity. We are not speaking of blind faith, for that is another way of giving your power away to someone else, their teachings and rules. In your material world, faith is built through actions and positive outcome, a function of the mind filtered through the heart. The heart is both a magnetic and radiating vortex and is the true source of human power. Your Sacred Mind holds the seed thoughts of your past and the future, and it is your source of the Divine will and power from our heavenly Father. Your seed thoughts for the future must be incubated within the Sacred Heart and the Adamantine Particles of Creator Light ignited by your love, and through your pure intention and actions they are manifested in the world of form. Abundance of all kinds is a natural manifestation when you are in harmonious attunement with Spirit and the Divine Plan for the greatest good of all. You must learn to function through the intellect of the Sacred Heart. As you strengthen the connection between your Sacred Mind and your Sacred Heart, you will begin to access the Wisdom of the Soul, your Higher Self and the multidimensional facets of your Self. Your Soul, your Higher Self, your guides, guardians and angelic helpers communicate with you through your Soul Self and your Sacred Heart. The whispers of Spirit in the unawakened become a mighty voice of loving wisdom and comfort as you awaken to the strength and majesty of your divinity. Many dear souls have asked, "How can we access more of the loving attributes of the Divine Mother and the feminine Archangels?" Your Sacred Hearts are beginning to blaze forth and you are aware that it is the loving energy of the Divine Mother that has been missing for so very long. The Divine Mother God and all the radiant facets of her Being have always been available to you no matter what other Divine mission and task she may be involved in. She, as our Father God, is omnipotent and omnipresent.

If it is your desire to experience more of the Divine Mother's love, attributes and qualities, we offer you the following suggestions. In a meditative state, see a beautiful crystal *pyramid forming in the fifth dimension (your Higher Self will determine the appropriate sub-level for your special Goddess Pyramid of Light). Envision the crystal table in the center with the Violet Flame blazing up from beneath the table. There is also a sparkling double-terminated quartz crystal hanging over the table with the uppermost point extending out of the top of the Pyramid. Place a number of crystal chairs around the table and then add any other items that you would like to have there. This is your personal creation, and you may envision anything you would like to have there, for this will be your sanctuary where you will come to commune with the Divine Mother and all her beautiful representatives. Indeed it is time to integrate to the fullest the aspects and qualities of the Divine Mother. Divine love, compassion, illumination, nurturance, gratitude, faith, hope and charity. These beautiful Ladies of Light will join you in your Pyramid, and they will leave a facet of their Essence there with you so that you may commune with them at any time you wish. Know that they will also radiate into the Etheric Replica of yourself that you will leave there on the crystal table the qualities and attributes that you desire to incorporate. Just remember, whatever you are given, you must use for the good of all in order to receive more. That is an immutable universal law.*

We gave you some of these affirmations a number of years ago; however, it is appropriate that we give them to you again at this time. While in your Pyramid of Light dedicated to the Divine Mother and her entourage, affirm in your words or as follows:

BELOVED DIVINE MOTHER, I ask you to join me in my Pyramid of Light and to gift me with your blessed loving energy so that I may be filled with the glory and power of your Divine Essence. I seek to integrate and portray your gentleness and your strength of Spirit, and to express your sweet, pure love in my daily life to any and all I meet. Open the portals of my Sacred Heart so that your pure love may blaze forth through me now and forever more.
I CALL FORTH THE BLESED LADY MARY, ARCHANGEL OF THE FIFTH RAY, for whom I feel such great affinity, to guide and sustain me in my quest for truth and creative power. I claim all the gifts that have been imprinted on my soul and within my brain structure and I gratefully manifest them in their highest form for the blessing of all. I am continually inspired to give birth to things of great beauty to delight and encourage others to do the same. I draw upon the laws of Creation and dedicate my

life in service to humanity.

I CALL UPON THE BEAUTIFUL LADY FAITH, ARCHANGEL OF THE FIRST RAY, to inspire me and lead me through unknown territory onto the path that leads to enlightenment. I will go forth in full faith, trust and knowledge that I am being led by my God Self, and I will be a shining example for all to see. I will show others that with courage and faith the impossible becomes possible, and by releasing that which may seem safe and secure when I am nudged to do so, I attain comfort and am blessed with riches untold. I will show the weak of heart that we can step off the cliff and soar among the stars.

I CALL UPON THE LADY CONSTANCE, ARCHANGEL OF JUSTICE/TRUTH, THE SECOND RAY, to fill me with the desire to know and experience the hidden wisdom of the ages. As I gain true knowledge and wisdom, and manifest it in my life, may I become an example and disseminator of higher truth, sharing it with all the seekers of the Light. I will give comfort to those who are discouraged and inspire those who feel defeated. I will be a courageous example for the faint of heart and give loving succor to those who do not feel worthy of love. I will honor and listen to the nudging of my Spirit and walk the way of truth and love.

I CALL UPON LADY CHARITY, ARCHANGEL OF THE THIRD RAY. I, who have known ignorance, bigotry and injustice, will be a shining example of unconditional love and pure intention. I will always endeavor to understand and forgive, knowing that each person is on their own sacred journey and must learn their lessons in their own way and in their own time. I claim the purity of my Divine Self and it shines radiantly for all to see and share in its warmth. I will share my gifts of abundance and I will be charitable in thoughts, action and deeds. I will personify the qualities of understanding, clear perception and Divine wisdom.

I CALL UPON LADY GRACE, ARCHANGEL OF THE SIXTH RAY, to fill me and infuse me with her glorious radiance. Make me a beacon for all to see so that they will know whom I serve as I use the Light of Spirit to heal, comfort and inspire. I will bask in the glow of her radiance and create such a brilliant aura of love that all whom I come in contact with will be blessed, and seeds of transformation will be planted and will come to fruition at the appropriate time. My spirit rejoices as I spread wide my influence of Loving Light.

I CALL UPON LADY AMETHYST, ARCHANGEL OF THE SEVENTH RAY, to be my inspiration. I claim the gift of the Violet Transmuting Flame, the Divine alchemical energy of transformation and transmutation. I will accept the challenge to be the full embodiment of the perfected masculine and feminine energy, showing all what it means to walk in power and strength while personifying love and compassion. I claim and pronounce my MASTERHOOD NOW!

I CALL UPON THE BELOVED LADY MASTER KWAN YIN to infuse me with the healing energy; love and compassion of her wondrous nature. Assist me to be a nurturer for all those who seek comfort, hope and inspiration. Allow me to be a Bearer of healing Light by which they attain wholeness in body, mind and Spirit. May all whom I meet and serve be infused with balance, peace and harmony.

I CALL UPON THE GODDESS OF LIBERTY to liberate me from any limitation that is keeping me from fulfilling my highest destiny. I assume the mantle of an inspired co-creator under the guidance of my Divine Self, and go forth in constant assurance of success. I know I am a teacher of the new, emerging wisdom and truth. May I never hesitate to speak my truth and share my wisdom when my Spirit leads me to do so. I accept the role of a gentle guide to all those who are led to me.

I CALL UPON THE LOVING GODDESSES OF THE DEVIC AND ELEMENTAL KINGDOMS to shower their radiant loving energy down upon the Earth, calming all the elements of nature and to join us in our efforts to heal our wounded Mother Earth. I petition them to work in unison with us once more to reclaim the beauty and perfection of the Earth. May we remember that we are stewards of the Earth and the animal, vegetable and mineral kingdoms were put under our care. May we walk in peace and harmony, honoring all our Mother/Father God's creations, from the lowest to the highest.

AFFIRM: I HEREBY DON MY SHINING CLOAK OF SPIRITUAL ARMOR AND ACCEPT THE GIFTS AND RESPONSIBILITIES OF AN ASCENDING MASTER OF COCREATION. I DEDICATE MY LIFE AND MY ALL TO THE GLORY OF GOD/GODDESS/ALL-THAT-IS, AND TO THE MANIFESTATION OF HEAVEN ON EARTH. AND SO IT IS!

Beloved ones, we ask you to love yourselves as we love you. We ask you to trust yourselves to make the right decisions with Spirit as your guide. We ask you to have faith in the future, and assure that it unfolds in perfect order by staying heart-centered and soul-focused. Many of you who have agreed to integrate the maximum amount of the higher frequency patterns of Creator Light are, at times, experiencing uncomfortable *symptoms and mood swings, but this too will pass as your physical vessel releases more and more of the impacted or negative energies from within. It was a very brave and unselfish thing that you agreed to and, as time passes, you will refine the physical vessel while you integrate more of your Divine Self. It is something that has never been done on Earth before and we honor you for being among the forerunners of this process. You and those like you are making it much easier for those who follow behind you. May the radiance of our Mother/Father God's Light pour down upon you. Know that you are loved beyond measure.*

I AM Archangel Michael and I joyously bring you these truths."

It is necessary that we all are 'opened' to receive God's love and many blessings. One way to do that is to cleanse and protect our body, mind, and soul. In life we cleanse our bodies when we shower or take a bath but we many times ignore our mind and soul. Why not multi-task and do all three at the same time. An excellent way to do so is when you take a bath or shower; you imagine in your mind that you are being bathed in a golden light of protection and love. You don't want to imagine a white light since the opposite of white is black and you don't want to attract any negative energy. When you take a bath or shower you want to release the negatives and protect yourself with a golden ray of light. At first it might be helpful to place something gold in your shower such as a bar of soap, wash cloth, or anything else with a gold color.

When you are cleansing your body with soap imagine you are removing negative energies from your body. Take in some deep breaths through your nose and exhale through your mouth. These are cleansing breaths to bring in positive energies and removing the negative energies. Imagine the water running over your body as being a golden ray of love and protection. Imagine this love and protection extending beyond your body by a few feet where you are now encased in a bubble of love and protection. The next day repeat the process and do this on a daily basis for God's protection from negative energies that you might encounter as you go through your day. By doing this you will feel more confident and in balance. You may want to use these words or any other words that you feel comfortable using after you take your cleansing breaths by saying "By these golden rays of light I am receiving God's protection and blessing to manifest love, health, happiness and prosperity." Repeat this three times.

There is also an awesome and powerful prayer that one can use to connect in the World Pyramid of Light in the high fifth dimension. By saying this prayer you will be able to eventually unite with your spiritual brothers and sisters from around the world:

"BELOVED FATHER/MOTHER GOD, I ASK FOR MY HIGHEST GOOD, THE GREATEST GOOD FOR THE EARTH AND ALL HUMANITY."

Breathe in the LIGHT, and breathe OUT the sacred Adamantine Particles of Creation activated by your unconditional loving energy.

BREATHE IN LIGHT**
BREATHE OUT LOVE**
BREATHE IN LIGHT**
BREATHE OUT LOVE.

The Infinity Breath exercise will enhance your efforts and increase the personal benefits you will derive. This blessed elixir will be used to assist humanity and the Earth; it will reinforce the determination and dedication of the righteous, dedicated souls, and will gradually cut off the resources of those who are only interested in power, control and domination of the masses. Also while in communion with your Father/Mother God, radiate your gratitude and heartfelt thanks for the many blessings that are being bestowed upon you. Not so much with words, but with an outpouring of love from within the core of your sacred heart.

In this Appendix the Archangel Michael speaks of the Father/Mother God. If man was created in the image of 'his' holiness, then it is also true that woman was created in the image of 'her' holiness. The Divinity is comprised of the masculine and feminine self. Here are some words to ponder and chew upon.

"As we grow up, we learn that even the one person that wasn't supposed to ever let us down probably will. You'll have your heart broken and you'll break others' hearts. You'll fight with your best friend or maybe even fall in love with them, and you'll cry because time is flying by. So take many pictures, laugh too much, forgive freely, and love like you've never been hurt. Life comes with no guarantees, no time outs, and no second chances. You just have to live life to the fullest, tell someone what they mean to you and tell someone off, speak out, dance in the pouring rain, hold someone's hand, comfort a friend, fall asleep watching the sun come up, stay up late, be a flirt, and

smile until your face hurts. Don't be afraid to take chances or fall in love and most of all; live in the moment because every second you spend angry or upset is a second of happiness you can never get back." Author - unknown

Your greatest discovery will be to find the secrets of God.

Seek out the Truth and the doors to Heaven will open.

The opposite of love is indifference.

The opposite of hate is understanding.

Holy Number Three
(The Trinity)

Embrace the healing properties of the Trinity in all aspects of your life.

Embrace the Trinity in Politics, Marriages, Prayers, Governments, Legal Partnerships, Spiritualism, and the list goes on and on…

Embrace the concept that everything, everything permeates from the God Source; the God Source is the heavenly consciousness.

The Holy Trinity of Love is the God Source, the Heavenly Father God and the Heavenly Mother God.

Humans will find Peace, Love, and Prosperity on Planet Earth when the warring religions of Judaism, Islam and Christianity find Understanding and Acceptance.

Embrace the Healing Properties of the Three-sided Triangle as a Pyramid.

The God Source is the power and the energy that permeates outwards throughout the many heavens and the many galaxies of all the Suns and all the planets and its beings.

The Trinity is the Unifier from the God Source.

Embrace the I AM dear God Masters.

APPENDIX 2 – ANGEL TECHNOLOGY
PART 1

LIVE KRYON CHANNELLING
"Needed Science for the Times"

This live channeling was given in Albuquerque, New Mexico. (Feb 14th, 2010)
To help the reader, this channeling has been rechanneled [by Lee and Kryon] and added onto, to provide even clearer understanding. Often what happens live has implied energy within it, which carries a kind of communication that the printed page does not. So enjoy this enhanced message given in Albuquerque, New Mexico.

Greetings dear ones, I am Kryon of magnetic service. Again we are here in a way that may seem strange to many. I want you to get used to hearing this voice and understanding the reality that is here. Perhaps you might ask yourself, *"Is this real?"* You might say, *"Kryon, I'm having a hard time believing that you're really channeling, that the voice comes from the other side of the veil. It's just so difficult!"* If that's what you're saying today, Human Being, I will say that you are blessed to be so honest with words coming from the struggle to work out of the three-dimensional box you are in.

Dear one, if you ask the right questions of your own Higher-Self, of your own belief, of your own psyche, you then start have things revealed that you didn't expect. For it indeed is a quantum experience on the other side of the veil. My partner [Lee] and I are linearizing this conversation for you. This is a quantum experience and that means that language is only a small part of it. The audio that you hear and the words seen on the page are only a portion of it.

In the past, we have spoken of something called the third language. This third language, identified some time ago, is not a language in linearity. It is instead a language of the *catalyst of the three*. We use the three in numerology to represent a catalytic *action* number. That is to say that all of you have the ability to receive what is being given at a level which is quantum, and not a language such as words on a page. Even the reader of this particular message can ask for a quantum experience and then be in the session with those who are in the room in real time.

We're going to give you some science. We've chosen, perhaps, an odd place for that [Albuquerque, New Mexico]. But we really haven't, for we think in a quantum way. We wanted to come to this place and honor those who built this building [The Indian Center]. We want to honor the ancestors who are here, listening. We've come to a very quiet place in the stillness of the southwest in order to give a message of clarity, and purity, so that others will also receive it in this fashion.

Science for today

When we give a scientific message, I ask my partner to go very slow. Some of the things we speak of now have been revealed to him, and some have not. So I asked him to proceed slowly, for it will be heard and read clearly and much will be seen around it. For what follows in this message is not just esoteric. There will be practicality presented and there will be physicists looking at it... and that makes my partner nervous.

This message is not necessarily a long one, but one which you have to hear. It's about the environment and science. So let us start with some assurance and positive news. Let us review one more time that what you are seeing in weather changes on this planet have not been created by Humans. What you have called global warming is not global warming at all, and I say it again: It is part of the cycle that always was. This information is not new, and we told you these things some years ago when the idea of warming first was presented, and fear was the result. We also called out the weather changes you are seeing now, back in 1989 when my partner began this journey with me. Long before the idea of warming was popular, I was telling you to expect this cycle.

The North Pole has melted several times and come back several times. It is waxing and waning. The water evaporation cycle [what Kryon called the water cycle] is the way Gaia works. However, this time it appears to be here sooner than expected, and that is alarming to many. If you were to ask Gaia right now to come in to this place, Gaia would give this message: *"Humans have not caused this."* Could it be any clearer? I give you this information so there would be no alarm sounded regarding it or actions taken that might be in response to a false idea.

However, at the same time I tell you that there is a mandate to change how you create your energy. What you put into the air is significant, for it is a hazard to your health. What you put into the air is significant, for it is a hazard to your health. What you put into the air hurts Humanity, not necessarily Gaia. Gaia is far more resilient than you think. Gaia adjusts in ways you don't expect, and faster than you expect. Your contribution to pollution is insignificant when compared to volcanic eruptions of the past. Gaia takes care of Gaia, and the process is not new, or a surprise. However, for humanity we say, "Clean up the air and you will live longer." It's not about stopping a weather cycle that you have created. Hardly! It's about common sense for life.

It's going to get colder. That's one of the subjects of today. You're going to need more energy to combat the cold, and we have given you advice in the past regarding this and one of them we wish to revisit today. For it is time for you to think out of the box of three dimensions when it comes to some of the things that we have discussed with you.

You think in a straight line. You don't necessarily think past certain concepts, but rather you assume things that then create straight line thinking. At the same time I give you this information, I will also tell you that this particular concept is already known on the planet. It is the way of it. We do not give you something that has not already occurred to a Human Being. Free choice is what we have told you is the operative word. So in order to honor this free choice attribute, the things presented today must have already occurred to a Human Being before we will deliver a message like this. This creates a situation where the Humans are manifesting it, not just using hints from Spirit.

When these insights are received by humanity, they normally *land* as inspiration on the planet in more than one place at a time. That is to say, epiphanies of discovery happen all at once, usually three to four places in order to assure that they will not be lost. It's like this: The vibration of the planet is like a big door that opens and closes with the vibration of an enlightened or non-enlightened humanity. If you choose to close this door by creating a low vibration of the planet, then information, invention, and discovery are lost. They actually go away, since humanity doesn't even care to look! However, when the vibration becomes higher, the door opens and discovery and invention just "lay there" ready to be seen. So Spirit does not dole out inventions, but rather the system you have created allows for it. For high science is always there no matter what, but the Human Beings on the planet temper how much of it becomes available by how high the planet vibrates with human consciousness. This explains how you have lost so much science in the past 50,000 years. There were societies who actually were far more quantum thinking than anything you currently have today.

There is an actual irony here in that you have higher tech *inventions* today, but far lower conscious of understanding. You have marvelous computing power that only is programmed for 3D! Later this will be funny to you.

There is tremendous energy available to you directly from the earth, and it's free. It is not what you call free energy, for you have to build an extractor to get it. But it's everywhere; its forever (you don't use it up) and it's called *geothermal energy*.

It's all below your feet, not really that far away and its natural *heat*. It's hot enough for you to drill down and create steam. If you can create steam through natural process of thermal energy, then you can drive steam turbines and create electricity. That will create the power you need to survive some harsher winters and to heat a home, but it may be the cleanest in comparison to the methods that pollute the air. If you can create the electricity itself in a very efficient way, it becomes far more viable for everyday use.

Using steam, there are other ways to create electricity as well. Humanity is fond of very elaborate steam engines, and you've been using them a very, very long time. Today's nuclear reactors are simply very expensive steam engines. You heat water using nuclear reactors and create steam with that heat, which then drives your turbines. So we're giving you something to think about. For nuclear power, as clean and good as it is, has bi-products which are dangerous and you know this. Geothermal, although very clean, can also be dangerous. So now we open the discussion of something new.

If you can drill approximately five kilometers into the earth, you will find enough heat to make a steam engine work. Now, five kilometers to you is not all that far as measured in a straight line along the surface of the earth. Many of you actually walk that distance to school and work and realize that it's not far. But if you're going to drill that distance, technically it becomes difficult and dangerous for the driller, but can be dangerous for the planet. On the way down through the crust of the earth to the five kilometer mark, you go through pockets of attributes... releasing gas perhaps; releasing fire, perhaps, releasing water, perhaps. If nothing else, sometimes you interrupt what we call the integrity of the lubricant of the shale itself. What I am saying here is you might even advance the potential of an earthquake, all by drilling down only five kilometers.

So now I'm going to give you the answer of how to make steam without drilling so far down, and it requires thinking "out of the box" of what you have always assumed. All along you're thinking that you're going to drill down and put a pipe in the earth with water in it. You put water in, and get steam out. However, what if I told you that you only have to drill down a fraction of that distance, and you will find enough heat to boil fluid! You'd say, "Impossible." This feature exists over the hot spots of the earth, which have heat very close to the surface, but those attributes don't exist in most places we're asking you to drill. The answer is not to use water. It's time to marry the highest technology that you have on your planet, with things you didn't expect to marry them with, and this is thinking out of the box.

This is the kind of thinking that is becoming a little more quantum, seeing the entire picture instead of just seeing what you think it should be, or what you are used to. There are solutions here, and some already know what they are. There is elegant chemistry that will boil at a fracture of the temperature that water will, and this is the answer. Learning to use those substances and those fluids with this chemistry within a geothermal closed system machine, this doesn't have to drill down five kilometers. How about two kilometers? Using this known chemistry it will be possible to drill only a fraction of the distance, and get the heat that you need for steam.

So we tell you this because you're going to need to do this. If you heed this advice, you'll find that the timing and the synchronicity of discovery is at hand. That is to say, you will understand it all and realize that the elements will fall together and you will get your steam engine. And it won't take five years to build and it won't be dangerous and you don't have to cover it with a shell. Much easier. It won't belch smoke. It won't pollute, and you don't have to worry about being next to it. Think about it... natural heat from Gaia that is forever! It will create electricity you're going to need to heat homes and businesses... because eventually it's going to get colder. That's number one.

What Humanity needs the most right now

We're going to give you one other insight: This is not new, in that the following information was known, then inappropriately sold and pocketed by industry. Since the idea is already known, I'm going to give it to you here so that the public can see it and anyone with synchronicity who listens to, or reads this message, will understand it. Even you sitting in the chairs will understand the concept, but the scientists and the physicists will then have to implement it. We would not mention it here unless it is very timely.

The resource that humanity is going to need the most as the population grows, as the weather changes, is what you probably already had guessed: Fresh water!   Already it's becoming scarce. You will notice the snow is falling more and more in the wrong places, and often in areas that have no infrastructure to capture the runoff.   The reservoirs and aqueducts are built for the old energy with the old weather patterns. As the population grows, water will be the issue.

The New Desalinization Answer

Here is one immediate answer. It is a profound thing when the earth is mostly water, yet you cannot drink it! The answer is to use the sea and the ocean, and covert it. The ocean, of course, is not fresh water, so you have to ask how to extract the salt.

Desalinization exists today in a very inefficient way. Large amounts of water have to go into vats of containment and sit there while heat is used in various ways. There are various systems, some of them steam, some of them not, all requiring heat to take out the salt. It takes a long time. It's expensive and not efficient. Therefore it is not tenable to desalinate for an entire city. Instead, only places that simply have no fresh water at all have a system like this. It becomes a necessity of inconvenience and expense instead of a good solution.

Now, I'm asking you to think out of the box and I'm going to give you the answer of how to desalinate water in a new way. My partner, I want you to go slow here.

Most of the largest cities on earth are on the coastlines of the ocean... very near water. This is because over time those coastal areas were places where trade could happen with ships and ports. So you end up with the largest cities being on the ocean. It's a good place to start, is it not, to get water for them, from the sources which they can simply look at and use? The answer is not that difficult, but it requires something that has not been considered.

The highest technology you have today has to do with the smallest of the small. You call it nano-technology. It is chemistry and even chemical machines, extremely small, taking the form as what you would call robots. These ultra small, molecular sized robots exist today, and are at the pinnacle of your new inventive efforts. Even now, your science is considering how to insert them into the Human bloodstream to seek out and kiss disease... as an enhancement to the white blood cells that you currently have. That's how small the nano-particles are.

Naturally there are objections to this, since it seems to alter the Human body. It doesn't, any more than any supplement that is not naturally created, which you have learned can help you with pain, disease, chemical balance, or even to sleep at night. So it joins forces with the kinds of science that has been given to Humanity to help keep you alive. Remember, that although we teach that a Human Being can use their own consciousness to do that, there are millions who will not believe it, or not interested in that. So science takes up the slack, so to speak, and there is much today that is known to assist the quality of Human life that is not metaphysical. This is a balance, and it is proper and appropriate. Still there are those who let their own child die, rather than use science to help balance a disease. They believe that anything that is not given from God is not appropriate. It's time to fully understand that good science is simply the discovery and implementation of the way God created the Universe. Used with integrity, it is appropriate, God-given, blessed, and was allowed to be discovered due to a higher-vibrational Earth. In other words, you earned it! Therefore to throw it away or call it evil is not to understand it.

A man is very thirsty. He is very religious and prays for water to be given him. Along comes another man with water, and offers it to him. The thirsty man rejects it, saying that he expects it only from God and will wait. He dies thirsty; never understanding the synchronicity of God is through other Humans! Learn to appreciate science that is given to Humanity for this reason.

Nanotechnology is becoming smarter. Science is learning to make the robots intelligent through chemistry, through logic, through electronics. It's like the logic of a computer, which can cleverly help you to do many things. It doesn't think for you, but rather it assists you in tasks you can't do yourself. These tiny robots can help desalinate water.

I'm going to give you a task: You're going to build desalination plant where the water never stops flowing, and where salt can be removed in real time, and a by-product created that you had no idea about. The water never has to rest and never has to be cooked. There is no heat involved at all. Using nanotechnology, the water goes in one end of the machine, and it comes out the other in a steady flow. In—salty, out—fresh, and ready then for standard purification.

The first stages of the system require that you release enough nanotechnology robots assigned to find the dissolved salts and attach themselves to them. Here is the secret, however: every single robot is magnetized! I am the magnetic master, after all.

All of the salt then becomes magnetic, with tiny little nano robots on to all of it. On to the next stage: Flowing into the next area, the water is exposed to tremendous, huge electromagnets, pulling the salt out of the water completely and totally, because the salt is now magnetic! Out it goes. Over simplified, perhaps, but this is the way of it. No heat is involved.

Now the by-product... you won't believe it! Oh, and this will be controversial when you discover it. Magnetic fields applied to water often create water that is quite healing. Do you see where this going? What a device that might be! It would be quantum, you know, because it uses magnetics. There would be those who will say that magnetically treated water is bad for you, since you are altering it in a way that is not understood. They don't realize the amount of energy that other Humans have gone through to find the healing waters of the earth! Now you get a bit of that in desalinating water! There will be no proof either way of what is happening, so that will make it controversial. All people will know is that fewer people are getting sick!

So this is what we wanted to give you today. This is what we wanted to have recorded today in this way, so that you might hear it and it would be published. I wish to tell you what we see in the future, based on the potentials you have developed. We're not going to give a timeframe, for there is none.

The Future of Science

The information I'm about to give you can be two generations away, maybe even three. But it all has to do with quantum invention. Physicists, listen. I'm going to give you something you already know, and it's possible. It involves another field of science but it opposes everything three dimensional you've ever learned. Humans are funny. Even in the highest math and geometry, everything is defined in a straight line. Therefore Humans just love to define a circle as a polygon with an infinite number of straight lines. That's funny! It's almost as though a circle didn't exist in nature, and the Human has to create a formula using a straight line object for it to exist. Interesting, isn't it? I'm just giving you the Human straight line bias, and its fun to look at. Bubbles have always been around. They're beautiful, you know? They're natural, you know? The circle is a natural occurring event in space, as well... think planets. But humans want this shape to be an infinite number of straight lines.

Like cartoon characters on a page, the stick figures find a few three dimensional properties in their two dimensional lives, and they "prove" them by creating an infinite number of stick figures to explain the shape.

What you already suspect is that gravity and magnetism all naturally bend. They don't go straight, and they never have. What about light? It doesn't either. When affected by the other two, it bends also. That should tell you something. Nothing is really a straight line at all! The only straight lines around are the brains of Humans. {Angel Kryon joke} You're not using the right kinds of math either, and we told you that long ago. There's elegance to math that is quantum and if I begin to tell you about it, even in the simplest terms, it's going to seem overly complex.

The New Math is Coming

{Author comment-glad I'm not in high school} Quantum math uses something that is going to be discovered and we're going to give it a name: influential numbers. These are numbers that do not have empirical values, but instead have values that are influenced by the numbers around them. Four is not a four. Four is modified because of the numbers that sit next to it, as in a formula, or in linearity as in counting. Each time a formula is manufactured in a quantum state, the numbers within it are all influenced by the others around it. This is because all of the numbers in that formula are modified by the numbers that are next to them. They're influential numbers. If four is used in a linear way, it is affected by the five, or by the three. They all influence the numbers next to each other, as seen in the conceptual sense. The reason is that a quantum reality is one that is never linear or has the attributes that you think are "normal". {Author comment-if you get audited by IRS try using this theory... afterwards chose the top bunk}

However complex, it is not random, and there is indeed an elegant system... a beautiful thing when you find out the attributes and see the consistency of the change. Chaos does not look like chaos when you understand the "chaos rules." Eventually, when you see this, you will then have the formula for a circle being a whole number, not an irrational number as it exists today. It won't be pi. Instead, it will be "pi solved." We ask the physicists to work it backwards if you have to, in order to get a whole number of pi. That will give you a hint and what has to be done with the rest of the computations.

Imagine mathematics with influential numbers! For each number is not empirical but influenced by the one around it. I'm giving you high math now, and here's how it's going to serve you: Because when you start to understand it, you're finally going to understand what I'm going to call the Holy Grail of Physics. That's a human term {Kryon wink}.

In your straight-line thinking, in your bias, you have many 3-D formulas, don't you? And when you look at the basics of physics, you talk about matter having mass. In those things which have mass you've figured out the atomic structure and density. You are proud of the consistency of the formulas, based on what you see around you, and you think they're static, don't you? You think there is a formula for everything, and it explains how things move and react. "If it has a certain atomic density and mass, then it weighs this or that in certain gravity. You've got it all figured out.

Indeed you have! But only in 3-D. So as soon as you become quantum with these formulas, they all stretch and become different. All this to tell you yet again, that it is possible for you to alter the mass of any object in existence. It doesn't matter how large or small or how dense it is. You can alter the mass of it, and therefore (pause..) the effect gravity has on it. There is no such thing as anti-gravity, only the control of mass. So whatever formula you have in 3D that tells you how much something should weigh, can be then changed by controlling the mass of the object in question. Therefore you are not changing gravity (which is really a quantum product of two other forces), but of the mass of an object. And it has to do with controlling the atomic density, or apparent density as seen by gravity.

In Yugoslavia, there's a famous workshop. Historic it is, for it belongs to the man who thought out of the box, Tesla. In that workshop, there are marks on the ceiling made by the objects that took off from his workbench and went straight up! They shattered, hitting the ceiling hard! Nikola was frustrated, for he had discovered the creation of mass less objects and didn't know how! He thought out of the box... the only one in existence to ever give you a blueprint on how alternating current might work. Oh, it's more than 3-D. Study it, for it is elegant.

All of this that Tesla did was created by magnetic, and this was also the basis behind the experiment in his workshop. However, in Tesla's time there were no computers or any of the finite instruments you have today to measure or create tiny fluctuations in magnetic fields. He accomplished the creation of altering the mass of an object, but he couldn't control it, and didn't know exactly how he did it. Frustrated, he was. By the way, he's back. I'm not going to tell you where. Maybe he will read this and know what to do next?

Clever, it is how magnetic fields can be arranged around magnetic fields. Even solutions (fluids) can be magnetized to create clever shaped fields within fields...sometimes at right angles to each other, sometimes not, to give you a condition that will create a change in mass. None of these things are out of the purview of Human development. How long it'll take? We don't know. That's up to you. But do you understand what it will change? Everything! It means that the things of science fiction are finally yours. What you called anti-gravity is simply an object with controllable mass. It'll float no matter how big. It's doable. Maybe it's time to implement it?

"Kryon, why do you tell us about these things?" With this we close. The answer is that we want you to stay here. All of this is given in love. We want you to stay here! And you're not going to have much luck with that unless you start thinking more quantum, unless you start accelerating the inventions and put some of the politics out of the way. But the countries which must do this are the ones who have the highest technical abilities and they also have the highest influential structures that are in the way of it all. {Authors note—I can relate to that in my energy project} It is time for the population to understand this and turn the physicists loose and not strap them with those things which are political, or industrially or efficiently "appropriate". Perhaps you don't know what I speak of, but they do.

In the process of this, there will be live extension; in the process there will epiphanies'; in the process you might even find that this message was accurate and true. Somewhere down the line, if you do, then you've got a puzzle, don't you, physicists? Don't you? If you're listening to this, you've got a puzzle, because who is it who is speaking from the other side of the veil, giving you information that is true and real and scientific? At some level, you're going to have to say *it's real.* At some time in the future you're going to have to admit that the spiritual and the science is allied, and that the energy that created the earth and the magnetic and the gravity and all of the things you studied, is a piece of you... since the creator is inside of each of you. Then maybe you'll open up?

It all has to do with this puzzle: Is it real or not? Is Kryon real or not? Is love real or not? Well, some of you know, because you've sat in the presence of the creator today who loves you. This family on my side of the veil loves you. It's a wonderful Valentine message, isn't it? So we say to you, dear ones, that all of the things that we talk about, whether they're scientific, or have to do with your Akash, or your core soul, or a Higher-Self, are given for one reason: to make the life on this planet easier. It's so you may discover the compassion that is the glue that puts together with creation, that changes the earth itself, for the shift is upon you.

What you call the 2012 energy is already here, having arrived approximately 1998. Let this be what it is supposed to be, a time of high consciousness, of scientific evolution with integrity, with an economy that is a re-emerging with integrity, with government that slowly changes old energy. There is a new paradigm occurring, with things that you would never put together in the past. This is an oxymoron – cannot exist together – integrity and government – integrity and insurance – integrity with banking. A new paradigm is upon you, and this shift is difficult. We have the warrior and the worker in the chairs in front of me. They know it because that's why they came: the Akash is alive and well in you, dear ones, and you know who you are. I know who you are. And I celebrate each, each one.

And so it is

Kryon

APPENDIX 3 ANGEL TECHNOLOGY
PART 2

LIVE ANGEL KRYON CHANNELING
"The Great Scientific Bias"

This live channeling was Given in the Washington DC area on November 7, 2009 and reprinted with permission.

Greetings, dear ones, I am Kryon of Magnetic Service.

Quickly it occurs does it not, the transition between Human Beings and one who is channeling a message from beyond? Perhaps it is a little too quick for those who would be in judgment about what is taking place here? But what my partner did not tell you is that there is no actual transition, since I'm always "under the surface" with him. This is his choice to have the energy of me in this way... to be able to flip back and forth in the messages of love between him speaking and me speaking. So we say to you, Human Being, which any of you can get to the place where there is little or no transition between you speaking and your Higher-Self speaking.

What I wish to speak about this day is difficult to define. I let my partner come up with a title for this channeling, for humans enjoy that. They want to realize a "compartmentalization of expectation." They wish to have some kind of identity process on everything they do, so I'll let him do it. For what I'm going to speak of is perception of dimensionality like I never have before. I wish to give you some of the mechanics of it, and a little bit about how it works, and also a little bit about what my partner calls the creation of *the wild card...* those things that you don't expect or don't believe in. So I have to start with an example.

Let me introduce you to Henry and Mary, they are cartoon characters, stick figures on a piece of paper. They are two dimensional. Of course, they are intelligent, since this is a parable. {Kryon smile}Their lives are not complicated, and they are simple stick figures. They have everything figured out. They even have love. The two dimensionality of their lives is all they have ever known, and they are pleased with it. They know the parameters of the piece of paper they're on, and they are happy with them. That's all they have ever had. They know what they can do and what they cannot do. Henry and Mary are satisfied and content with their reality.

Along comes a free thinker, one who has been drawn a little different. This odd character begins to speak to both of them about the potential of a third dimension... the idea of "up and down". He speaks of 3D instead of 2D, as they currently enjoy. It's the beginning of the concept of a kind of reality that they have never seen, and one they don't feel they participate in, nor can they really understand it.

Let's look at what Henry and Mary do with this information. First, they do not comprehend it. It's a little too high-minded for them. Second of all, it is outside of their reality, so they're not really that interested. They don't have to use it, so to them it's conjecture and so they don't believe it really is important or exists. It becomes a fantasy of science, something that will never pertain to Henry and Mary, who after all, are 2D drawings on a piece of paper.

There are many who sit and read this 2D piece of paper that is similar. Anything out of your 3D reality doesn't interest you. Not by choice, but because you are part of the paradigm that always was... a paradigm in 3D that you have lived all your life. It's a reality that is difficult to think beyond, and many really could care less about studying it. After all, what's wrong with the reality they are in? It works.

The new shift that is upon you is one of quantumness. It is going to require Human Beings to understand more about what is around them, which is invisible to them, but which is very real. They must come to an understanding, and therefore a belief, that not all things are viewable and understandable within 3D thinking, and that there is so much more that is actually part of their world, but requires a logic beyond what they are used to in order to comprehend it.

The best way I can begin this study in the time allotted is to take you on a journey and give you some information. There will be some things in this message that will be interesting to those who love science. To others who are not science minded, it might not relate, but they can still participate in the analogy that I'm giving, and understand the lesson.

I wish to take you to a real place, but for today, it must be only in your creative mind. The place is real, but you can't go there at the moment... not yet. The interesting thing is that each of you has actually been where I'm taking you, when you were not on Earth. It was before you were ever a Human, and we spent time here. It's an unbelievably beautiful place. The view is, shall say, unearthly. I want to take you just outside and above your own galaxy, looking at the spiral from above. Come with me for a moment. Pretend for a moment that the pressures of space and the temperatures don't apply to your Human body. None of these things matter, for you're in a protected bubble that is your spiritual self. All together, we go and we watch this magnificent sight.

As a Human Being, you're stuck with the silence of space, not understanding or even appreciating the fact that every single star sings a song. I hear them all. Silence to you is a symphony to me. For the vibratory rates of the light that is emitted from the stars all combine into a chorus, a manipulation of vibrational sonority that is beautiful. The universe sings to me, for I am quantum. The parts of you that are quantum are beginning to broach past the three-dimensional parts. That meld, that confluence, is going to create paradigms of thought that are different from any others on the planet. For there has been no time on the planet like this one, where you are asked to think out of the box of your comfortable reality, and go beyond the wall of your natural bias. Look at your galaxy with me for a moment. The beautiful spiral of it, is all moving slowly together as one... rotating slowly like a plate of lights. Take it all in.

I give you science today. I give you knowledge today that will only come about and be known within your future. And because of the transcriptions that are taken today, there will come a time when you will point to this particular message and say, *"Kryon was right."* And when you do, when the science confirms what I tell you today, I want you to look at the entire message. Because then your belief factor will also know that I speak truth when I speak about your relationship to Spirit, to the creator in you. I'm right when I talk about what is in front of you and your future.....

"As goes one, goes the other," you'll say, *"therefore I will pay attention to all that is said."*

Looking at the Galaxy

It's beautiful, isn't it, as we are suspended here above your home Galaxy? In what you call the silence of this moment,, looking at the galaxy moving so slowly, spirally all together as one, it's unbelievable, unearthly, and spectacular beyond words. Now I take you inside and tell you a little bit of what's happening that is a mystery to your science. There are odd things out here that don't fit earthly paradigms or rules. They don't fit *your* physics.

Henry and Mary, the two stick figures on the page, had scientists also. They had their 2D laws for physics, and that's all they needed. Everything worked just fine as long as they stayed on the page. You have four laws of physics, because you're in technically in 4D, and those laws work just fine. Those laws have proven themselves over and over, and as long as you stay in 4D (which you call 3D), they will always work.

Here's an esoteric question for you. Take a look at the stick figures Henry and Mary. How many laws of physics are there really for the 2D characters? Is there a whole set that encompasses multi-dimensional reality, or just enough to satisfy 2D? The answer should be obvious. Physics is complete no matter how you perceive it. Therefore Henry and Mary are only aware of, believe in, and are using, 2D, but all the laws are still there... ready to be discovered. 3D may not be something the stick figures understand, but it sits there ready, anyway. So extend that thinking and let me ask you this, Three-dimensional creature: If I told you there were six laws of physics, covering a dimensionality that you don't see, how many are there for you? The answer is the same as Henry and Mary. There are more than you know about, even if you are only aware of, and actively using, the four that you have.

Do you see? The four laws you have, work fine. There is nothing wrong with them, but there are more, and that's why we take you here above your galaxy to show it all to you, and to present something that astronomers also can see. Look: Something is weird with the way the galaxy is moving. Did you notice?

We've given you the two additional laws of physics before, and this is not the time to explain them again. But when you get into an inter-dimensional realm, you're looking at multi-dimensional energies that must contain more information than your current physics. You have four laws now. Call them Newtonian, Euclidian, Einsteinium if you wish. These are the ones that brought you to where you are today. But now gaze with me at your spiral galaxy for a moment and watch it move. It does not move like your solar system.

The laws you have of *objects in motion* carry with them a three-dimensional bias of consistency. Your science looks for empirical laws and they find what they believe is true for everything. But what they don't realize is that there is a bias applied. It only works in one direction... in 3D. If you apply the rules only on that one playing field of time, you can apply linear mathematics and figure out what you need from that. It's all in a straight line, all forward, never changing, always the same. You might say your science is *biased in simple consistency!*

"Kryon, what's wrong with that? Sounds fine to me!" Here comes the free thinker who is saying: "Inter-dimensional things do not apply to 3D logic or bias. The laws if inter-dimensional weak and strong forces are beyond 3D understanding, and may even seem to be chaotic and inconsistent."

Let me give you a further explanation. Your solar system works like you expect it does. Within the kinds of physics you have applied to the way things move in space, you have objects that are closer to the sun that move faster, like Mercury, for example. Then there are objects further away from the sun that moves slower (the outer planets). The laws of orbital mechanics are in play. The distance from the sun develops into the 3D laws of orbital mechanics based upon the rules you have discovered for gravity, mass, distance and speed. And the rules are correct... for 3D. Again, it lets you send spacecraft to the planets, to be so precise, to meet them in orbit, to take pictures and analyze them.

But look for a moment with me right now...*this is not the way your galaxy is moving.* It's in an elegant motion that defies the *law of the inverse square* (a law that defines how energy dissipates with distance from the source). It defies the basic laws of gravity and force. It defies the simple, biased, singular attributes of the way things move in space. Look at your galaxy with me. Watch it spin. It's almost like it was on a platter. Everything moves together. Everything! It's all rotating at the same speed, relative to the center...like a giant wheel that is all connected. This giant platter behaves like all the stars are pebbles, and are somehow glued to the fabric of space, all moving together.

How can that be? What are you seeing? Let me give you a hint and a clue: we've spoken about the weak and strong inter-dimensional forces which are undiscovered laws of five and six of physics. The way your galaxy moves is all about what's at the center of the galaxy, and displays these forces. You think it's a black hole, but it isn't. There's far more to it than you would imagine. Have you noticed in physics there is always polarity? From the smallest atomic structure to the largest, there is always polarity. You also see this in magnetic. It's also hiding in gravity. It's a staple of energy everywhere, everywhere. There are always two kinds of energy, and they work against and with each other to create dimensional reality. Matter itself is one polarity of reality, and anti-matter is the other. Always look for the push and pull, for it will show the way to the answers to the most perplexing issues of physics.

At the center of every galaxy there are "the twins." The twins are in the middle of the Milky Way as well. You've got two energies: One pushes and one pulls. However, you see it in your perception as one giant Black Hole. You assume the gravity of the Black Hole is somehow gripping that spiral and making it spin and making it spin together in an unusual fashion which violates all the laws of Newton. It's not so. What's happening in the center of your galaxy is beautiful. It is an elegant inter-dimensional force that is not gravity, which spreads through the entire region of your entire galaxy, a force that glues it together in a way that you do not have laws to explain...yet. In addition, there is something hiding that science is only now beginning to wrestle with.

All this explanation, to get to a place of logic for you that will broach a very big issue. Simply stated it is this:

When you step into inter-dimensional physics, and this includes the energies of what you call spirituality, you will find something you didn't expect: Consciousness...*physics with an attitude.* The inter-dimensionality of your galactic center has consciousness. It has to. Anything inter-dimensional is aligned with creation. I'm speaking of things you don't understand. These are high minded, sometimes unbelievable attributes that haven't really been broached in this way before. When you break the linear logic wall down from what you expect in linear physics, you're going to run up against things that don't make sense to your bias. They won't make sense... not just because they're in a quantum state, but they contain something else that "consistent 3D science" does not accept...intelligence in physics.

Your science is very proud of the Big Bang Theory. They have it all figured out and they have a timeline for it. This is really funny to us! How can you have a timeline for a quantum event? There is no time in a quantum state, yet they have it all figured out. They've even figured out that there's a residue they can measure that proves they're right. How clever of them!

Let me ask you something, if you smell that wonderful residue of bread cooking in the kitchen, what does that tell you? Does it say, "Bread was cooked here four billion years ago" or does it say, "It's being cooked now"?

It's the basis of straight line thinking in a singular time dimension that smells the bread and calculates how long ago it was cooked! There is no understanding that the quantum event of the "Big Bang" is still happening.

It explains the energy of Universal expansion. It even begins to explain the "energy of what you can't see." The "residue" they measure is the proof of the reality of an event still in progress as you see it in 3D, but an event that *is the reality of creation,* within a quantum state.

Look at what a 3D mismatch the current theory is: How could everything have come from nothing, and then at a speed greater than the speed of light, instantly expanded, violating every law of current physics, to create the current mass of the universe in a nano-moment? Yet the basis of singular thinking lets all that happen in the time of an instant... and they have it all figured out. They should all be celebrating with Henry and Mary! {Kryon humor}

Let me tell you something I have never, ever described to you before. The center of your galaxy spit out matter that is you. Science has it backwards. The twins in the center of your galaxy lead to the twins in the center of all the other galaxies. Million of them; billions of them. They're all connected in a way you cannot fathom outside of space, outside of time, like strings between friends who have a consciousness. Not the kind of intelligence and consciousness that you see in your brain, no. Instead it's benevolence, an intelligent glue that postures the universe in love. I told you that you wouldn't understand all of this. This is high-minded, high thinking, and many are simply not ready for it.

{Author note: The author believes the twins in the center of the galaxy may actually be Bert and Ernie, the loveable characters from Sesame Street™.}

The Gaia Effect

Let us go to something else. Life on the planet, and the way it was created, has become controversial because there are those in science who must linearize it all. Darwin gave you the possibilities of an evolved life system. He showed how it might work, perhaps, in a random selection of biology over and over through billions of years, creating what you have now. But then, enter *the Gaia Effect.*

Scientists are looking at earth history and they're starting to see something very bothersome to other scientists: There may be a consciousness that has created life. Naturally, true science does not want to think this way, for 3D straight thinking of your current science does not allow for rules outside the box of total consistency. The real irony here is that *singular consistency bias* does not allow for *creator bias.* Could the universe be biased toward life? In this irony, the Human is biased due to limited dimensional thinking, and the Universe is biased in love. {Author note: Scientists and governments at one time believed the earth was flat, and they were willing to put to the gallows those who disagreed...mankind has not evolved much since those days.}

The controversy goes like this: Earth history shows that life continued to be created and destroyed on the planet through four billion years. It started and it stopped and it created life itself and destroyed itself over and over. Whereas life was once looked upon as an "against all odds" attribute of the planet, and nowhere else in the Universe, it now is seen as having been created again and again!

Some say, *"Well, that's a random event happening."* Really? What are the odds after life had destroyed itself, of that incredible randomness striking again? How's that for evolution? Something that didn't work... returning! What do you think about that? Scientists are beginning to consider *The Gaia Effect*, as a consciousness coming from somewhere, somehow, that is biased to create life. It's outside of the purview of what you would call chance. Over and over it happened, until the planet it got it right. Photosynthesis was the answer, for it created a balance... plants and trees to consume the byproduct of life. So finally, the balance began.

It took a long time for that, but life was always created again until the "system" got it right. Even when the system snuffed life out, it returned! Even when the earth was barren of life because it hadn't worked out, it was created again up to five times. Science is starting to see this and is wondering how it is that earth seemed *biased to create life.* Some say there's a consciousness; some say that that is not true... there couldn't be, just couldn't be.

But there is, dear one, and it's an inter-dimensional consciousness that glues things together. Because when you get into an inter-dimensional state, you're starting to touch the face of God, the creative energy of the universe, and one that is indeed, biased in love.

Geological Surprises – Rethinking time

There are those who study the way the earth geologically came about, and again, in their straight-line thinking, they are biased.

They are biased because they look at erosion patterns, they look at the way things used to be, and then they apply specific universal laws to everything on the planet from then on. Well, there are some surprises: Have you heard the latest? How long did it take to cut the Grand Canyon? How many millions of years would the water have to trickle by in order to cut the canyon as it stands today? One million years, two million? It's still posted on the placards on the historic sites of how long it took. But now geologists are starting to change their minds because they have discovered other attributes that don't make sense. Now they're assigning a timeline of approximately three hundred years!

What happened to their logic? What they're now seeing is a *wild card*. That is to say there was no trickle of water. Instead, there was a sea that emptied into it... a ferocious torrent of water that cut the rock over a much shorter period of time. Outside the paradigm of thinking, it is, and accurate it is. You see where I'm going with this? It is the consistent biases that keep you in a straight line rut like the 2D figures on the piece of paper. You've got to start thinking out of the box and look for what else there might have been. So I've given you the Grand Canyon story, so that you can absorb the next one.

The Unspoken Geology of Lemurian Existence

I've told you some odd things about the planet, and geologists always roll their eyes. For Kryon gives you information that is often "geologically impossible," they say. I told you about Lemuria. I've told you the original Lemurian civilization was centered on dry land at the base of the highest mountains on earth, measured from the bottom to the top, which is now Hawaii. It is one big mountain with several peaks, and the peaks are what now stick out of the water today, which you call the Hawaiian Islands in the middle of the Pacific Ocean.

In the days of Lemuria, we told you that the land around the base was dry. Geologists laugh. It's in the middle of the Pacific Ocean? How could that be? I'm going to tell you how it could be. First, you must understand that geologically, 50,000 years ago is not a significant enough time for something like plate tectonics to have an impact on this attribute. 50,000 years is actually very little time in geology... yet the water level at that time was more than 400 feet lower than it is now. This is because you were in the process of a water cycle which we have discussed before. So that's one of the attributes that came into play. However, the other attribute is the biggest reason, and one we have never spoken of before.

The mountains of Hawaii slowly move over what is called a *hot spot,* that is to say it slowly moves over a tremendous volcanic core of activity that has existed there for millions of years. 50,000 years ago this *hot spot* was in the process of a giant "bulge" that actually gradually lifted the floor of the ocean around the Hawaiian mountain, more than six thousand feet. That is to say the mantel of the earth bulged enough due to volcanic pressure, to lift those mountains higher than they are now, to create a relatively small area of dry land that contained the mountain of Hawaii. When the lava was released, and it was, the bubble slowly deflated. This took several thousand years, without a cataclysmic eruption, as it was slowly released itself on the peaks of the mountain and poured into the sea, building yet more and around Hawaii. This created a situation where the base of the Hawaiian mountain was above sea level for a while. The slow release caused the bubble to subside, and Lemuria slowly was flooded. This is the story we told you originally, and the reason the Lemurians became sea faring, and moved to many other places.

Convenient, it is, for the doubters, that all evidence of Lemuria has been destroyed as it should be. It makes you wonder. It makes you wonder if these things might be so. But a linear thinker will tell you that this can't be so, since they have never seen evidence of it in history. You haven't seen that kind of bulge before, therefore we have the same "Grand Canyon" effect, where the truth lays hidden due to biased consistency. What you never saw is therefore not possible.

By the way, the evidence is indeed there of the bulge, for the striations of the ocean floor still show an odd symmetry around the mountain, giving hints that it was once stressed upward through volcanic influences, and then subsided. There are also bones of animals at those depths, buried deep, that would tell a biologist that what is on the ocean floor in the middle of the Pacific Ocean, was once exposed to sunlight...about 50,000 years ago.

Divine Creation – The Proof is in the Odds

Let me tell you about creation. Astronomers are starting to talk about *Intelligent Design.* Now we're getting somewhere, since they're starting to understand that the quantumness of the universe might indeed have consciousness. Against all odds, you live in a parameter, an attribute in space that statistically continues to be "against all odds". You are in a universe created for life! If you could throw the dice of physics and create a universe, it would never come up this way. Never. Statisticians have said that it's out *of the possibility of chance...* yet you sit in an earth teeming with life. You sit in an universe teeming with life. There is life on the planets around you, but you just haven't found it yet. Microbial it is, and it represents the beginning attributes of single-celled life. It's all there. You'll see. Take a trip to Europa (moon of Jupiter), and look around a little in the ocean. You'll see. Life is absolutely the way of the universe...everywhere. You'll see. And it's against all odds that it happened, and science is now seeing that. It is so out of the statistical model of the creation of any universe, that they have labeled it *Intelligent Design.* There has to have been a plan.

In the middle of your galaxy, the twins exist, pushing and pulling inter-dimensional energies that literally have an intelligent complement to them. All the stars move together in unison with it. Forces that are way beyond gravity are involved. It's an inter-dimensionality that glues the galaxy together, and that is something that I want to speak of because it has to do with your future.

Your Future

The futurists of your society have a tendency to look at *what was,* and then project *what will be.* Do you see the straight line thinking? In a bias of consistency, they say, *"Because of this, therefore, there will be this."* They're looking at a constant model of old energy, and in their projections, never giving it a chance to change. They are denying the very ability of Humanity to move past *what was.*

What is it that has been consistent on the planet regarding consciousness? Let's name the attributes: War, poverty, suffering, drama, a repeat of the same, a repeat of the same. Fractals of time that come and go and come and go, which create a consciousness that repeats and repeats and repeats.

Now you can see the bias, and why it's there. For anything that stays in the same cycle is expected to stay in it forever. This is also echoed in your physics. The more quantum you become, the less consistent you will be in thinking this way. That is to say, eventually you will *expect* things to happen that have not happened before. You are in a shift that is allowing for it, and all around you, things are changing. Listen: You cannot apply *last year's rules* to peace on earth. Is it possible? Yes... more than possible, it's the most probably outcome that we can give you.

What do last year's rules tell you about healing your body? They say it's incurable? It isn't. What do last year's rules tell you about the fear that is being generated over the shift you are in? Does it tell you that you're going to be covered by water? Well, if you apply the rate at which things are melting and then you project all this into the future, you apply the discourse of poor science... then of course you will be! But that's awfully consistent of you, isn't it? You see what I'm saying? You're not giving any allowance for the *wild card.* You're not giving an allowance for the fact that this planet is moving into an entirely different magnetic attribute. The sun is cooperating; the universe is cooperating; it's almost like the twins can see who you are!

The twins are physics, a magnificent pushing and pulling of an inter-dimensional attribute which we cannot explain even explains to you. The twins are not God. The twins are a result of a God-biased universe, and an inter-dimensional physics that you are only beginning to discover and question. Your science is only beginning to see it. The Gaia effect, Intelligent Design, the way the earth was put together, the way there was no accidents that you're here, against all the odds... that ought to add up to something in your logic.

You are in the middle of a tremendous shift that you've asked for, that it's time for! It's not one that's going to destroy you! You don't have to fear it. It's one you're in control of as you're becoming more quantum. You're starting to understand that the consistency of fear, of hate, of disappointment... is beginning to change. If you want to be consistent with things, know this, that the love of God is the most consistent and persistent thing on this earth and in the universe. Consistent, it is! So persistent that it would not stop until life was created, and until love was discovered.

The Consciousness of Kryon

We wanted to paint a picture today. It was mostly scientific, partly a puzzle, to show you that your current 3D logic is not expanded. It's not the kind of logic you're going to need to move into the future. We told you to *expect the wild card.* Expect things that have not happened before. Change history by thinking about future things which may be evolutionary and represent wild cards themselves. Can you recognize some of those wild cards in your very immediate past? How many times do we have to give you these things to look at? None of the quatrains of Nostradamus are accurate today. Books have been written about the tremendous upcoming war with Islam. Well, someday you can read them and laugh, because it's not happening that way. That entire scenario is based upon a consistent, unchanging consciousness on earth, where everything repeats in an expected old pattern, and it isn't!

Are you the expected pattern on earth, or are *you* the wild card? You see, there are things coming that you didn't expect. I know these things for I see the potentials that are not openly available to you. It's the consciousness which is "baking in the oven" that is working right now in ways that you do not expect. This is not future fortune telling. It is instead just stating the facts of the potentials of the minds on the planet... where they're going and what they are thinking.

I want you to leave this place with hope. We saved this message for this particular group. It's an advanced message, and it does not fall on the ears of those who were just here for the first time or in the energy for the first time. It falls on the ears of old souls. Don't you remember this? Remember this with me, for you expected it. That is why you are here, and that is why you will return.

Finally, this: I was with you at the wind of birth, each of you. Before you slipped into this planet, before the angels stood around the bed and sang to your mother at the joy of your birth, I was there. Right before you came again, I inquired like I always do, "*Is this really something you want to do? Look at the potentials, and the hardships, the disease and sorrow of being Human. Do you really want to go back?*" You looked at me like you always do and said, "*Send me in. I can hardly wait to get back and finish what I started.*"

Now you have some of the first signs you've ever had since you were a Human, that this planet can move into graduation, vibrate higher and become part of a confluence of energy that you've only dreamed about... and you're sitting on the edge of it.

I am Kryon, lover of humanity. That is the truth I give you today. I give this message in order to instill in within your hearts and in your minds, the hope that these things are so and that they are true. Perhaps some of you today will leave here differently than you came because of this. And so this particular message will be given again in a different form for a different crowd, but every bit as loving and poignant.

I am Kryon. And so it is.

APPENDIX 4 - THE WILL OF THE PEOPLE v. THE WILL OF GOVERNMENTS

In writing this book the best has been saved for last. Everything that has been written is to prepare you for this last segment of the book. By now you might have tried those spiritual exercises to lift your spiritual awareness to a higher level. This book was written to be very informative and open up the veil for you. The angels chose the name of the title for this Appendix. They woke the author up early in the morning so that you the reader will hear these last words.

Humanity has had to live with the plaque of serving the will of the governments. History has repeated itself over and over again with repressive governments. Mankind (which includes women) has welded its power over the masses in the governments that have been designed. A gift that God has bestowed upon the human race is that man would live their lives and all their dramas under Free Will. Because of Free Will God does not judge mankind. The will of the people have in most cases been subservient to the will of governments. Now there is also the Will of the Divinity. It is the Will of God that mankind will enter a period of peace and prosperity. All of you agreed to take part in this new era of peace. There are many who are in government service had agreed that they will open up this door. Unfortunately, there are some who now weld much power but because of greed, corruption and a thirst and lust for power have reneged on their promises and the glory of God.

Beloveds many of you have fears that the world will end on December 21st, 2012. We want to assure you that your planet will not be destroyed by anything celestial. You are not alone in this universe. Governments across the planet have kept from the people the existence of Star Beings. These people have been watching over your planet since the dawn of time. Humans are only in the kindergarten of what they can achieve as a society. The Star Beings are PhD graduates. They have helped and walked among you over the centuries. However, because of free will they have not intervened when humanity has created human atrocities. The Star Beings do have the right to intervene should humanity try to destroy itself with nuclear weapons.

The Star Beings have offered new technologies that would benefit mankind if they would be willing to end nuclear proliferation. Your governments have said no. Your governments have blocked the efforts of the Star People to make themselves known worldwide. Many of you have seen and photographed our vessels in your skies. The Star Beings have come in peace and they listen to the Angels. When they arrive do not listen to the media hype of the Star Beings as alien invaders. They will help you in your nuclear disasters. The governments now are trying to downplay the significance of the December 21st, 2012 date. Humanity has the power to co-create your own destiny. The world will not end on this date. However, this is the earth date for karmic Judgment Day. The Angels have been determining those with a good heart to those who have evil in their heart. They have been doing so for several years and they will complete their mission on December 21st. Look at these Angels part of a heavenly Census Bureau. This census is almost complete.

The dark side of the Illuminati has held control over the populations. They have also been instrumental in your geophysical events and weather manipulations for a destructive effect. The proponents for a New World Order, because of their work with the darkness, are actually creating a New World Disorder, which benefits no one – not even themselves. The death toll, property damage, financial loss and other damages have created many hardships for people. Many of these people who participate in the darkness have refused the Light that was being beamed to them. None will escape the consequences of their thoughts, intentions, and actions in the higher "spiritual court" in their life review. They will experience every moment of their Earth lifetime. That process will include their feeling the identical feeling of every person whose life they have touched in any way whatsoever, and in many cases, that number is in the millions. Your concept of hell will never come close to what these individuals will endure in life review or the primitive conditions that will exist in their next lifetimes. You see in the end the universe will sort things out.

God judges no soul and God will not judge them. However, the people will when they are identified and held accountable for what they have done. Most will deny all accusations, others will admit the truth for immunity or reduced sentences in helping to convict others, and some will escape justice by dying prior to the conclusion of their case or trial. None will escape the higher "spiritual court".

Your Masters of the Universe are making plans and taking actions to further their causes such as world domination and instilling submissiveness of the people to those in power. They governments are doing so because they think they are accountable to no one. God has one law and that is the Golden Rule – treat others the way you want to be treated or expressed another way; do unto others as you would have them do unto you. Beloveds you have all heard of this Golden Rule. Do you really understand the meaning and why God does not need to judge anyone? He knows you will eventually return to the Oneness. Those who have committed atrocities against humanity have already given their permission to experience the pain of all they have touched in their lives. They have agreed to experience the pain of others for they have asked – I want to be treated the same way by those I have helped and injured. That is karma. Their prayers have been answered.

It is my desire and hope that this book has been rewarding to you as we all embark on our journey together for a better world. If enough people visualize a new world union built on trust, understanding, integrity and love, then maybe we can stop the insanity in the world. May peace, prosperity and happiness follow you and your loved ones, always!

Robert Hostetler

www.ingramcontent.com/pod-product-compliance
Lightning Source LLC
Chambersburg PA
CBHW060242290526
45789CB00001B/157